Commonhold – The New Law

Commonhold – The New Law

DN Clarke MA, LLM (Cantab), Solicitor (Hons)
Professor and Dean of Law, University of Bristol

JORDANS

2002

Published by
Jordan Publishing Limited
21 St Thomas Street
Bristol BS1 6JS

British Library Cataloguing-in-Publication Data
A catalogue record for this book is available from the British Library.

ISBN 0 85308 774 1

Typeset by Jordan Publishing Limited
Printed and bound in Great Britain by Bell & Bain Ltd, Glasgow

To my brother

RICHARD JOHN ALAN CLARKE, Solicitor,

and for all with an interest, professional or otherwise, in property law matters

in the hope that this introductory volume will assist them

TABLE OF CASES

References are to paragraph numbers.

TABLE OF STATUTORY INSTRUMENTS AND OTHER LEGISLATION

References are to paragraph numbers.

Statutory Instruments

European Legislation

Overseas Legislation

TABLE OF ABBREVIATIONS

AGM   annual general meeting

CCS   commonhold community statement

CLRA 2002   Commonhold and Leasehold Reform Act 2002

EGM   extraordinary general meeting

IA 1986   Insolvency Act 1986

GLOSSARY

The Commonhold and Leasehold Reform Act 2002 (CLRA 2002), Part 1, contains a large number of defined expressions, and a helpful index to where most of these definitions are found is contained in s 70. Additionally, the meaning of standard expressions in both property and company law is adopted. Thus, a defined word or expression in the Law of Property Act 1925, the Companies Act 1985 or the Land Registration Act 2002 applies to the use of the same word or expression in the CLRA 2002 unless the contrary intention appears: s 69(3).

EXPRESSIONS DEFINED IN THE STATUTE

The following are the more important expressions listed in the index in s 70 and specifically defined in the CLRA 2002. (Those relating to limited use areas and to termination statements are not indexed in s 70.) The meanings set out are not exact reproductions of the (sometimes convoluted) statutory wording. The section numbers referred to indicate where the definition can be located in the CLRA 2002.

Common parts: Every part of the commonhold which is not for the time being shown as a commonhold unit by the commonhold community statement: s 25(1). The title to the common parts is vested in the commonhold association.

Commonhold: This is specifically defined as the land specified in the memorandum of association in relation to which a commonhold association exercises functions: s 1(1). More generally, it is the name for the special form of freehold land ownership for a community of freeholders known as unit-holders bound together as members of a commonhold association and collectively subject to the provisions of the commonhold community statement.

Commonhold association: A private company limited by guarantee (with £1 as the guarantee) with a specific object of exercising the functions of a commonhold association in relation to defined land: s 34.

Commonhold community statement (CCS): The document in a prescribed form delimiting by plans and description the extent of the commonhold units and making provision for the rights and duties of the commonhold association and the unit-holders: s 31.

Commonhold land: This exists once the freehold estate is registered as a freehold estate in commonhold land – which necessarily requires the same land to be specified in the memorandum of a commonhold association and to be regulated by a commonhold community statement. The commonhold association documentation and the commonhold community statement must filed at the time of the application to register: s 1(1).

Commonhold unit: One of at least two parcels of land within the commonhold, the extent of which are defined by the commonhold community statement: s 11.

Developer: Technically, any person who makes an application to register a freehold estate in commonhold land: s 58(1). But the term only has relevance when such a person carries on development business and prepares a commonhold community statement conferring development rights on the developer.

Development business: Those matters listed in CLRA 2002, Sch 4.

Insolvent commonhold association: One in relation to which a winding-up petition has been presented: s 50(2).

Joint unit-holder: One of two or more (maximum four) individuals who are together registered, or entitled to be registered, as proprietors of the freehold estate in a commonhold unit: s 13.

Limited use area: Any part of the common parts which has restrictions on its use in the commonhold community statement: s 25(2). The restrictions may either be to the classes of person who may use it or the kind of use to which it may be put.

Register: The register of title kept under s 1 of the Land Registration Act 2002: s 67(1). Commonhold will not be implemented until the Land Registration Act 2002 is in force and the Land Registration Act 1925 repealed.

The Registrar: The Chief Land Registrar.

Residential commonhold unit: A commonhold unit is residential if provision is made in the commonhold community statement requiring it to be used only for residential purposes, or for residential and other incidental purposes: s 17(5).

Succession order: An order under s 51 in relation to an insolvent commonhold association for a successor commonhold association to be registered as proprietor of the freehold estate in the common parts.

Successor commonhold association: An association formed to take over the common parts and responsibilities of an insolvent commonhold association and having the same land specified as the insolvent association: s 50. The object of both companies will be to exercise functions in relation to the same land.

Termination application: An application to the Registrar that all the land in relation to which a particular commonhold association exercises functions should cease to be commonhold land.

Termination statement and termination-statement resolution: A termination statement sets out the commonhold association's proposals for the transfer of the commonhold land and how the assets are to be distributed: s 47(1); the termination-statement resolution is a resolution approving the terms: s 43(2).

Transfer of unit: A transfer of the freehold estate in a unit, whether or not for consideration, whether or not subject to any reservation or other terms and whether or not by operation of law: s 15(1).

Transitional period: The period between registration of the freehold estate in the land as a freehold estate in commonhold land and the time when a person other than the applicant for registration becomes entitled to be registered as proprietor of one or more but not all of the commonhold units: s 8(1). A transitional period occurs only when there is an application to register without unit-holders.

Unit-holder: A person entitled to be registered as the proprietor of the freehold estate in a commonhold unit.

Winding-up resolution: A resolution for voluntary winding up within s 84 of the Insolvency Act 1986.

EXPRESSIONS APPEARING IN HEADNOTES OF THE STATUTE

A number of important expressions are used in the headnotes to sections of the statute, but are not separately or specifically defined and so are not statutory terms.

Commonhold assessment (headnote to s 38): The commonhold service charge, being the amount of estimated income required to be raised annually from unit-holders to meet the expenses of the association.

Registration with unit-holders (headnote to s 9): An application to register a commonhold which includes a list of the commonhold units and gives, in relation to each unit, the prescribed details of the proposed initial unit-holder or joint unit-holders. As a result, the commonhold is 'activated' immediately.

Registration without unit-holders (headnote to s 7): An application to register a commonhold where the applicant remains the sole registered proprietor of the all commonhold land during the transitional period. There is therefore no 'activation' of the commonhold at registration.

Reserve fund (headnote to s 39): Funds to finance the repair and maintenance either of the common parts or of the commonhold units and required by regulations to be included in a commonhold community statement.

ACTIVATION OF A COMMONHOLD

This is not a statutory term at all. It is used in this book to describe the moment when a commonhold community comes into being. This occurs when the commonhold association is entitled to be registered as proprietor of the freehold estate in the common parts (and the Registrar has a duty to make such registration without an application being made), the rights and duties conferred and imposed by the commonhold community statement come into force and any lease of the whole or part of the commonhold land is extinguished. Where there is a registration with unit-holders, activation occurs on registration: s 9(3). Where there is a registration without unit-holders, activation occurs at the end of the transitional period, that is, whenever after registration a person other than the applicant becomes entitled to be registered as proprietor of the freehold estate in one or more, but not all, of the commonhold units: s 7(3).

CHAPTER 1

COMMONHOLD – THE RATIONALE

A NEW FLEXIBLE FORM OF LANDHOLDING

A community of freehold owners

1.1 The Commonhold and Leasehold Reform Act 2002,[1] Part 1 introduces into English law a new form of landholding, which has been given the name commonhold. Although commonhold as such is unique to the law of England and Wales (both as to its nomenclature and in the way it is embedded into our registered title system), it is, as a wider concept, already well known and established in other common-law jurisdictions. In North America, the land tenure is known as condominium. In Australia, New Zealand and Singapore, it is established as strata or unit title within the Torrens system of registration. The commonhold system now enacted for England and Wales builds on the experience gained in those other jurisdictions.[2]

1.2 Commonhold was chosen to describe the new system of land ownership as a recognition that the emphasis is on co-operation between a community of freehold owners living within a defined area.[3] The core feature is two or more freehold owners each having title to properties (known as units) within the land registered as an estate in commonhold land. Each such freeholder has title to a commonhold unit and therefore has exclusive permanent ownership of a specified piece of property. Co-operation between the freeholders within the commonhold community is necessary because of the interdependence of obligations, the use of shared facilities or the existence of some common interest. Co-operation is achieved through the medium of the commonhold association, the corporate body in which the shared facilities of the commonhold, known as the common parts, are vested. A commonhold will require each of the unit-holders to make monetary contributions by way of commonhold assessment to maintenance of shared facilities and to the welfare of the community as a whole and will impose obligations on them.

---

[1] Abbreviated in this book to CLRA 2002.

[2] The relationship of commonhold to strata title and condominiums is more fully discussed at **1.33**.

[3] *Commonhold, Freehold Flats*, Report of a Working Group, 'the Aldridge Report', Cm 179, July 1987, para 1.9.

The need for flexibility

1.3 Commonhold is a vital and necessary new form of land holding for the twenty-first century. Modern society demands flexible legal solutions in a wide variety of situations where citizens need to live and work in close proximity. The high cost, and scarce availability, of land for businesses and homes demand that many facilities should be shared. The most obvious shared facility is a common roof. Blocks of residential flats, whether purpose built or converted from larger older buildings, have become not only homes of necessity for those at the lower economic end of the scale but also homes of choice for those on higher incomes wishing to live in the heart of our big cities. However, it is not just the sharing of the external structure of buildings with common access ways and services that makes this new land tenure desirable. Increasingly, there is demand for what may be termed 'up market' communal residential facilities such as shared swimming pools and leisure and sports facilities. Living in a community can also offer opportunities for increased personal security through the employment of security personnel or systems, the benefit of which residents or businesses can share. The establishment of condominiums and strata title schemes in overseas jurisdictions has provided considerable flexibility in a large variety of development situations. Commonhold will provide the same flexibility and choice in England and Wales.[4]

1.4 Commonhold is often perceived primarily as the long-term solution to the difficult and still outstanding problem of long residential leases – it is certainly viewed in that way by many occupants and residents in such leasehold schemes. However, the opportunities offered by the new system of commonhold go far beyond providing merely a new form of landholding for residential flat occupiers.[5] In other jurisdictions, condominiums and strata title provide an alternative and sometimes the preferred and even usual method of providing traditional homes. They also permit the setting up of mixed developments involving both residential and commercial elements; and give an alternative form of tenure to the well-established commercial lease at market rent in exclusively commercial developments where there are shared facilities.

The essential features of a commonhold

1.5 An estate in commonhold land consists of a group of freehold titles and each such title is a commonhold unit with one additional title for the common parts. The unit may be residential (a flat or a house) or commercial such as a

---

[4] But there are aspects of the legislation that unnecessarily limit that flexibility, at least for the present – see, eg, **2.17**, **4.20** and Chapter 13.

[5] Sadly, there is little prospect of many conversions of existing leasehold developments to commonhold as the legislation now stands; at present, commonhold is principally designed for new developments. See further **13.14**.

shop, office or light industrial unit. Each of the freehold owners, known as unit-holders, will also automatically be a member of a corporate body known as the commonhold association. This association will have title to the freehold of the common parts and communal facilities and have the responsibility for their management and upkeep. Membership of the association is limited to unit-holders, who therefore have control of it. They may delegate management to agents on their behalf and the directors of the association need not be members of the commonhold. Through the commonhold association, all communal facilities of the commonhold, the common parts and the external structures of multi-occupied buildings are maintained for the benefit of all. The association must be a company limited by guarantee, but special rules will apply to it. All commonhold associations will have a statutory form of memorandum and articles so that each association will have the same basic structure and rules. A separately incorporated commonhold association is required for each commonhold.

1.6   A purchaser or other transferee of a commonhold unit will succeed to the vendor's membership in the commonhold association. Each unit-holder for the time being has a stake in the communal property[6] and a voice in ensuring that the communal facilities are properly maintained and utilised for the benefit of each and all of the unit-holders entitled to use them.

1.7   The other essential feature of every commonhold will be a local law applicable to the community in question. These rules and regulations are embodied in what is termed the commonhold community statement (CCS). This foundation document makes provision for the rights and duties of the association and the unit-holders, contains the definitive plan for all of the units and sets out the management rules. It is the central governing document of the development.[7]

THE INADEQUACIES OF THE EXISTING LAW

1.8   This new system of land ownership has been made essential by the current inadequacies of the law which fails to meet the needs of communal living and working.

---

[6]   This interest cannot be properly described as a share, since the commonhold association will always be a company limited by guarantee and not limited by shares. But a lay unit-holder may sensibly describe the interest held in the communal property as a share in it.

[7]   The description given by Lord Irvine of Lairg LC in the Second Reading debate on 5 July 2001, HL Deb, Vol 626, col 886.

Positive obligations cannot be enforced in freehold land

1.9   Until the implementation of commonhold,[8] there are only two choices to a developer of any property. A title to a property either has to be freehold, the closest form to absolute ownership within English law, or the development has to be way of leasehold – namely, giving the purchaser of the property a right of occupancy for a fixed period of time.

1.10   There has never been any theoretical difficulty with the sale of a freehold of part of a building. There is a long history of 'flying freehold' in certain well-known cases[9] and both the common law and the Law of Property Act 1925 specifically permit the horizontal division of land into freehold units.[10] But communal ownership of property by combining a series of freehold titles into a mutually interdependent association has never been a practical solution. The essence of any interdependent and communal development scheme is the existence of a series of cross-obligations between the owners for the repair and maintenance of property and for the payment of money by way of service charge to support those communal obligations. Sadly, English property law was never able to develop so as to permit these obligations to be enforceable by and against the freehold owners for the time being of the property concerned.

1.11   The principle taught to generations of law students and quaintly known as the rule that a burden of a positive covenant does not run with the land proved to be inconvenient and ill-suited to the needs of twentieth-century life. It was established in the case of *Austerberry v Oldham Corporation*[11] in the nineteenth century. At the time there was very little demand for the development of a property by way of communal freehold ownership. The case itself involved an attempt to escape liability imposed by statute. It had nothing whatever to do with the situation of enforcement of mutually beneficial obligations between adjoining land-owners. Indeed, in earlier cases where there was a degree of mutual interdependence, the courts had permitted positive obligations to be enforced by the owners of the land for the time being,[12] but the decision in *Austerberry* prevented any further development of that idea. The result was that the horizontal division of freehold land became impractical. Although there is a well-known list of possible devices which seek to circumvent the problem in freehold land, none of them is satisfactory.[13]

---

8   Implementation of the Act will be at least 12 months from date of Royal Assent (as announced by Baroness Scotland of Asthal: HL Deb, Vol 633, col 691 (15 April 2002)) and will also be after the Land Registration Act 2002 is brought into force to avoid having to draft land registration rules for commonhold twice. See **1.35**.

9   The most well known are in Lincoln's Inn. See also Tolson (1950) 14 Conv (NS) 350.

10   Law of Property Act 1925, s 205(1)(ix).

11   (1885) 29 Ch D 750.

12   *Morland v Cook* (1868) LR 6 Eq 252; *Cooke v Chilcott* (1876) 3 Ch D 694.

13   See Megarry and Wade, *Law of Real Property* (6th edn, 2000) paras 16-019–16-026.

1.12   The common law thereby prevented sensible arrangements between adjoining freehold owners. In *Rhone v Stephens*,[14] an agreement for the repair of part of a shared roof of a property, once in common ownership but now divided between two separate freehold owners, was rendered unenforceable. One owner could ignore the obligation entered into by the predecessor in title relating to repair of the roof. Similarly, when an estate of houses was subject to the right to buy legislation, a subsequent purchaser of a property on the estate did not have to pay a modest maintenance charge which went towards the upkeep of the estate's communal facilities.[15] Ultimately, it is the link between the inability to enforce positive covenants and obtaining mortgage funding that is the key problem. Older flying freehold properties[16] and even more modern freehold flats do exist,[17] but if modern lending institutions will not lend on standard terms on such freehold titles, then leasehold is the only realistic alternative.[18]

1.13   *Rhone v Stephens* was a challenge to the basis of the *Austerberry* principle. It was argued that it should be overturned judicially. The House of Lords made it clear that it was no longer possible for a remedy to be established by judicial intervention and specifically stated that it was up to Parliament to change the law. Commonhold is the legislative answer. It enables freehold units to exist with enforceable mutually interdependent obligations[19] and is, in part at least, a response to the inadequacies of the common law.[20] It is a fresh solution and opportunity for the twenty-first century.

Shared ownership is not possible

1.14   In some overseas jurisdictions (where the common law is similar to that in England and Wales and the rule limiting the enforcement of positive obligations is the same), it has nevertheless been possible to use freehold ownership where there are shared facilities and mutual obligations by having a shared ownership of the common facilities. This is achieved either by having the whole property held by owners in common[21] or by having the common

---

[14]   [1994] 2 AC 310.

[15]   *Thamesmead Town v Allotey* [1998] 3 EGLR 97.

[16]   It is not uncommon to come across older cottages or terraced homes, some part of which lies above or below the adjoining property.

[17]   Particularly, apparently, in Brighton and Scarborough.

[18]   The open market value of freehold flats is often lower than leasehold because of the difficulties.

[19]   There will be wider opportunities in standard freehold land if and when covenants are replaced by land obligations. But the recommendations made in 1984 in Law Commission Report No 127 have been abandoned.

[20]   It is only a partial response because obligations can only be enforced within each commonhold. A wider solution, such as that offered by proposals for land obligations, awaits fresh examination by the Law Commission.

[21]   As happened in Australia prior to the advent of strata title and, more recently, in New Zealand, when a former single residential section is sub-divided for multiple occupancy.

parts held by the individual freehold owners of the properties as owners in common.[22] Thus, each of the freeholders having a shared interest in the common parts takes an equal share in the title to the common parts and, through the shared ownership, can enforce obligations against fellow co-owners.

1.15   In England and Wales this device, which is not ideal in any event, has not been possible. The Law of Property Act 1925 abolished the legal tenancy in common[23] and further limited the number of persons who could hold title to land to four, holding as trustees.[24] A shared ownership of common parts has not been a practical proposition in England and Wales.

The limitations of leasehold

1.16   The consequence of this situation is that developers have been forced, like it or not, to use the device of the lease. Covenants within leases can be enforced, not only between the original parties to the lease, but also between successors in title who become landlord and tenant under that lease. The drafting of such covenants gives the ability to enforce obligations and therefore the ability to secure finance from property lenders for the purchase of leasehold homes and businesses.

1.17   Contrary to some of the wilder and more extreme statements,[25] leasehold as a tenure and form of land holding is very valuable and has a number of important functions which will continue long after commonhold is widely established. The essence of a lease is a division of ownership and occupation of the land for a fixed period of time. Wherever there is such a genuine division, leasehold tenure is rightly valued. The classic example is whenever a tenant pays a market rent for the occupation of the property in question. Whether that tenant is a periodic residential tenant paying an occupation rent or a commercial tenant paying the open market rent for a 10- or 25-year full repairing and insurance lease, the principle is the same. The landlord has made an investment in freehold property and is obtaining an income return by granting a lease or tenancy for a period of time. Both parties to the lease benefit. Neither the residential tenant nor the commercial leaseholder has to find the capital value of the land. Instead, the open market rent can be met from a regular income while the landlord gets a fair return on a capital investment. Whenever such a genuine division of ownership is desired, leases and tenancies will continue to be the preferred form of tenure.

---

[22]   As is the case with blocks of leasehold flats in Hong Kong.

[23]   Law of Property Act 1925, s 34(1).

[24]   Trustee Act 1925, s 34(2).

[25]   Leaseholds have been described as 'feudal', most notably in the document 'An End to Feudalism', even though the leasehold estate was always outside feudal tenures – hence its survival. Calls for the 'abolition' of leases by residential long leaseholders conveniently ignore the fact that leases are vital in the commercial sector and very useful in a wide variety of other situations.

1.18 The problems arise because leaseholds have been pressed into service as the only practical solution where that division of ownership and occupation is not necessarily appropriate. This is particularly true with long residential leaseholds of flats in England and Wales. The purchaser of the flat is paying a large capital sum[26] and regards the property as a home and an asset which is 'owned'. The use of the lease is primarily a device to ensure that the positive covenants and obligations can be enforced. In the most ideal schemes, which are found in many parts of the country, the form of the conveyancing results in no real division of ownership and occupation. The freehold of the residential block of flats, rather than being held by an outside landlord, is commonly vested in a corporate body, often a company limited by shares or by guarantee. Such a company is usually incorporated as a residents' management company. All the flat leaseholders become shareholders in, or members of, the company and, through that membership, have a say with their co-owners in the enforcement of the landlord's obligations and in maintenance of the common parts. Usually, such leaseholders enjoy the benefit of long leases, commonly for a term of 999 years, at a very nominal rent or for no rental payment at all.[27] Such schemes look remarkably similar to the essence of the new commonhold regime. However, even in such situations difficulties and problems can arise.

1.19 The scheme is only as good as the lease and documentation that has been provided by the developer of the unit. It is now quite common to find that the documentation, often drafted some decades ago, contains inadequate covenants that do not satisfy the most demanding of would-be mortgagees. Each development may have slightly different provisions and covenants so that any purchaser or transferee of a flat must carefully scrutinise the lease in question before proceeding. There is no guarantee that each lease in the same development is identical. The corporate body is subject to all the usual company law rules, particularly relating to the filing of returns and annual accounts. It is sadly all too common for such residents' management companies to fail to file the necessary accounts and returns and to find they have been struck off the register.

1.20 In London and the South East of England and areas of high housing demand, it is much less usual for lease terms to be as long as 999 years. It is also much less usual for the freehold to be transferred by the developer of the property into the hands of the tenants, through the medium of a tenants' management company, once the development is complete. Instead, the freehold reversion to the residential flats may be retained by the developer

---

[26] Technically, as a premium for the grant or assignment of the lease. The sum paid as a premium will be very close to the value of the freehold interest (assuming it was available). The rent reserved is often a nominal sum and always very low in comparison to the open market rent for the property.

[27] If they do not have such very long terms, the control of the freehold enables them to grant fresh leases to each leaseholder.

(which may be a long established landed estate or a charity). In other situations, the developer will sell the freehold reversion on to an individual (or company) who is in the business of investing in freehold property reversions. The legitimate interests of such lessors are often in conflict with those of the leaseholders. This gives rise to what is known (by leaseholders at least) as the tyranny of the outside landlord.

1.21 It does not matter that the vast majority of such outside landlords are highly reputable companies and organisations, which may run their freehold reversions and perform their leasehold obligations to a very high standard. More pertinent is the fact that the occupiers of the residential long leases resent the fact that decision-making and control of the repair and upkeep of their homes rests with a person (or corporate body) who has a very different set of interests in the building from those of the residents themselves. It can be argued (perhaps with some force) that decision-making by a reputable estate landlord may result in a more harmonious community than when the decisions have to be agreed upon by a large group of leaseholders. But that argument is lost. The abuses perpetrated by the few have fatally undermined confidence in the use of long leaseholds as a method of providing homes.

1.22 A further problem is that in many such instances the term of the lease, rather than being 999 years (or other period effectively equivalent to freehold), is more frequently a term of 125 years, 99 years or even for lesser terms.[28] This gives rise to the problem of the wasting asset. As the term of the years remaining on the lease reduces, so the value of the capital asset falls accordingly and it declines very rapidly once the position is reached where it is difficult to obtain mortgage finance to purchase the lease in question.

1.23 The final and linked issue is that of management and control. The landlord of a block of long residential leasehold properties has – or had, prior to legislation culminating in the CLRA 2002[29] – control over repair, maintenance and insurance of the property. Although the exact powers would be determined by the terms of the lease, it is likely that those terms would have been primarily fixed with the interests of the lessor in mind. Moreover, the ability to decide whether – and on what terms – fresh leases were to be granted to existing leaseholders similarly lay with the freeholder. The scope for abuse of the dominant position was considerable.

1.24 The response of the legislature to practices which have disadvantaged leaseholders has been to provide a host of measures in various pieces of legislation to combat the perceived abuses. A considerable number of rights

---

[28] The shorter lease term, combined with the fact that the rent may be more than a nominal figure, gives the freehold reversion the value that is attractive to investors.

[29] The new statutory right to manage, contained in Part 2, Chapter 1, of the CLRA 2002, is exercisable by qualifying tenants who do not need to pay or prove fault or inadequate management to take over control of their affairs. The result may be that freehold reversions to residential long leases become very unattractive to property investors.

have been granted to residential long leaseholders over a period of time. Thus, long leaseholders may now have all or any of the following significant rights:

(1) the right of first refusal to purchase the freehold reversion when the freehold of the blocks is sold;[30]

(2) the right to be consulted and to challenge the reasonableness of the service charges with the requirement of more than one estimate;[31]

(3) the right to appoint a manager on certain grounds where there have been breaches of management obligations;[32]

(4) the right to apply for the grant of a new lease at a peppercorn rent for an additional 90 years;[33]

(5) the right to collective enfranchisement, namely the ability for the leaseholders to get together and buy out the freeholder;[34]

(6) the right to a management audit of accounts;[35] and

(7) the ability to apply to vary the terms of the leases when they are inadequate.[36]

1.25 This list is not exhaustive. More changes have been made in the CLRA 2002, extending and adding to many of these rights.[37] The result is a highly complex system with jurisdiction split between the High Court, county courts and leasehold valuation tribunals.

1.26 It is undoubtedly the case that long leaseholders, dissatisfied with the problems they have experienced, have been highly vociferous in pressing for the introduction of commonhold. They want their capital investment to be the purchase of a freehold property, rather than being forced into purchasing a flat with a leasehold title. They particularly resent the practice of leasehold titles of up to 99 years with an outside landlord. Commonhold also meets the aspiration of management control, particularly in relation to insurance and repair. The persistent risk of forfeiture of a lease and inadequate lease terms will not be concerns for a commonholder.

---

[30] Landlord and Tenant Act 1987, Part I (as amended)

[31] Landlord and Tenant Act 1985, ss 18–30.

[32] Landlord and Tenant Act 1987, Part II. Part III permits compulsory acquisition of the landlord's interest in limited circumstances.

[33] Leasehold Reform, Housing and Urban Development Act 1993, Part I, Chapter II.

[34] Ibid, Chapter I.

[35] Ibid, Chapter V.

[36] Landlord and Tenant Act 1987, Part IV.

[37] The rights to collective enfranchisement of flats, to a new lease of a flat and to the enfranchisement of houses are all extended and simplified in Part 2 of the CLRA 2002. There are extensive amendments of the provisions relating to service charges and a range of safeguards and amendments are introduced, particularly in relation to forfeiture.

Leases are no longer the answer for provision of homes for purchase

1.27   The CLRA 2002 marks, it is submitted, the end of the long lease as a suitable mechanism for the development of homes for sale. However suitable leases may be for provision of homes for rent, there is now no compelling reason why it must be adopted when flats are sold rather than rented and good reasons why it should not be used.[38] Commonhold now provides the mechanism by which developments of flats and homes with shared facilities can be sold with freehold title. Although it will remain possible for homes to be sold by way of long leases, there is really no longer an incentive for anyone – developer or a property company – to maintain an investment interest in the freehold reversion once a new development is complete. The new right to manage,[39] also introduced by the CLRA 2002, will permit the leaseholders to take over the management of any new leasehold development at any time. An individual leaseholder has the right to a new lease and the rent of any extended lease will be no more than a peppercorn. A group of leaseholders can immediately get together to collectively enfranchise and secure the freehold.[40] There is therefore every reason why new developments of residential properties for sale should now be either by the normal freehold route if there are no shared facilities or by commonhold where there are shared facilities and mutual obligations and a community is being created. Only in cases where there is a reason that commonhold is disadvantageous or will not operate effectively will leasehold remain a sensible choice.

THE BASICS OF COMMONHOLD

1.28   Before turning to a detailed analysis of the legislation, it may be helpful if the main principles of the new freehold estate in commonhold land are outlined by way of a sketch of the structure of Part 1 of the CLRA 2002.

1.29   A commonhold is a freehold community.[41] Within the boundaries of that community of separate freeholders, the commonhold is divided into freehold units (at least two), each unit being held by a freehold registered proprietor.[42] The remainder of the commonhold constitutes the common

---

[38]   Whether commonhold becomes the preferred mode for new developments will be a matter for the market to decide. For a comparison of the merits of commonhold when compared with long leases, see Chapter 13.

[39]   CLRA 2002, Part 2, Chapter 1.

[40]   The qualifying conditions for the grant of a new lease and for a collective enfranchisement have been simplified by the CLRA 2002. It is now very difficult, if not impossible, for a landlord to prevent long leaseholders exercising these rights.

[41]   A freehold estate in commonhold land (CLRA 2002, s 1) is initially a single title, but it will be divided up into a community of freehold titles consisting of a title for each unit and the common parts, vested in the commonhold association, all subject to the CCS. The division will occur immediately on registration where the registration incorporates existing unit-holders.

[42]   See CLRA 2002, ss 11–24.

parts,[43] which are vested in the commonhold association. This association is a private company limited by guarantee and its only members are the freehold registered proprietors of the units within the community.[44]

1.30 This community is bound together by a 'local law' drafted when the community was established and based on standard basic provisions, the key provisions of which will be identical in each commonhold. This local law is known as the commonhold community statement (CCS).[45] The closest analogy in the current law is perhaps the standard draft lease designed for a multi-tenanted residential or commercial building. At present, that standard draft lease is the template for separate documentation for each leasehold unit. By way of contrast, the CCS is a single document, on the registered title, that contains the fundamental rules of the community. The exact extent of each unit will be delineated by precise plans[46] attached to the CCS; the remaining area of the commonhold constitutes the common parts. By definition, having one document will ensure that the same rights and obligations apply to each unit-holder and that those rights and duties affect a new unit-holder in the same way as they did the former one.[47]

1.31 Unlike a leasehold community, the members are always in control of their own destiny. Within the statutory limits, they can change the provisions of the CCS, updating it and moulding it to meet changing circumstances. The community is controlled by its members (through the medium of the commonhold association in general meeting). The directors of the association may either be members, elected from their own number, or they may be professionals or other outsiders appointed by the members to run the community on behalf of the association. Whether the directors are members or professionals, they will have an overriding duty to manage the common parts on behalf of the unit-holders and to ensure that their rights as freehold owners are fully observed.[48]

1.32 A freehold estate in commonhold land is created out of a standard freehold registered with absolute title. It arises by a form of second registration with the onus on the promoter of the estate in commonhold land

---

[43] See CLRA 2002, ss 25–30. Section 25(1) defines common parts as every part of the commonhold which is not for the time being a commonhold unit in accordance with the CCS.

[44] CLRA 2002, s 34 and Sch 3. The only other members, to begin with, are the original subscribers and (if desired) the developer.

[45] See CLRA 2002, ss 31–33.

[46] The plans attached to the CCS will be the basis for the Land Registry titles for each unit and the division of the units from the common parts – see CLRA 2002, s 11(2) and (3).

[47] CLRA 2002, s 16(1). In other words, *Austerberry v Oldham Corporation* cannot apply to these freehold units.

[48] CLRA 2002, s 35 imposes on the directors a duty to exercise their powers so as to permit or facilitate, so far as possible, the exercise by each unit-holder of his rights and his enjoyment of the freehold estate in the unit.

to provide the completed documentation at registration.[49] There are two separate routes after registration, one designed for new developments[50] and the other for conversions from existing titles where there are already existing unit-holders.[51] In each case, the site of the commonhold will normally be 'legally cleared' of pre-existing mortgages or leases, either by the holders of such interests consenting or, in the cases of some leases, by way of extinguishment of those leases and payment of compensation.[52] The 'special statutory attributes'[53] of this new form of freehold title thereafter ensure that owning a commonhold unit will be quite unlike a standard freehold. A purchaser buys into a community, its culture, regulations, duties and benefits. The community and the commonhold title will persist until steps are taken to restore the underlying standard freehold title. Thus, the CLRA 2002 provides that there may be a voluntary liquidation of the commonhold association.[54] A majority of the unit-holders (at least 80%) must agree termination provisions (for example, division of proceeds of sale). Upon such dissolution, the commonhold association takes over the all units and becomes registered with a standard freehold title. In other words, the commonhold can collapse back into standard freehold if the unit-holders wish, for example, to sell the property for redevelopment.

1.33 Commonhold is a distinct name, but the concept is derivative. New South Wales established strata title in Australia and there is now over 40 years of experience in Australian jurisdictions.[55] In very simple terms, the strata title schemes[56] are founded on definitive registered plans with extensive statutory rights, statutory regulation of management and a high degree of standardisation.[57] The first attempts to draft commonhold drew heavily on this antipodean experience.[58] The CLRA 2002, however, also reflects North

---

[49]   The local regulatory law, namely the CCS, which includes the definitive plans, and the memorandum and articles of the commonhold association are the two key documents but there must also be all necessary consents – see CLRA 2002, ss 2–5.

[50]   CLRA 2002, s 7.

[51]   Ibid, s 9.

[52]   Ibid, ss 3 and 10. But see **3.46** and **3.52**.

[53]   This phrase was used in the Commonhold Bill drafted in 1996 and is not in the CLRA 2002. But it sums up the nature of commonhold.

[54]   CLRA 2002, ss 43–49. There are also compulsory winding-up provisions where the commonhold association is insolvent.

[55]   The legislation began with the Conveyancing (Strata Titles) Act 1961 (NSW). There are currently three NSW statutes regulating strata schemes, of which the more important are the Strata Schemes (Freehold Development) Act 1973 (NSW) and the Strata Schemes (Management) Act 1996 (NSW). See also the Body Corporate and Community Management Act 1997 (Queensland).

[56]   Particularly those found in the states of Australia, and in New Zealand and Singapore.

[57]   The Singapore Land Titles (Strata) Act is a good example of this model.

[58]   See especially *Commonhold – a consultation paper (with draft Bill annexed)*, Cm 1345, 1990. The introduction (para 1.2) states that the aim was for a high degree of standardisation, with 'virtually all' obligations laid down by statute or statutory instrument, 'reducing to an absolute minimum the need for conveyancers to consider the rules applicable to essentially similar arrangements'.

American experience with condominiums. There is a long history in the United States of community associations. Although every state now has a condominium property act, the legal foundation for a community association remains the governing documentation drafted for the site in question. Commonhold, as set out in the CLRA 2002, has been designed to operate within our own registered land system and, as such, still has features in common with strata title. But the insistence upon each scheme having a separately drafted CCS, with the common parts vested in a specially incorporated commonhold association, retains the traditional English reliance on documents and has more in common with the structure of a condominium.[59]

IMPLEMENTATION AND EXTENT OF THE NEW LAW

Implementation

1.34   As is now usual with complex legislation, the CLRA 2002 will be brought into force in stages by statutory instrument. In the case of Part 1, relating to commonhold, the appropriate authority is the Lord Chancellor.[60]

1.35   The commonhold legislation will not be brought into force until the autumn of 2003 at the earliest. The Minister announced to Parliament that implementation would be at least 12 months after Royal Assent, which occurred on 1 May 2002.[61] There are many regulations to be drafted and published prior to the legislation being brought into force.[62] Moreover, it has been made clear that implementation of commonhold cannot take place until the Land Registration Act 2002 is first brought into force.[63] The target date for that is understood to be October 2003. A possible date for commonhold to be implemented is therefore 1 January 2004.

---

[59] However, in the Queensland system, each strata title now has a 'community management statement' which has some similarity to the CCS. This has been described as a 'management tool', which tells the story about the scheme and defines its nature (Janes, *The BCCA for everybody* (Herd and Janes, Brisbane, 1998)).

[60] CLRA 2002, s 181(1) and (4)(a).

[61] Baroness Scotland of Asthal: HL Deb, Vol 633, col 691 (15 April 2002).

[62] Some 26 sections of Part 1 of the CLRA 2002 refer to regulations or rules on about 18 major topics.

[63] The CLRA 2002 assumes that the Land Registration Act 2002 is in force (see, for example, s 65). In any event, it would make little sense to amend or add to the Land Registration Rules 1925 only for them to be replaced by a new set of Land Registration Rules under the Land Registration Act 2002.

Extent

1.36   Commonhold extends to England and Wales only.[64] Since Part 1 relating to commonhold binds the Crown,[65] it will be possible for the Crown as freeholder to apply to register an estate in commonhold.[66]

---

[64]   CLRA 2002, s 182.

[65]   Ibid, s 63.

[66]   This is made feasible by the Land Registration Act 2002, s 79(1), which permits Her Majesty to grant a fee simple absolute in possession to Herself. An estate in demesne, or allodial, land must (ibid, s 79(2) and (3)) be registered at the Land Registry.

CHAPTER 2

THE NATURE OF COMMONHOLD

KEY FEATURES

Embedded in the land registration system

2.1 The Commonhold and Leasehold Reform Act 2002,[1] Part 1 is the culmination of a 15-year process, during which time commonhold proposals have been through many different forms. Although overseas experience has been influential,[2] the final form of commonhold is very firmly designed for the registered land system of England and Wales. Commonhold is embedded within the land registration process. It can only be created out of registered freehold land and involves a further or second registration of land that already has freehold registered title.[3] A freehold estate in the land is registered as commonhold if the Registrar is satisfied that the requirements for registration have been met. Commonhold land is created at that point.[4]

Basis of commonhold is documentary

2.2 A freehold estate in commonhold land rests on the basis of certain key statutory documentary requirements. These requirements are designed to ensure that the fundamental features of the planned community are in place and that all persons with substantial interests in the property[5] concerned consent to the establishment of that community. The developer or promoter

---

[1] Abbreviated in this book to CLRA 2002.

[2] The early commonhold proposals took the experience of strata title systems in New South Wales as their starting point, while the final form of the CLRA 2002 now also reflects lessons from North American practice with condominium systems – see **1.33**.

[3] Or is, at least, entitled to be so registered.

[4] The centrality of the concept of commonhold as a community is emphasised by the CLRA 2002 providing that a reference to commonhold in Part 1 is a reference to the land in relation to which the commonhold association exercises functions: s 1(2).

[5] The policy of the CLRA 2002 is to require consents of freeholders, long leaseholders and chargees and mortgagees – see s 2 and the discussion at **3.28–3.38**. The registered proprietor of a leasehold estate in the whole or part of the land granted for a term of more than 21 years will have to consent but the consent – formally, at least – of tenants holding terms for less than 21 years is not required.

of a commonhold who is a registered proprietor of the land will be entitled to the commonhold registration if:[6]

– a commonhold association has been established satisfying the statutory requirements and the land in question is specified as the land in relation to which that commonhold association is to exercise its functions;
– a commonhold community statement (CCS) exists to regulate the relationship between the commonhold association and the unit-holders who will be purchasing into the community development; and
– all necessary consents are forthcoming and accompany the application.

2.3 There is therefore no particular requirement as to the nature of the physical structures or of the buildings within the commonhold. These can be entirely separate units, or linked units, or contained within a single structure. The architect thus has complete freedom as to the nature and form of the construction on the commonhold land. There is no list of physical attributes that a commonhold development has to satisfy.[7] The commonhold can be as large as is desired (although the present form of the legislation has limitations that suggest that very large commonholds will not be usual) or it may be as small as two commonhold units with limited shared facilities; however, three or more units is desirable.[8] It is the registered title that is the conclusive identification that a particular parcel of land is a freehold estate in commonhold land.

Freehold estate
2.4 A core feature of a commonhold is that it is a form of freehold estate. Commonhold could have been enacted as a distinct third legal estate in land alongside freehold and leasehold.[9] There was some recent debate on this issue,[10] but to create a distinct and third estate in land would have necessitated major revision to the basic principles of the Law of Property Act 1925 and no doubt many hundreds of consequential changes to other legislation. It was therefore more convenient to create commonhold as a sub-species of freehold. Moreover, it was also politically more expedient to provide for commonhold as a form of freehold title and thereby avoid any suggestion that

---

[6] CLRA 2002, ss 1 and 3 and Sch 1, considered more fully below.

[7] 'One cannot identify a structure as part of a commonhold community by merely looking at it' – Rosenberry, *Commonhold Ownership in England and Wales*, Blundell Memorial Lecture, 2001.

[8] A relatively common example would be the conversion of a house into two flats. Whether commonhold is entirely suited for just two flats is questionable because if the two members disagree, since they each have one vote each in the association, there will be an impasse.

[9] See, for example, Clarke (1995) 58 MLR 486 at 496.

[10] In the consultation process prior to the issue of the Draft Bill and Consultation Paper in August 2000 (Cm 4843). Although defining commonhold as a species of freehold, the August 2000 consultation did seek views as to a limited right to have commonholds based on leasehold land.

commonhold was in any sense an inferior estate. However, commonhold is so completely distinct from a normal freehold title that it is better seen as a distinct form of land holding, if not strictly a separate estate in land. Title to a commonhold unit will probably (and, it is submitted, rightly) be regarded as quite different from a standard freehold title.

THE STATUTORY DEFINITION

Essential features

Registered freehold with absolute title

2.5　A commonhold is created out of land that has been previously registered as freehold with absolute title at HM Land Registry.[11] Such land becomes commonhold if the freehold estate is further registered as a freehold estate in commonhold land.[12] The creation of a commonhold community is fundamentally based on this subsequent registration process.

A commonhold association exercising functions

2.6　The second requirement is that, at the time of such registration, the land registered as commonhold is specified in the memorandum of association of a commonhold association as the land in relation to which the association is to exercise functions.[13] Therefore, there must exist, at the time of the commonhold registration, a private company limited by guarantee, registered at Companies House with the statutory standard memorandum and articles of association relevant to a commonhold association and formed with specific land in mind. The land to be registered as commonhold must be the land specified in the memorandum of association as the land in relation to which the commonhold association is to exercise functions.[14] The commonhold land and its commonhold association are indissolubly linked. Indeed, throughout Part 1 of the CLRA 2002, a reference to commonhold is a reference to the land in relation to which the commonhold association exercises its functions (and not, as might be expected, to the land registered as commonhold).[15]

---

[11]　Or, at least, land in respect of which application for registration with absolute title has been made and the Registrar is satisfied that the applicant is entitled to be so registered: CLRA 2002, s 2(3)(b).

[12]　Ibid, s 1(1)(a).

[13]　Ibid, s 1(1)(b). A commonhold association has the meaning given to it by s 34: s 1(3).

[14]　The necessity for the commonhold association to specify the land over which it will exercise its functions will mean that it is unlikely that it will be possible to purchase an 'off-the-shelf' ready-formed association. See further **4.6**.

[15]　CLRA 2002, s 1(2). By defining commonhold in this way, later changes to the number of units, or boundaries of units, are accommodated more easily.

A commonhold community statement

2.7 The third essential feature of the statutory definition is that at the time of registration there must be a CCS, which is the governing document or local law of the community. This will be drafted and prepared in advance of registration by or on behalf of the person seeking registration of a commonhold.[16] It will be based on the statutory template[17] and many of its provisions will be found in all commonholds. It must set out in the prescribed form the rights and duties both of the commonhold association and of the unit-holders who will be contemporaneously registered as first unit-holders or in due course purchase into the commonhold community.[18] Although the CCS may not come into force at the time of registration, and will not be in force until one or more persons[19] is entitled to be registered as a unit-holder,[20] it must be in a completed form at registration. It must be ready to come into force at the due time.

Prior preparation and planning

2.8 A commonhold can only be established where there is a clear vision of the community to be established. Careful planning and preparation is required, not only of the necessary documentation, but also in respect of finance, planning permission and related matters. Even where the commonhold is being established out of an existing development, with commonhold units replacing long leaseholds in a block of flats, the actual creation of the commonhold by registration will be the culmination of a long preparatory process. This process will include the formation of the commonhold association and the completion of the CCS. The registration of the commonhold will be one of the last steps in the process and certainly not the start of it.

Unregistered land

2.9 Although it is not possible to establish a commonhold on unregistered title, there should be no insuperable difficulty in developing a commonhold where all or part of the title has yet to be registered. In the case of new development, it will be almost inevitable that the land will be subject to first registration of title, for example, when a developer purchases the land. On completion of this initial purchase transaction, the land will usually be

---

[16] This will be the registered freeholder (or freeholders if the application related to more than one title). The person who makes the application is also the developer as defined.

[17] At the time of writing, there is only a draft form available.

[18] CLRA 2002, s 1(1)(c). Where there is a registration with existing unit-holders under s 9, the rights and duties come into force immediately on registration – see **3.21**.

[19] Other than the applicant for registration of the commonhold.

[20] See CLRA 2002, ss 7(3)(c) and 9(3)(e).

registered first with a normal freehold title.[21] A subsequent registration process will establish the commonhold in due course.

2.10 Potential title difficulties might be encountered in relation to an existing leasehold development where all the leaseholders wish to join and convert their titles and property into a commonhold community.[22] If they have recently purchased the freehold reversion to their long leases, perhaps by a collective enfranchisement, then they will have no difficulty (in title terms) in establishing the commonhold. The freehold reversion will (by definition) either be registered at the time of purchase or be subject to first registration on completion of the enfranchisement. It is, however, possible that the leaseholders purchased the freehold reversion many years ago, perhaps at a time when compulsory registration of title did not apply. In such a case, the freehold may remain vested in a management company with unregistered title. Indeed, the existing long leases, or some of them, may not yet have registered title. In such cases, it will be necessary to apply for first registration of the freehold reversion or satisfy the Registrar (as a preliminary step) that it is vested in a person who is entitled to be registered with freehold absolute title.[23] It should not, however, be necessary for any of the long leases that remain unregistered to go through this process, provided all the leaseholders consent to the establishment of the commonhold.[24] This is because the parties will agree that the all the long leases, whether registered or not, will be replaced by the freehold of a commonhold unit on the establishment of the commonhold.[25]

Two or more parcels of land

2.11 It is perfectly possible to establish a multi-site commonhold on two or more parcels or areas of land which are not contiguous.[26] All that is required is that the memorandum and articles of association of the commonhold association specify that the association is to exercise the commonhold functions over all such land and that one CCS applies to all the land in

---

[21] It will be possible merely to satisfy the Registrar of entitlement to be so registered and proceed immediately with the application to register the freehold estate in commonhold land under CLRA 2002, s 2 – see **3.8**. But in the case of a recent purchase of an unregistered development site, for example, preparation for the commonhold application may take longer than the 2-month period allowed to complete a compulsory registration of title under Land Registration Act 2002, s 6(4).

[22] Such an application will be made under CLRA 2002, s 9. For a fuller discussion of the difficulties facing those who wish to convert from an existing leasehold development to commonhold, see **13.14**.

[23] CLRA 2002, s 2(3)(b).

[24] For consents required to secure registration, see CLRA 2002, s 3(1) and the discussion of consents needed by lessees at **3.41–3.42** where the position of holders of leases granted for more than 21 years but with unregistered titles is examined.

[25] Any lease of all or part of the commonhold land is extinguished on activation of the commonhold in any event – see CLRA 2002, ss 7(3)(d) and 9(3)(f), and **3.64–3.71**.

[26] CLRA 2002, s 57(1).

question.[27] Thus, a single commonhold can be created from (for example) two parcels of land on opposite sides of a road or, indeed, where there are other properties separating the two parcels of lands concerned. The practical issue will be whether the two or more areas of land concerned are so close, or otherwise so united, as to share in a community development with mutual obligations and shared facilities. If there are no substantial shared facilities or mutual obligations between the two or more parcels, then it is unlikely that a single commonhold will be appropriate. In such cases, it will be preferable to establish two distinct commonholds.

Two or more titles

2.12   An application can be made jointly by two or more persons, each of whom is the registered freeholder of part of the land to which the application relates.[28]

LAND WHICH CANNOT BE COMMONHOLD

2.13   There are a limited number of situations where land cannot be registered as commonhold.[29] Two of these are significant. There cannot be a commonhold based on leasehold title and there can be no 'flying commonholds'.

Leasehold land

2.14   Since, by definition, commonhold can only be registered on the basis of a freehold estate it follows that there can be no possibility of a commonhold being established on land with leasehold title – even if the leasehold estate is due to survive for many more years than the expected life of the commonhold.[30] A freehold estate cannot be carved out of a leasehold estate. This absolute exclusion of the possibility of the commonhold being established on leasehold land follows naturally from the twin requirements of defining commonhold as a sub-species of freehold and requiring a further registration of an existing registered freehold title. Yet it is by no means obvious that there would not be a market for commonhold communities established on leasehold land. Certainly, in New South Wales, legislation subsequent to the original establishment of strata title now permits strata title

---

[27]   CLRA 2002, s 57(2).

[28]   Ibid, s 57(3). Regulations can make provision to this effect.

[29]   Ibid, s 4 and Sch 2.

[30]   A leaseholder will always have to secure the freehold estate before an application can be made, either by purchase by private treaty, by exercising a statutory right to enfranchisement or (rarely) by enlargement under Law of Property Act 1925, s 153 if the statutory requirements are met.

communities based on leasehold title.[31] One area where there might have been such demand within England and Wales is in relation to developments that now occur through the medium of leases of bare sites with ground rents. Certainly, in the commercial context, there may have been room for commercial commonholds established on titles with 125-year long leases with ground rents payable to a local authority which wished to retain long-term development control.[32] Such a possibility is precluded by the legislation in its present form.

Flying freeholds – the grounded rule

No 'flying commonholds'

2.15 A 'flying freehold' cannot be the basis of a commonhold community. There can be no 'flying commonholds'. The CLRA 2002 provides that an application for the registration of a commonhold cannot be made wholly or partly in relation to the land that is above ground level ('raised land'), unless all the land between the ground and the raised land is the subject of the same application.[33] This provision gives expression to what is known as the 'grounded rule'. This rule was proposed by the Aldridge Committee in 1987[34] and has been a feature of all the subsequent commonhold proposals, as well as the CLRA 2002.

2.16 The grounded rule suggests that each separate commonhold be a logical and viable property, no part of which is above or below other property held either on separate freehold or leasehold titles or even belonging to another commonhold. This allows management to be simplified and ensures that whenever a commonhold is terminated the property can be redeveloped or rebuilt. But perhaps the most cogent reason for excluding, at least for the time being, flying commonholds is that the present law, as we have seen, does not permit the mutual enforcement of freehold covenants between adjoining freehold owners.[35] The CLRA 2002 only provides a solution to the

---

[31] The Strata Schemes (Leasehold Development Act) 1996 (NSW). But it seems that only about 15 strata title developments have so far been registered by virtue of this New South Wales statute.

[32] In the consultation, *Commonhold and Leasehold Reform, Draft Bill and Consultation Paper*, Cm 4843, August 2000, p 85, para 2.3, views were requested on the possibility of commercial commonholds based on leasehold tenure.

[33] CLRA 2002, Sch 2, para 1(1). The use of the phrase 'raised land', defined as land above ground level, suggests that an estate in commonhold land can exist where there are subterranean freehold titles below ground level, perhaps in a basement, which are not part of the commonhold. Such a situation is unlikely to be attractive, nor are there obvious commercial advantages to suggest it is likely to be done deliberately. This interpretation of the definition led to concerns that the foundations of a building containing a commonhold community could be excluded from it – see HC Deb, Vol 381, col 648, Report Stage (11 March 2002). See further **3.12**.

[34] The Aldridge Report, op cit, p 1, n 3, paras 3.12–3.15.

[35] See **1.9–1.13**. So it would not be possible to guarantee enforceability of obligations between the commonhold and the freehold titles which would be below it.

enforcement of mutual obligations within the commonhold itself and between unit-holders for the time being.

The need for greater flexibility

2.17   In the long term it is likely that the legislation will be amended to permit greater flexibility. Indeed, repeated attempts were made during the passage of the legislation to modify the absolute rule against flying commonholds.[36] The aim was to allow a residential commonhold to exist in a building where there was retail or office use below the residential units. It was claimed, with some force, that if this were not possible then a harmonious blending of residential homes with offices and shops would be severely compromised.[37] Such an amendment would have required express statutory provision to allow the necessary positive covenants between the commonhold and the business use on the lower floors to be enforced by and against successors in title. The Government was, understandably, not prepared to countenance piecemeal reform in this way. Notwithstanding earlier reports proposing reform of the law of covenants and the introduction of a new property interest, the land obligation,[38] the Law Commission is reconsidering the matter afresh. Until its views are available, it is not considered desirable or sensible to permit positive covenants to be enforceable by successors in title by virtue of a specific statutory provision in this particular situation alone. Flying commonholds therefore have to wait for a wider reform of the law.[39] Until then, it will not be possible to have either one commonhold on top of another or a commonhold sitting on top of a commercial or other development on the ground or lower floors of a building.

2.18   This restriction against flying commonholds (which, at least at present, is necessary) is likely to constitute a significant hindrance to the development of commonholds in existing or newly developed mixed-use buildings. A commonhold existing separately from and above the retail or office use in the same building is not possible, nor is a single multi-use commonhold an attractive proposition. The legislation provides for a commonhold with only a single class of unit-holder, with each unit-holder having an equal say in the

---

[36]   See, for example, the debates in Grand Committee on the 2000 Bill, 20 February 2001, col 18 and during the Lords parliamentary stages on the 2002 Act – see HL Deb, Vol 627, col 498 (Committee Stage), Vol 628, col 469 (Report). Concern was also expressed in the Commons, at Second Reading (HC Deb, Vol 377, cols 444–445), but the Government rejected suggested amendments (Standing Committee D, First Sitting, 15 January 2001, cols 23–25).

[37]   Lord Kingsland, HL Deb, Vol 627, col 498; Mr William Cash, Standing Committee D, col 24.

[38]   Law Commission Report No 127, 1984.

[39]   Lord McIntoish of Haringay, Vol 627, col 500. The Law Commission Report 1984, which recommended the introduction of land obligations, will not now be enacted. The Minister indicated that the Law Commission's new recommendations, when available, will be the subject of wide consultation and be treated very seriously. But there is, clearly, no commitment to legislate at present. See also Standing Committee D, cols 24–25 (Mr Michael Wills).

management of the commonhold association.[40] Although this may be an acceptable limitation for commonholds which are purely residential, in the case of mixed-use commonholds it is likely to produce considerable difficulties.

2.19 Overseas experience suggests that commonholds are particularly desired in cities. Especially in city centre locations, the most economical form of land use often requires the ground, and sometimes some of the lower floors, of a multi-storey development to be dedicated to commercial and retail purposes, while the upper floors are dedicated to residential use. There are two sensible statutory solutions to deal with mixed-use commonholds and developments of this nature. The first is to permit one commonhold on top of another so that there is a commonhold community for all the retail occupiers on the ground and lower floors and a separate commonhold community for the upper residential floors. This is not possible under the current legislation, as we have seen, because of the inability to have two commonholds, one 'flying' above the other, with mutually enforceable obligations. The alternative approach is to have a single commonhold divided into master and subsidiary sections. A master commonhold would consist of the whole structure, including the retail and commercial uses together, and regulate the shared obligations in relation to the building such as the external repairing and maintenance obligations and any access that both the commercial and residential sections share. There would then be subsidiary commonholds within the master association, one relating to the commercial element with its commercial concerns and the other relating to the residential element. During the final consultation prior to the Bill which was introduced in 2000, there was serious discussion whether the legislation should indeed provide for a commonhold to be divided in this way between a master commonhold and subsidiary associations.[41] Such a provision would have assisted in mixed-use developments. Unfortunately, it was decided not to complicate the legislation by making such provision.

2.20 It is possible that, in the future, the legislation may be amended both to permit flying commonholds if land obligations are introduced into the law and also to allow master and subsidiary commonholds. Until then, however, there can be only one single, unified commonhold, which must be constructed to ensure that all the development above ground level is included within the commonhold.

---

[40] See **4.16**.

[41] See *Commonhold and Leasehold Reform, Draft Bill and Consultation Paper*, Cm 4843, August 2000, p 88, para 3.3. Such terms are drawn from condominium experience. But the same approach is found in strata title schemes. It is possible in New South Wales to have a number of strata title schemes in the same building, one for the residential element perhaps on the upper floors, one for any commercial element on the lower floors and one for the retail units on the ground floor – see, for example, Ilkin, *Strata Schemes and Community Schemes Management and the Law* (LBC Information Services, Sydney, 3rd edn, 1998), p 60.

2.21 It should be noted that the grounded rule does not prevent an established commonhold from later extending upwards. Rooftop extensions and roof conversions by a commonhold association will be possible. An application for the addition of land to a commonhold may therefore be made wholly or in part in relation to raised land, if all the land between the ground and the raised land forms part of the commonhold to which the raised land is to be added.[42]

Agricultural land

2.22 An application cannot be made to register land as commonhold if any part of the land is agricultural land. This is defined as agricultural land within the meaning of the Agriculture Act 1947; land comprised in a tenancy of an agricultural holding within the meaning of the Agricultural Holdings Act 1986; or land comprised in a farm business tenancy for the purposes of the Agricultural Tenancies Act 1995.[43] It is unlikely that it would ever be appropriate or desirable to establish a commonhold based on or including such agricultural land, but this provision ensures that it cannot be done.

Contingent freehold titles arising by statute

2.23 These forms of freehold title cannot sensibly be the basis of an application to establish a freehold estate in commonhold land. Contingent freehold titles do not occur very often but there are a number of enactments dating from the nineteenth century which provide that land is to revert to the original grantor on the happening of certain events. It is these forms of contingent title that cannot be the basis of an application for a commonhold.[44]

2.24 An estate is contingent for the purposes of the CLRA 2002 if (and only if) the estate is liable to revert to or vest in a person other than the present registered proprietor on the occurrence or non-occurrence of a particular event and the reverter or vesting must occur by operation of law as a result of one of those enactments.[45]

2.25 The situations covered are land originally conveyed for use as a school;[46] certain land compulsorily purchased;[47] sites conveyed or given for the establishment of certain literary or scientific institutions;[48] and sites

---

[42] CLRA 2002, Sch 2, para 1(2). Such an application would be made in accordance with s 41 – see **10.35–10.43**.

[43] Ibid, Sch 2, para 2.

[44] Ibid, Sch 2, para 3(1).

[45] Ibid, Sch 2, para 3(2) and (3).

[46] Under the School Sites Act 1841.

[47] Under the Land Clauses Acts. By virtue of Interpretation Act 1978, s 5, Sch 1, this expression means the Land Clauses Consolidation Act 1845, Land Clauses Consolidation Acts Amendment Act 1860 and any Acts for the time being in force amending the same.

[48] Under the Literary and Scientific Institutions Act 1854.

originally conveyed or given for established places of worship.[49] In case there are further enactments creating such contingent titles, the CLRA 2002 does provide that regulations can add an enactment to the list or remove one from it.[50] It should be noted that the provisions relating to contingent titles relate solely to those arising by virtue of the listed enactments and not to any contingent title which is made or arises under a conveyance or other transfer of land.[51]

Land which is already commonhold

2.26   Land which is already commonhold land cannot be registered as part of another commonhold.[52] There is no process to enable land which is part of one commonhold, even if part of the common parts, to be transferred from one established commonhold to another.[53]

NO BUILT RULE

2.27   It is worth noting that there is one aspect of earlier Commonhold Bills which is not in any way a requirement in the CLRA 2002. The Aldridge Committee proposed that commonhold legislation should include a rule that all parts of a commonhold must be structurally complete before units were transferred by the promoter to unit owners. This was referred to as the built rule. It was a feature both of the draft Bill published in 1990 and of the Bill that briefly made an appearance in Parliament in December 1996.[54] The rule was designed as a measure of consumer protection to ensure that a purchaser of a commonhold unit could rely on all the common facilities being in place and being structurally complete at the time of the purchase. A further advantage claimed for it was that such a rule would ensure that the total number of units was fixed at the time of the first sale, so that the financial viability of a commonhold could be ensured. There would be no risk of fewer units than originally planned being built and therefore no risk that the percentage charge applicable to the first unit sold might be increased. It was also thought that there would be greater accuracy in conveyancing because the

---

[49]   Under the Places of Worship Sites Act 1873.

[50]   CLRA 2002, Sch 2, para 3(4).

[51]   Any such titles are unlikely to qualify for registration with absolute title anyway.

[52]   CLRA 2002, s 2(1)(b).

[53]   It is necessary for the commonhold association of the established commonhold to agree to remove the land from the commonhold, amend the CCS and the articles and memorandum of association and register the change before the land removed can be included in an application to register a separate commonhold.

[54]   Clauses 9(1)(b) and 19 of the 1990 draft Bill; cl 3(3)(a) of the 1996 Bill.

physical boundaries of all the units would be clearly ascertainable and the plan of the development could be checked against the existing boundaries.[55]

2.28 However, the built rule as so envisaged would have caused considerable difficulties. It meant that there had to be complex phasing proposals for larger developments, without which developers simply would not have been able to operate. If they were unable to have the financial assistance of a stream of sales as the development progressed, there is no doubt that developers would have continued to construct properties for sale by way of leasehold rather than commonhold. In other words, the abandonment of the built rule as originally envisaged ensures that there can be proper financing of commonhold developments by the developers and promoters of the schemes. The CLRA 2002 is also more flexible in the rights it gives to developers, which may include the ability to change details of units as the development proceeds.[56]

2.29 The omission of a built rule may have been influenced by the fact that it probably would not have provided significant consumer protection in any event. Thus, in New South Wales, where a desirable development is planned and on the drawing board and demand for the planned strata title units is high, schemes have been developed (notwithstanding legislative restrictions) whereby units can be sold 'off the plan'. Such sales are also common in England and Wales for current developments by way of long leases, so it is important that commonhold units can be pre-sold and completions take place even if some of the facilities do not yet exist.

2.30 Some of the consumer protection which it was envisaged would be provided by the built rule is now given instead through the CCS. This comes into force on the sale of the first unit. Although the physical structure and facilities of the completed commonhold do not have to be complete at the time of the sale of the first unit, a CCS must conform to certain minimum requirements. It will have to set out the total number of units envisaged, provide the definitive plan of the development and the boundaries of the proposed units, and state the percentage share that each unit has to contribute to the commonhold assessment.[57] The omission of the built rule as such from the CLRA 2002 should not be a concern and would appear to make it more likely that commonhold will be embraced by developers.

---

[55] The CLRA 2002 ensures that this aspect continues since the CCS must delineate the boundaries of the units with precision and by reference to a plan at first registration – see s 11(2)(b) and (3)(a). But developers may reserve the right to alter these – see s 58 and Sch 4, para 6, and **8.18**.

[56] See the discussion of developer's rights at **8.9–8.12**.

[57] This is, however, subject to developer's rights – see Chapter 8.

CHAPTER 3

CREATING AND REGISTERING A COMMONHOLD

GENERAL PRINCIPLES

3.1   The registration procedure for a commonhold is set out in ss 2 to 10 of the CLRA 2002, with further details contained in Sch 1. Further regulations are to be made, some of which at the time of writing exist in draft form.[1] There are three key general principles that will assist in understanding the registration process.

Registration and 'activation'

3.2   The first principle is that a distinction is made between completion of the registration of the commonhold and what may be termed 'activation' of the commonhold community. The registration of a freehold estate as an estate in commonhold land will occur as soon as the Registrar is satisfied with the documentation submitted.[2] Activation of the commonhold community occurs only when a person other than the applicant for first registration of the commonhold is entitled to be registered as the proprietor of the freehold estate in one or more, but not all, of the commonhold units.[3] Until that time, the commonhold association is not separately registered as the proprietor of the freehold estate of the common parts, nor does the commonhold community statement (CCS) come into force. This distinction is consistent with the concept of commonhold. While there is a single person entitled to the freehold of the whole of the land comprising the proposed commonhold community, it remains essentially a normal freehold title. The registration of a freehold estate in commonhold land indicates an intention to establish the commonhold by future sale or transfer of one or more of the units. However, until there is a community, which of necessity means two or more unit owners, there can be no functioning commonhold.

---

[1]   The registration procedure will be governed by Rules made by virtue of CLRA 2002, s 65, made by statutory instrument in the same manner as land registration rules under the Land Registration Act 2002.

[2]   CLRA 2002, s 2.

[3]   Ibid, ss 7(3) and 9(1). Note that 'activation' is not a term or concept used in the legislation.

3.3 Activation of the commonhold may occur at the moment of first registration. This will be the case whenever there is an application subject to s 9 and there are existing unit-holders on first registration.[4] In all other cases, the commonhold will be activated on the sale of the first unit.[5]

Distinction between registration with unit-holders and registration where there are no existing unit-holders

3.4 The delay in activation of the commonhold marks out the principal distinction between a registration process by a developer (where the units will be newly built or created by conversion of an existing building), who registers the commonhold before the sale of the first unit,[6] and a registration of an existing development with commonhold title where there is already occupation by the intended unit-holders.[7] The form, style and procedural requirements of the registration process will also involve rather different emphases where a developer is setting up a commonhold afresh. Where new buildings are planned, or the development involves conversions from existing buildings, the consent requirements (to establish the commonhold) will usually be relatively easy to satisfy.[8] Decisions about the detailed contents, and drafting, of the CCS will be under the control of the developer alone. By way of contrast, where many people are interested in the creation of the commonhold by virtue of prior occupation of the would-be units, it will be far more complex and difficult to obtain the consent of all the persons who must be involved. The necessary agreement for the establishment of the commonhold association will have to be obtained from a group of persons. Together, they will also have to resolve or agree (with their advisers) the exact content of the memorandum and articles of association of the commonhold association and settle the details of the CCS.

Registration marks the end of the process of creation

3.5 The final general practical principle to be borne in mind is that registration of a commonhold will not mark the commencement of the process of the creation of the commonhold community, but will be the

---

[4] CLRA 2002, s 9, which has a head note 'Registration with unit-holders'. The application must request that the section apply and submit a list of the proposed unit-holders: s 9(2). If the request under s 9 is inadvertently omitted, activation will still occur as soon as a person is entitled to be registered as the proprietor of a unit, which may occur contemporaneously.

[5] This will normally be the actual date of completion of the sale since activation occurs as soon as a person other that the applicant for registration of the commonhold becomes *entitled* to be registered as proprietor of one of the commonhold units: CLRA 2002, s 7(3).

[6] It is suggested that developers could choose to delay registration until the sale of the first unit and use the s 9 route instead – see **3.6**.

[7] Usually, they will be leaseholders seeking to convert to commonhold.

[8] Commonly, a developer in such a situation will have bought out all the persons with property interests in the site of the intended commonhold. But see the discussion at **3.46**.

culmination of a complex and often quite lengthy preparatory process. The community must be fully planned, the commonhold association established and duly incorporated and the CCS prepared in its final form before an application for registration can be submitted.[9] These requirements may be shortly stated, but considerable professional effort and expertise will be needed to achieve the desired result.

3.6 Indeed, in practice, it may often be convenient to delay application for registration of the commonhold for as long as possible. In the case of a new development, this will permit last minute minor adjustments to the CCS or to the detailed boundaries or design of the units. Only when the first unit is ready or nearly ready to be sold will it be necessary to submit the commonhold application.[10] In such a case, instead of registration prior to the sale of the first unit, it may be possible for the developer to consider the alternative route. Instead of prior registration subject to CLRA 2002, s 7, he might submit the application to register at the time of the first sale or sales and request that s 9 apply. He would need to include a list of the details of the proposed unit-holders, but this requirement may be met by submitting the names of the purchasers of the first unit or units sold, and the developer (or the developer's nominees) would be listed as proprietor of the unsold units.[11] In the situation where an existing group of leaseholders is seeking to change their titles to commonhold, the application for registration will be made only when every other aspect of the conversion process has been agreed or settled.[12]

APPLICATION FOR REGISTRATION

Application is by the registered proprietor

3.7 An application to register a freehold estate in land as a freehold estate in commonhold land is made by the registered freeholder of the land concerned.[13]

3.8 The registered freeholder must have a freehold estate with absolute title or must have applied for such registration and satisfied the Registrar that he is

---

[9] These are the documents required by CLRA 2002, Sch 1.

[10] Obviously, the land must be registered as commonhold, or the registration process must at least be commenced, before title can be made to transfer the first unit to be sold.

[11] The writer has pointed out this possibility to the Lord Chancellor's Department. It is now likely that regulations will nullify any advantages which might otherwise accrue to a developer who requests s 9 to apply.

[12] This will not only involve agreement on the documentation and the obtaining of consents but also preparation of the conveyancing aspects.

[13] CLRA 2002, s 2(1)(a).

entitled to be so registered.[14] If the land is registered, wholly or partly, with either freehold possessory title or (more unusually) with qualified title it will be necessary, prior to the application to register an estate in commonhold land, to make a successful application to upgrade the freehold to title absolute.[15]

3.9 If the registered proprietor consists of two or more persons holding the land jointly, then for the purposes of the application such joint tenants will be treated as the registered proprietor.[16] Applications will be possible by two or more persons, each of whom is the registered freeholder of part of the land to which the application relates.[17] Such applications will be governed by regulations yet to be made[18] but, taken together, the two or more freeholders must be the registered proprietors of the whole of the land to which the application relates. In cases where a commonhold is intended to be established on land currently owned by two or more persons, it will be a matter of judgement which of two procedures to follow. It may be more convenient to transfer the separate titles into a single title prior to the application for registration of commonhold. This will enable a straightforward application to be made to register the estate as commonhold land. Alternatively, it may be preferable to have a conjoined application made by two or more different proprietors who together comprise the proprietors of the land intended as the basis of the commonhold community.[19]

Land included in the application

Defining the extent

3.10 The extent of the land included in the application will normally be straightforward and not dissimilar to an application to register any freehold land. It will need to be the same as the land specified in the memorandum of association of the commonhold association[20] but more precisely defined as it appears that a postal address may suffice for the description in the memorandum.[21] It may be possible in a straightforward application merely to

---

[14]   CLRA 2002, s 2(3).

[15]   Or, at least, apply for the title to be upgraded and satisfy the Registrar that the applicant is entitled to be registered with absolute title: CLRA 2002, s 2(3)(b).

[16]   There is no specific provision in Part 1 of the CLRA 2002 to this effect, but see Interpretation Act 1978, s 6.

[17]   CLRA 2002, s 57(3). This provision will apply in a case where a group of persons holding freehold flats (as flying freeholds) join together to register a commonhold and convert their flats into commonhold units. Unanimity will be required. A maximum of four persons can be named as registered proprietors of the estate in commonhold land.

[18]   See CLRA 2002, ss 57(4) and 64.

[19]   Such a procedure would permit an easier separation of interests if it is decided not to proceed with the commonhold before the first unit is transferred.

[20]   CLRA 2002, s 1(1)(b).

[21]   See cl 3 of the draft in Appendix 1.

refer to the definition in the CCS and the plans attached to that statement. Regulations are likely to provide that these plans will provide the exact details on which the registration will be based.

3.11 The applicant will need to ensure that there is no part of the land included in the application which may not be commonhold by virtue of the statute.[22] In this respect there are a number of difficulties caused by the exact wording of para 1 of Sch 2 to the CLRA 2002. It reads:

> 'Subject to sub-paragraph (2), an application may not be made under section 2 wholly or partly in relation to land above ground level ("raised land") unless all the land between the ground and the raised land is the subject of the same application.'

The statutory purpose is summarised in the Explanatory Notes issued with the Act:

> 'Paragraph 1 forbids the development of commonhold at first floor level or above unless all the land below it and down to the ground is subject to the same application. This is to avoid the risk which attends "flying freeholds", particularly the problems of enforcing any covenants relating to access and support.'[23]

Land is not separately defined in the CLRA 2002, but the definition in the Law of Property Act 1925 which applies[24] is that 'land' includes land of any tenure, mines and minerals, and buildings and parts of buildings. There are a number of particular situations that could give rise to difficulty.

Basements

3.12 The wording makes it clear that a commonhold need not extend below ground level. An applicant need not therefore be concerned with exclusions for mines and minerals or with any railway tunnels under the land. However, it also seems possible for a basement below ground level to be excluded from the application even if it is an integral part of a single structure erected on the land. The use of the phrase 'raised land', defined as land above ground level, suggests that an estate in commonhold land can exist where there are other subterranean freehold titles below ground level, perhaps in a basement, which are not part of the estate in commonhold land. Such a situation is unlikely to be attractive nor are there obvious commercial advantages to suggest it is likely to be done deliberately. The exclusion of the foundations of a building containing a commonhold community and the vesting of a basement in a

---

[22]   CLRA 2002, s 4 and Sch 2 – see **2.13–2.25**. Moreover, and obviously, a commonhold cannot be established if any part of the land is already commonhold land: s 2(1)(b).

[23]   Explanatory Notes, para 310, p 65.

[24]   Section 205(1)(ix), applied by CLRA 2002, s 69(3).

separate standard freehold title raises exactly the same concerns about enforcement of repairing obligations as those that arise in any flying freehold.[25] Redevelopment could also be compromised.[26]

3.13   It also seems theoretically possible to have a subterranean commonhold with a title separate from the buildings above ground level. The concerns are similar, but from a different perspective. The legal relationship between the commonhold below and the buildings above in any situation where the foundations of the building encompass the basement commonhold will result in ongoing problems when those foundations of the structure need maintenance and repair.

3.14   In either case, difficulties may also arise in deciding what is and is not below ground level. The level may be not be the same at the front of the building as at the back. An artificial ground level may not be the same as that in the natural state of the land. All in all, it is unlikely to be sensible to take advantage of the statutory wording to create a commonhold that excludes basement areas or to seek to register an entirely subterranean commonhold.

Boundaries and overhanging buildings

3.15   The grounded rule means that the boundaries of a commonhold will be delineated at ground level. These will be no more precise than for any other registered title.[27] There appears to be nothing in the statutory wording which will inhibit registration of land as a commonhold when there are overhanging structures from adjoining buildings. Such overhangs, whether balconies, eaves or whatever, will not be raised land for the purposes of para 1(1) of Sch 2 to the CLRA 2002 because the application is not made in respect of it. Standard property rules will apply. Similarly, the fact that the building to which the commonhold application relates has balconies or other overhanging structures should not be a difficulty as there is no land between the projection and the ground.

'Flying freeholds'

3.16   It is quite clear that a commonhold must be grounded, and both the statute and the explanatory wording makes it clear that all the land between the ground and the raised land must be subject to the same application. There can be no 'flying commonholds'. However, not all of a building need be included in the application, a vertical division being always acceptable. So a

---

[25]   For example, if a building needed underpinning, the existence of a freehold title in the basement could cause significant difficulties.

[26]   Concerns that the foundations of a building containing a commonhold community could be excluded from it were raised in Parliament: see *Hansard*, Vol 381, col 648, Report Stage (11 March 2002).

[27]   The general boundaries rule, currently contained in r 278 of the Land Registration Rules 1925, and re-enacted in a different form in Land Registration Act 2002, s 60, will apply.

terraced property, or part of a large house now vertically divided, can become an estate in commonhold land.

3.17 The more difficult issue is whether a flying freehold can be left above a commonhold. For example, in an existing block of freehold flats, the question is whether the freeholders on the ground and some of the lower floors can establish a commonhold, including in their application all the flats between ground level and the top of the commonhold but not necessarily including all the flats in the building. On one reading of para 1 of Sch 2 to the CLRA 2002, this may be done on the basis that all the land between the ground level and the raised land *within the application* is included. It does not matter that there is other raised land above excluded from the application. The problem with this interpretation is that the members of the commonhold will have exactly the same problems with enforcing repairing and maintenance obligations by and against the freeholder above their units as they would have with a freeholder beneath. It is not obvious why a flying commonhold is not permitted but a flying freehold above a commonhold is acceptable. An alternative reading of this paragraph is to stress the words 'wholly or partly'. On this basis, it is not possible to apply to register even part of land above ground level unless all the land between the ground and the raised land above is included.

3.18 In normal circumstances, there will be no difficulty. Even in a large block of existing long leaseholders, the underlying freehold title will include the whole building, and all the land, and the registered titles, will therefore be subject to the one application. If, however, it is possible to exclude upper floors of a building from a commonhold, there is the prospect of a conversion from long leasehold without the consent or participation of every leaseholder – provided the dissident leaseholders who refused to consent to a conversion to commonhold are not on the ground floor (and are, ideally, on the top floor). However, it is doubtful whether it would ever be sensible to create a commonhold while leaving a flying freehold title above.

The better view

3.19 The better view of the wording of para 1 of Sch 2 to the CLRA 2002 is that there cannot be a commonhold application in respect of only some floors of a building. Where only part of a building is to be included, there must be a vertical separation from the rest of the structure. But even if the alternative interpretation is preferred, it will not be practical or sensible to create a commonhold leaving a separate freehold title or titles above.[28]

---

[28] Except, perhaps, where a group of existing owners of flying freehold titles in the same building wish to improve their position by creating a commonhold and cannot secure the consent of the owner of the top flat to participate in the scheme. Even then, the benefits are likely to be marginal.

Two different registration outcomes

3.20 There are two routes to commonhold registration. The documentation required differs only slightly, but the effect of registration is very different. The CLRA 2002 anticipates that 'new build' and redevelopments of existing buildings will be by an application to register an estate in commonhold land which is subject to CLRA 2002, s 7. The application is made by the freeholder, who is also the developer.[29] A developer can include in the CCS important development rights.[30] On such registration, the applicant continues to be registered as the proprietor of the entirety of the freehold estate in commonhold land.[31] There is, at that stage, no community so the CCS does not come into force.[32]

3.21 The alternative route of registration is where CLRA 2002, s 9 applies. This section is appropriate where there is a registration with existing unit-holders (according to the head note to that section). This route is clearly designed for 'conversions' from leaseholds where the long leasehold flats become the commonhold units, all the leaseholders consent and the consenting leaseholders already occupy the flats that are to become the commonhold units. Section 9 will apply only if a statement by the applicant accompanies the application requesting that it should do so. Such a statement must include a list of all the commonhold units giving in relation to each one prescribed details of the proposed initial unit-holders.[33] The consequences are then very different. On registration when s 9 applies, the community is activated immediately.[34] The commonhold association is entitled to be registered as the proprietor of the freehold estate in the common parts, each unit-holder or joint unit-holders are entitled to be registered as proprietor(s) of the freehold estate in the units and the CCS comes into force.

Documentation required – the four 'Cs'

3.22 The CLRA 2002 sets out the required documentation which must accompany the application[35] – the four 'Cs'.

---

[29] The developer is the person who makes the application under CLRA 2002, s 2. This will normally be a single freeholder with absolute title but it may be two or more such freeholders with separate titles who jointly wish to create a commonhold.

[30] By virtue of CLRA 2002, s 58 and Sch 4.

[31] Ibid, s 7(2)(a).

[32] Ibid, s 7(2)(b). There is therefore a transitional period – see **3.53–3.57**.

[33] Ibid, s 9(1)(b) and (2).

[34] Ibid, s 9(3) and see **3.63**.

[35] Ibid, s 2(2) and Sch 1.

1. Commonhold association documents

3.23   The application must include the full documentation relating to the established and registered commonhold association. It must also contain the commonhold association certificate of corporation.[36] If the certificate of corporation has been altered for any reason, the altered certificate of incorporation[37] must also be included. The memorandum and articles of association of the commonhold association completes the documentation required in this respect.[38] Establishment of the commonhold association is covered in Chapter 4.

2. The commonhold community statement

3.24   The commonhold community statement, the foundation of any commonhold community, is the second essential component of the application.[39] Since this document will form part of the registered title,[40] it must be in a final form as any later changes which need to be made will involve a process of formal amendment and alteration of the filed copy.[41] The process of drafting and completing a suitable CCS is discussed in Chapter 5.

3. Consents

3.25   The application must be accompanied by all of the relevant consents that the CLRA 2002 requires.[42] In the simplest of cases, it may be that the only consent required is that of the registered freehold proprietor who is making the application. However, it will be relatively unusual for this to be the case. Since there are a considerable number of significant and diverse issues relating to consent, these are drawn together in **3.28–3.48**.

4. Certificate by the directors

3.26   The final document required in connection with an application is an accompanying certificate[43] given by the directors of the commonhold

---

[36]   Under s 13 of the Companies Act 1985.

[37]   Issued under s 28 of the Companies Act 1985.

[38]   CLRA 2002, Sch 1, paras 2–4.

[39]   Ibid, Sch 1, para 5.

[40]   Ibid, s 5(1)(c).

[41]   Amendment of a CCS will be according to the procedure stated in it and amendments only have effect when registered in accordance with CLRA 2002, s 33. For the exceptional method of amending a statement as a consequence of rights reserved by a developer under s 57 and Sch 4, para 6, see **8.18–8.20**.

[42]   CLRA 2002, Sch 1, para 6. If the consent is not available, then the application can only proceed if there is instead either an order of the court by virtue of s 3(2)(f) dispensing with the requirement of consent or evidence of deemed consent by virtue of s 3(2)(e). In the case of a conditional order dispensing with consent, the order must be accompanied by evidence that the condition has been complied with – Sch 1, para 6(1)(b) and (2).

[43]   Ibid, Sch 1, para 7.

association. In essence, it will state that the documentation is in the correct form. Specifically, it must certify that:

(a)   the memorandum and articles of association submitted with the application comply with the regulations and requirements relating to the establishment of commonhold associations;

(b)   the CCS satisfies the requirement of the statute;

(c)   the application and the submitted documentation meet the requirements of Sch 2 to the CLRA 2002 (ie that none of the land is not permitted to become commonhold land);

(d)   the commonhold association has not traded;[44] and

(e)   the association has not incurred any liability which has not been discharged.[45]

3.27   It is unlikely that such a certificate will be offered by any directors who merely acted as nominees when the commonhold association was first formed. It will be better to ensure, therefore, when the commonhold association is set up, that the first directors are persons who are sufficiently involved with the establishment of the commonhold to be willing and able to give the necessary certificate. Alternatively, following formation of the commonhold association, directors must be appointed who can give the necessary certification on the application.[46]

ISSUES RELATING TO CONSENTS TO REGISTRATION

The statutory requirements

3.28   The consents of the following persons, where they exist in any particular case, are required.[47]

(a) *The registered proprietor of the freehold estate in the whole or part of the land*[48]

3.29   Since, by definition, any person having a freehold estate in the land will be making the application for registration of the commonhold, there should be no difficulty in obtaining this consent. However, the amendment of this

---

[44]   This requirement would appear to prevent an existing residents' management company from becoming a commonhold association.

[45]   All the costs relating to the incorporation of the association must therefore be discharged by the developer or applicant for registration.

[46]   There is a fuller discussion of the issues relating to the formation of the commonhold association in Chapter 4, see **4.6**.

[47]   CLRA 2002, s 3.

[48]   Ibid, s 3(1)(a).

subsection in Parliament[49] does emphasise that a specific consent in the prescribed form must accompany the application even though the application is by the same person. Even where there are multiple freeholders involved, as might be the case where all the proprietors of freehold flats in one block join together to change their interests to commonhold, each such freeholder will need both to be party to the application and to complete a consent form.

(b) *The registered proprietor of a leasehold estate in a whole or part of the land granted for a term of more than 21 years*[50]

3.30 Remarkably, it is not the consent of every person who is a leaseholder that is required but only consents of registered proprietors of leases granted for a term of more than 21 years. The period of 21 years was chosen specifically as the period that currently renders a lease subject to registration at the Land Registry.[51] Under this head, therefore, although consents may be required of registered proprietors of leases granted for more than 21 years but which have less than 21 years left to run, consents of persons who hold leases granted for less than 21 years or any unregistered leasehold interests (even if for terms of more than 21 years) are not required. It was a specific policy decision not to require consents of registered proprietors of leases granted for terms of more than 7 years even though leases for such terms are to become subject to registration of title.[52]

(c) *The registered proprietor of a charge over the whole or any part of the land*[53]

3.31 It will probably be common for the freehold land to be subject to a registered charge. A developer will almost certainly offer the land as security to assist in financing the development of a new commonhold. Where the application is being made by persons interested in an existing development who wish to convert from a long leasehold status, there may be no person as a registered proprietor of a charge over the freehold reversion. However, it will be very common in such cases for there to be registered proprietors of charges over the long leasehold units. In all such cases, the registered proprietor of each charge over all, or part, of the land concerned will need to consent to the application. There is no provision in the CLRA 2002, such as that found in the provisions relating to the grant of a new, extended, lease,[54] for any automatic transfer of charges from a long leasehold unit to

---

[49] Which had the effect of separating consents by freeholders and consents by registered leaseholders – see HL Deb, Vol 628, col 907 (Third Reading).

[50] CLRA 2002, s 3(1)(b)

[51] HL Deb, Vol 628, col 907.

[52] By virtue of Land Registration Act 2002, s 4(1)(c).

[53] CLRA 2002, s 3(1)(c).

[54] See Leasehold Reform, Housing and Urban Development Act 1993, s 58(4).

commonhold units within the development. Not only must fresh mortgages and charges be prepared for units in such circumstances, but also the formal consent of the existing chargees or mortgagees of the long leases is needed when application for the commonhold is made.

(d) Prescribed persons

3.32 Provision is made within the CLRA 2002 for consents to be required of any other class of person.[55] No regulations have been made at the time of writing, but there are two categories of interest, at least, which may be prescribed by regulation by virtue of this subsection.

3.33 First, consideration is being given to whether consent should be required of the beneficiaries of notices or cautions which are on the register at the time the application for a registration of a commonhold takes place.[56] Until a late amendment, the specific consent was to be required from any person who at the time of application was registered as a cautioner in respect of the whole or part of the land.[57] However, the Land Registration Act 2002 was enacted prior to the CLRA 2002[58] and the opportunity was taken to amend the latter in the light of the changes to the land registration process. Cautions against dealings will no longer be possible when the Land Registration Act 2002 is in force; the only cautions thereafter will be existing entries and cautions against first registration.[59] Third party interests requiring protection will be entered on the register by a notice. If it is thought that requiring consents of those entitled to the benefits of notices and cautions will assist in the resolution of title disputes before any application for registration, then such consents are likely to be prescribed. However, in practice, any cautions or notices that do exist on the title may well have to be resolved in any event and the caution cleared from the title before the application to register is proceeded with, whether or not consents are needed. It will depend on the nature of the notice or caution whether the consent of the cautioner, if forthcoming, is sufficient to make a commonhold application a realistic proposition or whether it is necessary to negotiate removal of the entry.

---

[55] CLRA 2002, s 3(1)(d).

[56] See the comments of the Minister, Mr Michael Wills, at Report Stage in the Commons – HC Deb, Vol 381, col 671 (11 March 2002). Notices or cautions might relate to a variety of interests, including estate contracts, options and matrimonial homes rights.

[57] This was the original cl 3(1)(d) of the Bill but was removed by Government amendment at Report Stage.

[58] It is almost certain that commonhold will not be implemented until the Land Registration Act 2002 is in force. This will ensure that it is not necessary to amend the Land Registration Rules 1925 and then promptly redraft new rules for commonhold in the light of the Land Registration Act 2002.

[59] The right to lodge a caution against first registration (ss 15–22 of the Land Registration Act 2002) is restricted and is not available to a person who is able to apply for registration of title – see s 15(3) of that Act.

3.34 Secondly, it is to be hoped that the consents of long leaseholders of leases granted for more than 21 years but which still have unregistered title will be prescribed. The consent provision only refers to 'the registered proprietor of a leasehold estate' and would not therefore appear to include lessees where their leases remain with unregistered title.[60] It would seem sensible to anticipate that lessees holding terms of leases granted for more than 21 years but which have not yet been subject to first registration of title would be prescribed as consents which must be forthcoming.[61] However, correspondence with the Commonhold Bill Team[62] suggests this is not currently planned. After consultation with the Land Registry, it was felt that the difficulties for the Registry in ascertaining where there are unregistered leases ruled out a requirement of consent from such owners. This stance may have to change. There is no reason why the consents of any unregistered leaseholder whose interest appears and is noted on the freehold title, and of any mortgagee of such a lease, should not be required.[63] The problems which might arise if the consents of known but unregistered long lessees are not prescribed are considered later.[64]

Consents which are not required

3.35 Consents are not required from the holders of leasehold estates granted for terms of less than 21 years, nor from the holders of an unregistered lease or charge. Two other omissions are worthy of comment.

(a) Certain legal interests

3.36 When introduced into Parliament, the 2000 Commonhold and Leasehold Reform Bill[65] contained a further requirement that the 'registered proprietor of any interest in whole or part of the land' would need to consent to registration. This was a curiously drafted provision since interests in land do not have a registered proprietor. In any event, it would have been very awkward to obtain the consent of all persons who had such legal interests in

---

[60] Although a question about this issue was raised in the House of Commons, it was not answered by the Minister. The question was asked by Mr Llwyd at Second Reading – HC Deb, Vol 377, col 471 (8 January 2002).

[61] The problem of unregistered leases granted for terms of more than 21 years will rapidly diminish as the measures to prescribe compulsory registration of title and encourage voluntary registration take effect.

[62] Letters to the author from the Lord Chancellor's Department, 16 March 2002 and 19 June 2002.

[63] Confining consent to those leasehold interests appearing on the freehold title would solve the problem in most cases but absolve the Land Registry from having to look further. The consenting unregistered leaseholder could be required to submit the title deeds (as if for first registration) but, rather than receive title to the leasehold estate, title to a commonhold unit would, as with all the other registered long leaseholders, be given in return.

[64] See the discussion of problems with consents at **3.41**.

[65] Ie the precursor to the CLRA 2002. This Bill was lost when the General Election of 2001 was called.

the land.[66] Fortunately, this provision was removed in the parliamentary proceedings on the 2000 Bill and was dropped from the text of the CLRA 2002 from the outset.

3.37   The consequence is that, although there are provisions relating to leases and registered charges, the persons benefiting from other legal interests – namely easements, profits and rentcharges – do not need to consent to the establishment of an estate in commonhold land. In this respect, commonhold is no different from any other freehold estate. Thus, any easement existing at the time of registration will continue to bind the land and must be accommodated within the commonhold development in the usual way.

(b) Overriding interests

3.38   It should be noted that the persons holding overriding interests over the land which is the subject of the commonhold application do not have to consent to a registration. Since, however, these are overriding interests, they will bind the commonhold land – except where the CLRA 2002 provides otherwise.[67] It is therefore incumbent upon the applicant for registration of a commonhold to make careful enquires and assessments of the position, particularly in relation to persons in actual occupation of the land. Some overriding interests, such as legal easements as to drainage and so forth, may or may not interfere with the planned commonhold development. Others, however, such as an option to purchase held by a lessee in occupation, would have to be dealt with prior to proceeding.

Form and effect of consents

3.39   Before the CLRA 2002 comes into force, regulations may – and certainly will – be introduced to make provision about consents.[68] These regulations may make provision prescribing the form of consent and the effect and duration of the consent, which may include the ability to bind successors – an important feature for promoters of the commonhold.[69] They may also provide for the withdrawal of consent (including provision to prevent withdrawal in specified circumstances) and there is power to provide that consent given for the purpose of one application is to have effect for the purposes of another application.[70] This provision will assist where an application for commonhold has to be resubmitted for any reason.

---

[66]   It would have been very difficult, for example, to get consent of every person with the benefit of an easement over the land.

[67]   Thus, if the overriding interest is an unregistered lease, it will be extinguished on activation of the commonhold – see **3.65**.

[68]   CLRA 2002, s 3(2).

[69]   Ibid, s 3(2)(a) and (b).

[70]   Ibid, s 3(2)(c) and (d).

3.40   Regulations may also make provision for consent to be deemed to have been given in specified circumstances and enable application to be made to a court to dispense with the requirement of consent.[71] On the face of the statute, these words seem wide enough to permit the regulations to allow deemed consent, or confer jurisdiction to dispense with consent in a wide variety of circumstances. It was pointed out in parliamentary debates that this could, effectively, override the inherent principle of unanimity for the establishment of a commonhold.[72] However, the Minister responded by asserting that the intention was to limit the dispensing power to situations where obtaining consent was impossible.[73] The articulated policy is that where consent is required but refused, a commonhold cannot be established. Consequently, regulations are not likely to modify that stated objective and permit the dispensing power to override objections in any way. Nevertheless, the CLRA 2002 gives no guidance as to when it would be appropriate to deem consent, nor as to the circumstances in which it would be proper for a court to be given power to dispense with consent. There are merely very wide powers for an order dispensing with consent to be absolute or conditional and for the court to make any such other provision as it thinks appropriate.[74]

Some problems with leases and consents

(a) Unregistered long leases

3.41   The failure to specify that consent should be given from all lessees of terms granted for more than 21 years is regrettable. There will be a category of unregistered residential leases granted for long terms at low rents, commonly 99 or 999 years. Such leases may have been granted at a time when the area in which they are situated was not, at the time of the grant, in an area of compulsory registration of title. There may have been no subsequent event to trigger first registration of title to such leases prior to the application for registration of the commonhold. It is to be hoped that consent of such lessees becomes a prescribed class whose consent is required[75] and, if this is done, the problems will largely disappear. What is the position, however, if the consent of such lessees is not prescribed by regulation?

3.42   The issue of consent is significant. All leases will be extinguished once the commonhold is activated.[76] Although all lessees may be entitled to

---

[71]   CLRA 2002, s 3(2)(e) and (f).

[72]   HL Deb, Vol 627, col 486, Lord Kingsland. The issue of unanimity of consent from all long leaseholders is discussed at **13.14**.

[73]   HL Deb, Vol 627, col 488, Baroness Scotland of Asthal. The example given was where a leaseholder could not be traced.

[74]   CLRA 2002, s 3(3).

[75]   This could be done by virtue of the power given by CLRA 2002, s 3(1)(d) – see **3.32**.

[76]   See CLRA 2002, ss 7(3)(d) and 9(3)(f), and **3.65**.

compensation for loss,[77] monetary recompense may be regarded
as inadequate compensation by long leaseholders whose consent was not
required to the extinguishment of their interests merely because title to their
lease happened to remain unregistered. The prospect of a conversion to
commonhold without unanimous consent is then a possibility. If the dissident
leaseholder has an unregistered lease, the application could proceed, simply
because the lease happens to be unregistered, without the consent of both the
unregistered leaseholder and of any mortgagee of that lease. An unregistered
dissident lessee can effectively be forced to convert to commonhold or accept
the alternative of unsecured compensation. The consequences for any
mortgagee of an unregistered long lease are seemingly ignored.[78] The case,
therefore, for prescribing consents from the holders of unregistered long
leases noted on the leasehold title is a strong one.[79]

(b) Tenants (for terms of less than 21 years) in occupation

3.43 A commonhold is a community formed to share facilities, and
undertake repair and maintenance of common parts. The community of
interest (which is a consequence of commonhold) cannot tolerate other forms
of estate within the commonhold – whether these are standard freehold or
pre-existing leasehold.[80] As a consequence, the site of the proposed
commonhold has to be 'legally cleared' of existing leasehold interests so that
there remains only the freehold fee simple which can then be the basis to
establish the commonhold on the freehold land. Therefore, a freehold
developer wishing to establish a commonhold will normally have to purchase
or negotiate the surrender of any existing leasehold interests. Alternatively, he
must obtain the necessary consents both of the holders, and of any
mortgagees or chargees, of the pre-existing freehold or leasehold titles in the
land. The process of obtaining those consents may result either in a release of
the interests concerned or in an agreement for a stake in the developed
commonhold. Logically, the consent of every such leaseholder or tenant and
every such chargee or mortgagee should be required. But, as we have seen,
this is not the case. Not every leaseholder or registered proprietor of a
leasehold estate is required to consent. Large numbers of leases and tenancies
(both residential and commercial) are granted on a periodic basis or for terms

---

[77] As discussed at **3.68**.

[78] The mortgagee of an unregistered lease does not appear to be entitled to compensation as the statutory
liability only extends to the 'holder' of the lease. This opens up the prospect of a complete loss of
security for mortgagees of unregistered leases. See the discussion of the compensation provisions at
3.70.

[79] If, as is suggested (see **3.34**), such consent also required proof of title, as if voluntary registration was
being sought, the consent of any mortgagee of the unregistered leasehold estate could also be a
prescribed consent.

[80] Only leases granted after the commonhold is established – see CLRA 2002, ss 7(3) and 9(3) – will be
permitted. Residential leases must meet prescribed conditions, one of which is likely to be that the term
is not more than 7 years (s 17), and non-residential leases only have effect subject to the CCS (s 18).

of less than 21 years. Such tenants and lessees will not need to consent formally to the establishment of the commonhold. If no steps are taken to negotiate with them, then their leases will be extinguished.[81] Yet they may still remain in occupation of part of the commonhold land at the time their leases are extinguished.

3.44 Lessees and tenants under short-term leases should have had to give their consent to the establishment of commonhold. These tenants will usually have no direct stake in the commonhold to be established. Such leases will commonly be at market rent. If they are residential leases, they may be protected by the Rent Acts or Housing Acts and, in any event (if a residential lease), possession can only be sought by court action. At the very least, better provision for compensation should have been made.

3.45 Consider the situation where a developer purchases a building to convert and upgrade to high-quality residential units by establishing a commonhold and selling the units with commonhold title. One or more flats may still be occupied by periodic residential tenants, perhaps with security of tenure. If the developer chooses to develop in the historically usual way of granting long leases at low rents, then he would have a choice. If unable to take possession proceedings, he would either have to negotiate with the short residential tenants for the surrender of their leases (no doubt by paying compensation for the surrender), or he could proceed (if it is physically possible so to do) to refurbish the rest of the building and to let flats on long leases. The small number of tenants would be left in place and their flats sold on long leases only when they were eventually vacated. When establishing a commonhold, the latter option is not available,[82] but there is no real reason why the developer should not be forced to negotiate with existing occupiers to obtain their consent to proceed or to purchase their interests.

3.46 It is also possible that commonhold could be used to 'winkle out' the short-term tenant with security of tenure. Perhaps a developer wishes to refurbish (say) a block of ten flats, nine of which are vacant, but one of which has a tenant (with some form of security of tenure). It does seem that the developer could proceed to apply (quite properly) for registration of the commonhold, ignoring the existence of that tenant, who does not need to consent to the registration. The developer would proceed to refurbish the other nine flats. On sale of the first commonhold unit, the tenancy is extinguished. Is the developer then able to take possession proceedings to remove that tenant and refurbish the last flat? The CLRA 2002 is quite clear. The lease is extinguished. The tenant would become a trespasser and have no right to occupy and a possession order could, on the face of the Act, be

---

[81] Negotiation to agree a surrender or to agree a substituted interest within the planned commonhold is the ideal solution.

[82] Perhaps it should be. Why could the developer not become the proprietor of the commonhold unit and the assured or Rent Act tenancy become a tenancy of the unit?

obtained. A court faced with a claim for possession of such a flat will be forced to consider the relevant earlier legislation (providing for security of tenure) in the light of the extinguishment of that tenancy under the CLRA 2002. Security of tenure may arise under the Rent Act 1977, the Housing Act 1988 or the Landlord and Tenant Act 1954. In each case, the court would have to consider the impact of the provision that 'any lease shall be extinguished' and it is by no means clear what the result would be. The tenant will certainly be entitled to compensation for loss.[83] But for (say) an elderly tenant, the prospect of having to struggle to claim through the courts for compensation may be a scant consolation for the loss of a home, so it is likely the security of tenure would still be claimed and the issue would be litigated.[84]

(c) Arranging for informal consent or securing prior termination

3.47 Where the only leases are registered leases granted for more than 21 years, no special legal difficulties arise because the registered proprietor of a leasehold estate in whole or part of the land must consent to the application.[85] If consent is not forthcoming, the application cannot proceed. Where consent is given, then, no doubt as part of giving the consent, the necessary arrangements will be made to deal with all the consequences for the parties concerned.

3.48 The more difficult situation arises where there are unregistered long leases or tenancies. In cases where there is actual knowledge of these leases (as will usually be the case), it is almost inevitable that it will be sensible to obtain the agreement of the lessees concerned to the application for commonhold. Such would be the case where a group of long leaseholders have enfranchised and seek to convert their long leases to commonhold. If one leaseholder's 99-year lease is unregistered, there will be no need for his formal consent to the application[86] but every reason for his full participation and consent to the process. Alternatively, negotiation of a surrender or other termination of the leases in question prior to the application for registration of the commonhold

---

[83]   See **3.69**.

[84]   A Rent Act tenant is likely to be in the best position. The most natural reading is that only the protected tenancy (not many will still exist!) would be extinguished by the CLRA 2002. This would leave the statutory tenancy – which is not an estate in land but only a personal right of occupation and therefore not a lease that could be extinguished – still in force and protecting the occupation – see Rent Act 1977, s 2. An assured tenancy would appear to be extinguished by the CLRA 2002. Section 5(2) of the Housing Act 1988 provides for the statutory periodic tenancy to arise if a fixed-term tenancy comes to an end otherwise than by order of the court or action by the tenant. So a statutory periodic tenancy might survive, although it is a legal estate in land and so could be described as a 'lease' which is also to be extinguished. A business tenant would appear to be in the weakest position. Section 24 of the Landlord and Tenant Act 1954, which provides that such tenancies shall not come to an end unless terminated as the 1954 Act provides, would surely have to give way to the later statute providing that 'any lease' is extinguished.

[85]   See CLRA 2002, s 3(1)(b).

[86]   Unless long unregistered lessees become a prescribed class of persons whose consent is required – see **3.34**.

will often be the more sensible course of action. Again, if one flat in an otherwise unoccupied block is held on an assured tenancy, it will be better to secure termination before the application for the commonhold is made.[87]

EXISTING MORTGAGES AT REGISTRATION

General principles

3.49 Although the consent of the registered proprietor of a charge over all or part of the land is required to establish a commonhold,[88] charges are not otherwise subject to special rules when an estate in commonhold land is registered. However, there is one situation where an existing charge can be extinguished, in whole or in part, by the statute.

New commonhold developments

3.50 A developer is likely to borrow against the security of the planned commonhold land. Such a loan will invariably be secured by a registered charge. The consent of any lender holding a registered charge over the freehold land will be needed for registration as an estate in commonhold land.[89] No doubt the terms of such consent will usually require that the security be maintained after registration as a commonhold by means of a registered charge over the commonhold land. When the first unit is transferred, the common parts of the commonhold will be vested in the commonhold association free of that charge.[90] The charge may thereafter continue only over the unsold units, provided always that the whole of each and any unit is charged. In the unlikely event of a developer's charge only extending to land that becomes part of a unit, then the charge is extinguished in relation to the part only.[91] No doubt each purchaser will require the charge to be released progressively as each unit is sold or transferred. When the last unit is sold, the charge entered into by the developer will terminate. The process will thus be very similar to existing freehold development practice.

---

[87] Although, as discussed, it would appear that it might be possible to proceed ignoring the presence of an unco-operative tenant with a short lease and then seek possession once the lease is extinguished.

[88] See **3.31**.

[89] CLRA 2002, s 3(1)(c).

[90] Ibid, s 28(3); ss 7(3)(a) and 9(3)(a) give the entitlement to be registered as the freehold proprietor of the common parts. Under s 9, the vesting of the land free of the charge will occur immediately on registration.

[91] Ibid, s 22(4), when the land becomes commonhold land. So if the charge related to the whole of a number of units and to part only of another, the charge would only be extinguished as it related to the part of a unit.

Conversions from long leasehold

3.51 Where a group of existing long leaseholders agree to convert to commonhold, they will need the consent of registered proprietors of charges both over the freehold title and over all the leasehold titles.[92] On registration of the commonhold, the leases will be extinguished and the registered charges over those leasehold titles will be terminated as a consequence.[93] So lenders will, as a price of their consent, normally require a substituted security over the relevant new commonhold unit. By way of contrast, any registered charge over the freehold reversion (if any) will probably have to be discharged prior to the application to register a commonhold. The consent of the lender holding such a registered charge will be required and it will not be possible to substitute a charge over the interest of the commonhold association over the common parts.[94] It is highly unlikely that the new unit-holders will accept a charge in respect of a loan that related to the freehold reversion being continued by charges securing the loan by apportionment over the new commonhold units.

Conversions from freehold flats

3.52 It will be normally better practice to follow a similar procedure to conversions from long leases, namely to terminate existing registered charges over leasehold flats and replace them with charges over what will become new commonhold units. However, it will be possible for a charge over a freehold flat to continue as a charge over the commonhold unit that replaces it provided that the charge relates to the whole of the unit. If, however, the charge relates to only part of a unit, when it becomes commonhold land, the charge is extinguished.[95] This provision reflects the rule that it is not possible to create a charge over part only of an interest in a unit. Since it is likely that the exact extent of a freehold flat may not be co-terminus with the defined extent of the commonhold unit,[96] it seems much better not to rely on the

---

[92] Consent is required of registered proprietors of charges over part of the land to be registered as a freehold estate in commonhold land.

[93] If the lease is extinguished, there is no longer an estate over which the charge can operate. But in the unlikely event of a registered proprietor of a charge consenting to registration but without agreement as to the consequences for the charge, the obligation to repay would remain.

[94] It is not normally possible to create a legal charge over the common parts except in relation to a legal mortgage approved unanimously by a resolution of the commonhold association – CLRA 2002, ss 28(1) and 29(1) and (2). However, such a resolution would not appear to be possible prior to registration of the commonhold as the directors of the association must certify at registration that the association has not traded – ibid, Sch 1, para 7(d). So it is not possible to arrange for a fresh charge of the common parts to take effect immediately after registration of the commonhold.

[95] CLRA 2002, s 22(1) and (4).

[96] Thus a commonhold flat is likely to exclude the external structures of the building in which it is located but a freehold flat may include them. The common parts of the commonhold may be defined to exclude structures, fittings or apparatus within the flat (such as service pipes, cable and conduits) – ibid, s 11(3).

ability for charges to continue at the time of registration of the commonhold. The redemption of any charge over the freehold flat and its replacement by a fresh charge over the commonhold unit will be better practice. It should be noted that where a charge is extinguished, it is only the security that is lost. The obligation to repay under the mortgage covenant will remain in force.[97]

THE TRANSITIONAL PERIOD

Rationale

3.53 Once an application for registration of a freehold estate in commonhold land has been made and the documentation required by the CLRA 2002 has satisfied the Registrar, then the Registrar registers the freehold estate as a freehold estate in commonhold land. However, a commonhold cannot operate until there is a community – namely, there must be more than two persons involved. A commonhold is activated and comes into existence as a community only when a person other than the applicant for registration becomes entitled to be registered as the proprietor of the freehold estate in one or more of the commonhold units.[98]

Definition and effect

3.54 The period of time between first registration as commonhold and the later registration of the first unit in a person other than the applicant is known as the transitional period.[99] This is defined as the period between registration of the freehold estate in land as a freehold estate in commonhold land and the registration of a person other than the applicant as a proprietor of one or more, but not all, of the commonhold units.

3.55 In the transitional period, the register of the commonhold land will not include the prescribed details of the freeholder of each commonhold unit since, by definition, this would be the same person as the applicant for registration as freeholder owner of the whole of the commonhold land.[100] The developer simply continues as the registered proprietor of all the estate in commonhold land, and the commonhold association is not registered as proprietor of the common parts.[101] Regulations may be made to provide that, during the transitional period, provisions of the CCS, of the memorandum and articles of the commonhold association or indeed any provision of the

---

[97] There is no express provision to this effect.

[98] CLRA 2002, s 7(3) – and see **3.63**.

[99] Ibid, s 8(1).

[100] Ibid, s 5(3).

[101] However, any reference in the CLRA 2002 to a commonhold association exercising functions in relation to the commonhold land still apply even if the time falls in the transitional period: s 8(6).

CLRA 2002 shall not have effect or shall only have effect with specified modifications.[102]

3.56 During the transitional period, therefore, the commonhold is effectively in suspended animation. It may be activated on the application of a person to register a unit or it may become stillborn and cease to exist if the applicant decides to apply for de-registration of the commonhold. The applicant continues to be registered as proprietor of the freehold estate in the whole of the commonhold land. The rights and duties conferred and imposed by the CCS do not come into force, unless regulations so provide.[103]

De-registration

3.57 The most significant point about the transitional period is that during this period it is relatively straightforward for the applicant to decide that a commonhold is no longer what is required. An application can be made to the Registrar for the land to cease to be registered as a freehold estate in commonhold land during the transitional period. If consents were required for the original registration as a commonhold, then the same persons will need to consent to the application for cessation.[104] If the consents (where required) are forthcoming, then the Registrar will arrange for the freehold estate to cease to be registered as a freehold estate in commonhold land.[105]

THE TITLE TO THE COMMONHOLD

Contents of the register

3.58 Each commonhold title will be in the basic form of any registered title to freehold land.[106] The proprietorship register of each unit will state the details of the registered proprietor to the land; the property register will describe the land with reference to the filed plan; and there will be a charges register. However, what is different is that each estate in commonhold land divides up into these component freehold titles. So each commonhold will have a series of freehold titles within it – one more than the number of units within it. The additional title is that relating to the common parts held by the commonhold association.

---

[102] CLRA 2002, s 8(2) and (3).

[103] Ibid, ss 7(2) and 8(2).

[104] Ibid, s 8(5).

[105] Ibid, s 8(4). The procedure permitting de-registration, although straightforward, will be costly in time and money.

[106] Ibid, s 67 provides that the register means the register of title kept under s 1 of the Land Registration Act 2002, and 'Registrar' throughout the Act is a reference to the Chief Land Registrar.

3.59 The Registrar must ensure that in respect of any commonhold land certain details or documents are kept in his custody and referred to in the register.[107] These are:

– the prescribed details of the commonhold association;
– the prescribed details of the registered freeholder of each commonhold unit;[108]
– a copy of the commonhold community statement (CCS);
– a copy of the memorandum and articles of association of the commonhold association.

3.60 The Registrar may arrange for additional documents or information to be referred to in the register and kept in his custody if they are submitted in accordance with any provision made by or by virtue of the CLRA 2002.[109]

Title during, and on termination of, the transitional period

3.61 During the transitional period, the registered proprietor will continue to be the freeholder who made application for registration. It is only when the commonhold is activated (by a person being entitled to be registered as freehold proprietor of one of the units) that the commonhold association is entitled to be registered as proprietor of the freehold estate in all the common parts of the freehold. At that point, the commonhold association is registered without further application being made.[110] There is also no register of the freeholder of each commonhold unit during the transitional period – this is not needed, as each unit would be registered in the name of the freeholder. However, on the termination of the transitional period, or in any case where an application for registration is made with existing unit-holders, then the commonhold title will contain the prescribed details of the registered freeholder of each commonhold unit.[111] In a development situation, units will be progressively transferred to purchasers. The first purchaser or transferee of one of the units will activate the commonhold and that purchaser will be listed in the commonhold title as the registered freeholder of the unit concerned. All the remaining units will appear in the name of the original freeholder.[112]

---

[107] CLRA 2002, s 5(1).

[108] These details, perforce, will not be on the register during the transitional period: ibid, s 5(3).

[109] Ibid, s 5(2).

[110] Ibid, ss 1(4), 7(3)(a) and (b) and 9(3)(a) and (d). Land Registry computers and procedures will need to be modified to cope with registrations required without an application.

[111] Ibid, s 5(1)(b) and 5(3).

[112] It is not yet clear whether the Land Registry will leave the unsold units in a single title in the name of the developer or set up separate titles for each unit in readiness for the eventual sale of these units.

Title where there are existing unit-holders at registration

3.62   In a situation where registration is being made with existing unit-holders, then the original application will be accompanied by a statement requesting that s 9 of the CLRA 2002 applies.[113] That statement must include a list of all the proposed commonhold units and give in relation to each one of those units the prescribed details of the initial unit-holder, or joint unit-holders where relevant.[114] On registration, the person specified in that list will be registered as proprietor of the freehold estate in the commonhold unit concerned or, where relevant, joint unit-holders will be registered as one of the proprietors of the freehold estate in the unit.[115] These entries will be made in the register without separate applications being made.[116] Each unit-holder will be entitled to registration with separate title to the unit concerned.

Activation of the commonhold

Establishment of the community

3.63   Activation[117] of the commonhold sets the community in motion. Activation occurs either on registration of the commonhold, if the applicant requests that s 9 should apply and supplies a list of the proposed initial unit-holders, or where a person other than the applicant becomes entitled to be registered as the proprietor of the freehold estate in one or more, but not all, of the commonhold units.[118] Only at this point do the rights and duties conferred and imposed by the commonhold community statement come into force.[119] Two or more unit-holders are now in place and the relationship between them and the commonhold association that has become registered as the proprietor of the freehold estate in the common parts is governed by that document.

Existing leases extinguished

3.64   Activation also results in any lease of the whole or part of the common land being extinguished.[120] A lease for this purpose is defined as a lease granted for any term and granted before the commonhold association became entitled to be registered as the proprietor of the freehold estate in the

---

[113]   CLRA 2002, s 9(1)(b).

[114]   Ibid, s 9(2).

[115]   Ibid, s 9(3)(a)–(c).

[116]   Ibid, s 9(3)(d).

[117]   This is not a statutory term.

[118]   See CLRA 2002, ss 7(3) and 9.

[119]   Ibid, ss 7(3)(c) and 9(3)(e).

[120]   Ibid, ss 7(3)(d) and 9(3)(f). It is likely that such leases will have been negotiated out of existence prior to activation of the commonhold by way of surrender or other termination – see the discussion at **3.67**.

common parts.[121] It will therefore include not only leases in existence prior to the application for commonhold but also leases created, if any, during the transitional period. Any leases granted in the transitional period will, therefore, be very precarious indeed.[122]

EXTINGUISHMENT OF LEASES AND PAYMENT OF COMPENSATION

Rationale

3.65 The importance of dealing with all leases of the whole or part of the land to be registered as commonhold, whether those leases are registered or not, and whether or not formal consent is required, is demonstrated by the consequence for leases once a commonhold is activated. As soon as a person other than the applicant for the initial registration for an estate in commonhold land becomes entitled to be registered as a proprietor of the freehold estate in one or more, but not all, of the commonhold units, then any lease of the whole or part of the commonhold land is extinguished by virtue of the CLRA 2002.[123] This extinguishment of all leases will occur immediately on registration of the commonhold land in those cases where there are already unit-holders at the time of the registration. In a new development, leases will be extinguished as soon as there is a transfer of the unit to a first purchaser.

3.66 The rationale of this extinguishment provision is clear and follows from the nature of commonhold. Commonhold is a form of freehold land and cannot be subject to earlier created leases. Moreover, the policy of the legislation is to restrict the type of leases that can be created after the establishment of the commonhold in respect of commonhold units.[124]

3.67 If the CLRA 2002 had provided that all lessees of land comprising of the whole or part of the commonhold land should consent to the application for commonhold, then there would be no particular difficulty. Negotiations would undoubtedly take place to cope with the consequences of the termination of the leasehold interests. In most cases, such agreement would involve an agreement to surrender or otherwise determine the leases prior to the application being made. In other cases, the application could only proceed with the informed consent of all lessees and tenants. However, consent is required only of registered proprietors of a leasehold estate granted for more than 21 years and not of every lessee.[125] The consequence is that an

---

[121] CLRA 2002, ss 7(4) and 9(4).

[122] There is no reason why the tenant will realise this unless title is deduced (which would be rare in the case of a short-term tenancy such as an assured shorthold) or the landlord's title is inspected.

[123] CLRA 2002, ss 7(3)(d) and 9(3)(f).

[124] Ibid, ss 17–19, and **6.17–6.27**.

[125] See **3.30**.

application can be made without the consent of an unregistered lessee; and, upon activation of the commonhold, that lessee's interest would be extinguished. In such circumstances, a right to compensation for loss suffered by the holder of an extinguished lease arises under s 10.

Liability for extinguished leases

3.68   The CLRA 2002 makes specific provision to cover the situation where a lease is extinguished[126] and the consent to the holder of that lease was not required by s 3.[127] The liability for loss falls upon the person whose interest was most proximate to the extinguished lease.

3.69   If the holder of a lease superior to the extinguished lease gave consent, then he will be liable for loss suffered by the holder of an extinguished lease. If there is more than one superior lease, then liability attaches only to the person whose lease was most proximate to the extinguished lease.[128] If there is no superior lease, then the person who gave consent as freeholder of the estate out of which the extinguished lease was granted will be liable for the loss.[129]

Problems with the compensation provisions

3.70   The difficulties with s 10 revolve not around what it says but what it fails to do. Although the form of these compensation provisions is now better than the original draft,[130] there is little in the statute to assist in resolving disputes.[131] There is no guidance as to how the loss suffered by the holder of the extinguished lease is to be calculated.[132] There is no special (let alone, simple) procedure established for claiming or recovering the loss in any straightforward or efficient manner. Moreover, it is the holder of the extinguished lease who must take action, which may be lengthy and expensive, to secure payment for loss suffered. Significantly, there is no provision for security to be provided when the commonhold is registered for those entitled

---

[126]   By virtue of CLRA 2002, ss 7(3)(d) or 9(3)(f).

[127]   Ibid, s 10(1).

[128]   Ibid, s 10(2) and (3).

[129]   Ibid, s 10(4).

[130]   Section 10 as it now stands was inserted at Third Reading in the House of Lords: HL Deb, Vol 628, col 909. In its original form, compensation was only payable by a superior leaseholder, if there was one, who had consented.

[131]   There is, additionally, no specific statutory authority to add to the compensation provisions by regulation.

[132]   Presumably, compensation will be the market value of the lease in question, but there will be difficult issues. For example, the lease may be unassignable yet have considerable personal value to the occupying lessee.

to compensation.[133] If the person liable for the loss has no assets from which the loss can be claimed, the unfortunate lessee may find not only that the lease is extinguished, but also that no compensation is forthcoming. Most importantly of all, any mortgagee of the extinguished lease has no apparent statutory claim for any loss suffered, as the liability only extends to losses suffered by 'the holder of the extinguished lease'.[134] Where the liability for loss falls on the freeholder, the holder of an extinguished lease will at least have the knowledge that the new commonhold land itself offers some security for the compensation claim.[135]

3.71   From the point of view of the would-be applicant for commonhold, it undoubtedly remains advisable to ensure that all leases are dealt with before the application is made. There is the safeguard that if a lease exists whose existence is not known, it will be extinguished once the commonhold commences. Yet the provision for extinguishment gives some encouragement to cavalier action where a single lessee whose consent is not required is the only obstacle to an application for registration as commonhold land. From a lessee's point of view, it shows the importance of considering protective action where the lease is not itself registered so that the lessee's consent is not required. If the application for registration of the commonhold has not yet been made, then an application to register the lessee's title (if an unregistered lease granted for a term more than 21 years) would give the lessee protection. In other cases, perhaps registration of a notice on the title or of a pending land action would be possible. If the application for registration of a commonhold has already been made and proceedings for securing compensation have commenced, registration of a pending land action to secure compensation for the loss suffered against the title freeholder who made the application might give some security for eventual recovery of the loss.

---

[133]   This was recognised in debates. The example was postulated of a person due to pay the compensation being insolvent. If that person is a company in receivership, it was suggested that a receiver could give consent as agent for the company, but that the liability for compensation remains the unsecured liability of the company in receivership. See Lord Goodhart, HL Deb, Vol 628, col 908 (Third Reading). The Government Minister promised to look into the issue but it was not raised again.

[134]   CLRA 2002, s 10(2). See also s 10(1)(b) which limits the application to cases where the consent of the holder of the lease was not required by s 3. Only if a mortgagee could be seen as a 'holder of a lease' would the right to compensation arise. This might be the case where the mortgagee is in possession but it is not a natural reading of the word generally.

[135]   But not after the common parts have been vested in the commonhold association and all the units have been sold or vested in new unit-holders.

MISTAKES IN THE REGISTRATION PROCESS

The situations covered

3.72 The CLRA 2002 contains wide powers to cope with the potential problems arising where a successful application has been made to register land as a freehold estate in commonhold land but such registration should not have occurred because there were deficiencies in the registration process. Three situations are covered by the Act.[136] These are:

– where the application for registration was not in accordance with the basic requirements of s 2. In some circumstances it is possible some of the documentation may have been missing and its absence overlooked. Alternatively, perhaps part of the land is already part of an adjacent commonhold;[137]

– where the certificate by the directors of the commonhold association was inaccurate. Perhaps, for example, the certificate wrongly certified that the commonhold association has not traded; and

– where the registration contravened any provision made by, or by virtue of, Part 1 of the Act relating to commonhold.

3.73 Where such deficiencies come to light it is not possible for a register to be altered by the Registrar under the Land Registration Act 2002.[138] The rationale would appear to be that to permit the standard processes to apply might undermine the whole basis of an established commonhold. Hence, a special procedure is provided. The situation can be dealt with only by application to the court for a declaration that the freehold estate should not have been registered as a freehold estate in commonhold land.[139] Such an application can be made only by a person who claims to be adversely affected by the registration and not by the Registrar or any other person.[140] If, however, the court is minded to grant a declaration, being satisfied that deficiencies have occurred, then there are wide powers in relation to the order that the court may make.[141] The court may make any order that appears to it to be appropriate. In particular, the court may choose to provide that the registration is to be treated as valid for all purposes, or it may provide for rectification of the register; or it may indeed provide for the land to cease to

---

[136] Under CLRA 2002, s 6(1).

[137] And so cannot be commonhold land: s 2(1)(b).

[138] Ibid, s 6(2). Alteration, under Sch 4 of the Land Registration Act 2002, replaces rectification under the 1925 Act. The Registrar's power to take action, including making or cancelling an entry where he considers it appropriate in connection with Part 1 of the Act, is subject to the restrictions of s 6(2): CLRA 2002, s 67(4) and (5).

[139] CLRA 2002, s 6(3).

[140] Ibid, s 6(4).

[141] Ibid, s 6(5) and (6).

be registered as commonhold land. If an order does include a declaration that the land should cease to be commonhold land, then the court has power to make a winding-up order in respect of the commonhold association.[142] There are powers to make an award of compensation to be paid by one specified person to another. There is power to require a director or other specified officer of a commonhold association to take any specified steps. It is specifically provided that these may include the alteration or amendment of a document such as the CCS or the memorandum and articles of the commonhold association. In making these orders, the court may apply, disapply or modify the provisions of the Land Registration Act 2002 relating to indemnity. These wide powers should ensure that persons who are disadvantaged or who suffer loss by virtue of an error in the registration process can be properly compensated.

---

[142]   Ibid, s 55, and **12.37**.

CHAPTER 4

THE COMMONHOLD ASSOCIATION

4.1 The incorporation of the commonhold association, the corporate body that will be registered as the proprietor of the freehold estate in the common parts of the community, must be completed before the application for registration of a commonhold can take place. Indeed, the incorporation of this company is likely to be the very first stage in the process.

CONSTITUTION AND FORMATION

A company limited by guarantee

4.2 A commonhold association takes the corporate form of a private company limited by guarantee.[1] The CLRA 2002 does not create a purpose-designed corporate vehicle for this purpose, as was once envisaged.[2] By utilising the existing corporate form of private company limited by guarantee, the primary legislation establishing the principle of commonhold was simplified. This simplification does, however, come at a price.[3]

4.3 Nevertheless, the statutory constitution of, and the regulations relating to, a commonhold association make it a very particular form of private company limited by guarantee. Special rules apply which make it essential that each commonhold association is designed and incorporated especially for the particular commonhold that is planned.

4.4 First, the name of the commonhold association will certainly be subject to regulations.[4] These regulations may provide that the name by which a commonhold association is registered under the Companies Act 1985 must satisfy specified requirements. It is likely that these regulations will always require the words 'commonhold association' to be included in the company name. This name will then have a special recognition, reinforced by the fact that the regulations will also have power to provide that any company other

---

[1] CLRA 2002, s 34. Except as otherwise provided, a commonhold association will be subject to the Companies Acts.

[2] For example, as created by cl 3 of the 1990 Commonhold Bill – see *Commonhold, A Consultation Paper (with draft Bill annexed)*, Cm 1345, p 46.

[3] See the discussion at **12.3–12.8**.

[4] The power is contained in CLRA 2002, Sch 3, para 16.

than a commonhold association may not include a specified word or expression.[5] In short, any person dealing with a commonhold association will know immediately from the name the nature of the corporate body involved.

4.5   Secondly, the CLRA 2002 provides that £1 is to be specified as the amount required from each member of the company as a contribution to the assets of the association in the event of it being wound up.[6] This nominal figure, identical for each member, is the maximum contribution due under company law from the members of the association for payment of debts and liabilities of the association.[7] Consequently, the memorandum of association of commonhold associations will always have to provide that the sum of £1 is the amount every member undertakes to contribute on winding up or within one year of ceasing to be a member.[8]

4.6   Thirdly, the commonhold association will have to be especially formed in relation to the closely defined parcel, or parcels, of land on which the commonhold will be established. It is unlikely to be feasible therefore to buy a ready formed commonhold association 'off the shelf'. It is almost certain that the company agents will prefer to incorporate the company with the exact details of the description of the land concerned to be inserted into the memorandum and articles.[9] If this is not done, it will be necessary in every case to amend the memorandum and articles immediately to make the necessary reference to the land before an application to register a commonhold can be made.

4.7   Fourthly, it may be advisable to have the promoters of the commonhold, or their solicitors or other agents, as the original subscribers to the memorandum of association. This is because the subscribers are the sole members of the association until the land specified in its memorandum becomes commonhold land.[10] They continue as the only members throughout any transitional period and only the developer can be entered into the register of members in addition to them.[11] It would seem advisable for the subscribers to be persons closely involved with the promotion of the commonhold, rather than company agents, who will not wish to have a continuing role after

---

[5]   CLRA 2002, Sch 3, para 16(b).

[6]   Ibid, s 34(1)(b) and (draft) standard memorandum of association, cl 7.

[7]   Under Companies Act 1985, s 2(4).

[8]   As in the standard form, see Appendix 1.

[9]   'Shelf' companies are much less common than they were in any event because custom incorporations can now be processed very quickly. Very soon, same day incorporations by electronic submission, without an extra fee, should be possible. Choosing a custom designed company will also reduce the costs of a later change of name and so forth.

[10]   CLRA 2002, Sch 3, para 5. There is no mechanism to change the membership or add new members until after registration has taken place. Any subsequent members can only be persons who are unit-holders.

[11]   Ibid, Sch 3, para 6.

incorporation is completed. The directors of the association must give a certificate when the association applies for registration and, at the very least, the directors at that time must be in a position to make that certification.

4.8 Finally, a commonhold association is subject to regulations[12] making detailed provision about the form and content of both its memorandum and the articles of association. Each commonhold association will be required to have adopted the elements of the standard form provisions of the memorandum and articles that are, in effect, compulsory as set out in those regulations.[13]

4.9 In one sense, a company limited by guarantee could be described as a fairly familiar corporate personality. Indeed, it will be known to property practitioners, since the company limited by guarantee is very commonly found in leasehold developments where the tenants take control of the freehold through the medium of their own management company. However, it is in fact a form of company that has had relatively little attention in either the academic or the practitioner literature on company law.[14] A number of points are worth emphasising.

- A company limited by guarantee is not suitable for business organisations and is usually used in situations where there is to be no distribution to members. In most cases this should not cause any difficulties, but it is possible to conceive of situations, such as a profitable sale of vacant land forming part of the common parts, where a distribution of profits is required.[15]
- It is, of course, a company subject to the requirements of the Companies Acts. A commonhold association is not exempt from filing annual returns, for example.
- It is a limited liability company. The only assets of a commonhold association are likely to be the common parts (vested in it) and funds in its bank accounts. Such monies will be raised from its members by way of commonhold assessment (service charge) and by way of levy to build up reserve funds. The limited liability status of the commonhold association has meant that it is subject to the normal processes of the

---

[12] CLRA 2002, Sch 3, para 2. The form of articles of association of a company limited by guarantee prescribed by the Companies Act 1985 do not apply: CLRA 2002, Sch 3, para 4(1).

[13] Schedule 3, para 2(2) provides that a commonhold association may adopt provisions of the regulations for its memorandum and articles, but para 2(3) adds that the regulations may include provisions that are to have effect whether or not they are adopted. Any provisions so prescibed are effectively compulsory and may as well be adopted so that the situation is clear on the face of the memorandum and articles.

[14] See, for example, *Palmer's Company Law* (Sweet & Maxwell, 25th edn), paras 2.008–2.013.

[15] This issue is discussed further at **4.17**.

Insolvency Act 1986 and special provisions have had to be made for those circumstances.[16]

4.10   Other jurisdictions have created special corporate bodies, rather than utilise an existing corporate vehicle. Such specially designed corporations need not necessarily have limited liability status, nor need they be subject to the Companies Acts. However, a purchaser buying into a commonhold will have to look to the Registrar of Companies as well as the Land Registrar. A creditor of the commonhold association will not be able to have direct recourse to the members and unit-holders for recovery of debts due from the association.[17]

Objects of the commonhold association

4.11   The CLRA 2002 requires the memorandum of association to state that 'an object' of the company is to exercise the functions of a commonhold association in relation to specified commonhold land.[18] In fact, the form of memorandum of association in the draft regulations[19] makes that the prime object of the company,[20] although the Act would appear to assume that a commonhold association could have other, equally valid, prime objects. The regulations, rightly it is submitted, provide only for powers that are subsidiary to the central objects of carrying out the functions of a commonhold association. The draft memorandum of association[21] contains no fewer than 37 subsidiary powers, but it clearly states that these are to be powers given in furtherance of the prime objects of the commonhold association but not otherwise. Consequently, although commonhold associations will have all the necessary powers to administer the property or deal with the freehold estate in the commonhold land in almost any conceivable way, the investment, lending and borrowing powers are all carefully designed to ensure that all the powers work only in fulfilment of the main objects. Each association will operate only in relation to its defined property.

4.12   All commonhold associations will therefore be working within the same confines. Each promoter will need to adopt all the provisions of the draft memorandum and articles where these are to have effect whether or not adopted – and this is likely to apply to the majority of the provisions contained in the draft memorandum and articles in the regulations. If these sections are omitted, then the regulations may include provision that they are

---

[16]   These are analysed in Chapter 12.

[17]   See **12.6**.

[18]   CLRA 2002, s 34(1)(a). 'Object' in relation to a commonhold association means an object stated in the association's memorandum of association in accordance with s 2(1)(c) of the Companies Act 1985: CLRA 2002, s 69(1).

[19]   At the time of writing, these are in draft form only.

[20]   The exact wording can be seen in the regulations in Appendix 1; see cl 3.

[21]   Ibid; see cl 4.

to have effect for a commonhold association whether or not they are formally adopted.[22] More importantly, any provision in the memorandum and articles is to have no effect to the extent that it is inconsistent with the regulations.[23] The regulations will have effect in relation to all memoranda or articles irrespective of the date of those memoranda or articles, subject only to transitional provisions of any new regulations.[24] This enables regulations to be regularly updated and ensures that all memoranda and articles of association meet the regulations that may exist from time to time.

Formation

4.13 A commonhold association will be formed under the provisions of the Companies Act 1985.[25] In addition to the delivery of the memorandum and articles, there will need to be the usual statement of the persons who are to be the first director or directors of the company and of the person who is to be the first secretary. As the directors have to give a certificate on application for registration of a commonhold,[26] it is important for them to be persons able and willing to give the necessary certification at the date of the application for registration of the commonhold. It has already been argued that the company will be especially formed and that the subscribers need to be more than nominees, so the first directors should also be persons involved in the formation, rather than company agents.[27]

4.14 The Registrar of Companies will not only have to be satisfied that all the relevant requirements of the Companies Act have been met in relation to the memorandum of association, but also that the memorandum meets all the statutory requirements of the CLRA 2002 and of all regulations made thereunder.[28]

Alteration of the memorandum and articles

4.15 Once incorporated, the commonhold association's certificate of incorporation and its memorandum and articles must accompany any application for registration of the land as a freehold estate in commonhold

---

[22] CLRA 2002, Sch 3, para 2(3).

[23] Ibid, Sch 3, para 2(4).

[24] Ibid, Sch 3, para 2(5).

[25] Companies Act 1985, Part I, Chapter I; s 1(2)(b) governs companies limited by guarantee.

[26] See **3.26**.

[27] The first directors could be the freeholder/developer, or his solicitor, agents, employees or other nominees. Alternatively, a specialist property company could undertake the work, continue involvement as the units are progressively sold and continue as agents for the commonhold if the unit owners are satisfied with their services. The commonhold association's registered office could then be the address of the property company and not at the commonhold.

[28] CLRA 2002, Sch 3, para 17. The statutory declaration of compliance under Companies Act 1985, s 12, includes a reference to the CLRA 2002.

land.[29] Consequently, any subsequent alteration of the memorandum or articles of association after registration of the commonhold has no effect until the altered version of the memorandum or articles is registered as the CLRA 2002 provides.[30] Any alteration must be made in accordance with the existing memorandum and articles of association. All alterations must themselves, of course, meet all the statutory requirements as to form and content. Alteration of the memorandum of association is governed primarily by the CLRA 2002 and the regulations made thereunder, as relevant provisions of the Companies Act 1985 do not apply.[31] Once the memorandum or articles have been altered, then the commonhold association must apply to the Registrar,[32] who arranges for an altered memorandum or articles to be kept in his custody and referred to in the register. The application must be accompanied by a certificate given by the directors of the commonhold association that the memorandum or articles as altered comply with the existing regulations.[33]

MEMBERSHIP OF THE COMMONHOLD ASSOCIATION

The principle of community equality

4.16   A commonhold is designed with an equality of interest between unit-holders in mind. This sentiment[34] embodies the principle that each member of the commonhold community has the same interest as any other. Each member has the same voice within the commonhold association. This principle means that it is not possible to have a commonhold association where some members have greater voting rights than others. Thus, in a commonhold which contains some penthouse flats or units and some studio flats or units, the owner of a penthouse flat has the same voting rights as an

---

[29]   CLRA 2002, s 2(2); Sch 1, paras 2–3.

[30]   Ibid, Sch 3, para 3(1).

[31]   By virtue of CLRA 2002, Sch 3, para 4(1), ss 2(7) and 3 of the Companies Act 1985 do not apply to a commonhold association. Section 22(2) and (3) of that Act are disapplied by CLRA 2002, Sch 3, para 15(2).

[32]   Under CLRA 2002, Sch 3, para 3(2). If the alteration has been by special resolution in accordance with Companies Act 1985, s 4, then the application for registration cannot be made immediately. Opportunity must be given for objection to the alteration under s 5 of the 1985 Act. The period during which an application for cancellation may be made must have expired without an application being submitted; or any application must have been withdrawn; or the alteration must have been confirmed by the court under s 5: CLRA 2002, Sch 3, para 4(2).

[33]   Ibid, Sch 3, para 3(3). The Registrar may make any consequential amendments to the register which he thinks are appropriate when it is amended: Sch 3, para 3(4).

[34]   There was no discussion on this issue in the debates on the CLRA 2002. In the debates in Grand Committee on the 2000 Bill, however, a Conservative amendment to provide for a company limited by shares was to give the 'advantage' of differentiating between unit-holders. The response was that the whole nature of a commonhold association is that it should be on a one member, one vote basis – see HL Deb, Vol 622, CWH 73 (Lord Bach agreeing with Lord Goodhart at CWH 6).

owner of a studio flat even if the capital value of each unit is very different. This limitation may in the long term be found to be inconvenient, but at the moment is reinforced by provisions in both the statute and regulations. Thus a commonhold association must, as we have seen, be a company limited by guarantee. It is not possible to have a company limited by shares with differential share holding. Moreover, in the unlikely event of the commonhold association receiving a windfall, it is not permitted to make any distribution to its members whether in cash or otherwise.[35] No guarantee of more than £1 can be stipulated in the memorandum and so it would not seem to be possible to vary voting rights by having differential guarantees.

4.17   The principle of one member, one vote within the association does not mean that unit owners must contribute to the cost of the community equally. The percentage contribution of each unit towards repairs and maintenance through the commonhold assessment may vary. The commonhold community statement (CCS) must make provision for percentages of any estimate to be allocated to each unit and it is clear that differential percentages for units can be stipulated, provided those percentages amount in aggregate to 100%.[36] Indeed, it is specifically provided that a unit may have a nil percentage contribution.[37]

4.18   Thus, a developer may be able to plan the community so that holders of larger interests actually hold two units rather than one. They will thereby obtain twice the votes within the commonhold association, since there is no limit in the legislation as it stands on the number of units that can be vested in the same person.[38] This opens up the prospects of commonhold units that are designed to give extra voting rights and not for reasons of utility. The CCS could create nominal units (perhaps of car parking spaces or garden areas), which carry no part of the commonhold assessment but are designed to give unit-holders of higher value units larger voting rights within the commonhold association.

4.19   It can be argued that to have each member duly represented in the company with equal voting rights is not a fair representation if those who pay more do not have any greater say, especially in decisions on financial matters. Equality of voting power could potentially cause friction in a community where there are (say) a relatively large number of units making a modest contribution to the cost of the community and a smaller number of larger units, each making a much greater percentage contribution. One can imagine a

---

[35]   See draft memorandum of association, cl 81. But for this planned provision, a distribution of profits would be possible: *Palmer's Company Law* (Sweet & Maxwell, 25th edn), para 2.008.

[36]   CLRA 2002, s 38(1)(d) and (2)(a).

[37]   Ibid, s 38(2)(b).

[38]   The extra votes would, however, only be exercisable on a poll (which will need the support of five members or one-tenth of the total voting rights) if the terms of the draft memorandum and articles are reproduced in the final regulations – see draft articles of association, cl 21.

situation where the larger number of unit-holders making a small contribution vote for a larger increase in assessment or reserve provision, despite the opposition of the smaller number of members making the larger contributions which may amount in total to well over 50% of the total assessment due.

4.20 Unless the principle of equality is changed or modified in later legislation,[39] it is submitted that it will always be a significant disincentive to the establishment of commonholds where units vary significantly in size or where the financial interests of members are very different. In particular, it is unlikely that mixed commonholds of commercial and residential uses will be regarded as feasible except in limited circumstances. In such a case, one or two commercial unit-holders, perhaps paying a considerable percentage of the costs of the commonhold community, could be regularly outvoted by a larger number of residential members who might together contribute only a small part of the total financial costs of the community. Commercial occupiers are unlikely to accept such a prospect with equanimity.

Register of members

4.21 As with all companies, a commonhold association will have the duty[40] to maintain a register of its members. However, it is particularly important in the case of a commonhold association that the register of members is kept constantly up to date as units are sold or transferred to new owners. This will enable each unit owner to participate in the affairs of the commonhold association from the earliest possible date. Consequently, regulations may make provision about the performance by a commonhold association of its duty to maintain a register.[41] The aim is to avoid inordinate delays in either deleting the name of the departing unit owner or entering the name of a new unit owner. In particular, the regulations may require entries to be made within specified periods.[42] If there is a failure to meet any requirement to register within a specified period, then a commonhold association and every one of its officers who is in default is liable to a fine.[43]

---

[39] The CLRA 2002 may be compared to cl 5 of the 1996 Commonhold Bill which fixed voting rights to be determined, in an admittedly complex way, by reference to the fraction of the service charge payable.

[40] Under Companies Act 1985, s 352. The (draft) standard memorandum of association, cl 6, requires that a register of members be kept which complies with regulations under the CLRA 2002.

[41] CLRA 2002, Sch 3, para 14(1).

[42] Ibid, Sch 3, para 14(2). The period may be calculated from any point in time, but particularly from the date a new unit owner notifies the commonhold association of the transfer or the date on which the directors become aware of any specified matter: Sch 3, para 14(3).

[43] By virtue of Companies Act 1985, s 352(5), applied by CLRA 2002, Sch 3, para 14(4). Liability for a continued contravention is to a daily default fine.

Restrictions on membership

4.22 The basic principle is that a person who is unit-holder within a commonhold must be a member of the commonhold association.[44] Conversely, a person who is not the unit-holder may not be. The provisions[45] giving effect to these principles are not well drafted in all particulars. Depending on the stage of the process of the establishment of the commonhold, the membership of the commonhold association will change. There are three separate periods to consider, namely:

- the pre-commonhold period beginning with the incorporation of the commonhold association and ending when the land specified in its memorandum becomes commonhold land;
- the transitional period (if any); and
- the subsequent period, when the commonhold is 'activated' and there are two or more different owners of two or more commonhold units.

4.23 In the *pre-commonhold period*, it is provided that the subscribers or subscriber to the memorandum shall be the sole members or member of the association;[46] therefore, unless the freeholder of the would-be commonhold land, or his solicitor or other agent, becomes the subscribers or subscriber to the memorandum, the members of the company until registration of the commonhold will be persons who may, as company agents, have nothing whatsoever to do with the establishment of the commonhold or the commonhold land. No doubt they will provide undated resignations to take effect at a later date but, if unconnected with the development, they may wish to have no further part to play after formation of the company.[47] Yet, at least until the commonhold is registered, the subscriber(s) perforce remain(s), perhaps for some time, as the sole member(s) of the association. For this reason, it is suggested that the subscribers should be chosen from among persons who have some connection with the freeholder or developer of the commonhold.

4.24 During *the transitional period*,[48] the original subscribers or subscriber to the memorandum continue to be members or the member of the association. The one difference is that the developer for the time being in respect of all or part of the commonhold is entitled to be entered in the register of members

---

[44]   CLRA 2002, Sch 3, para 7. The unit-holder need not agree to become a member of the association as s 22(2) of the Companies Act 1985 does not apply to a commonhold association: Sch 3, para 15(2).

[45]   Contained in CLRA 2002, Sch 3, Part 2, paras 5–15.

[46]   Ibid, Sch 3, para 5. One subscriber is sufficient but two or more are desirable. Companies Act 1985, s 22(1) applies to the subscribers as initial members: CLRA 2002, Sch 3, para 15(1).

[47]   Section 22(1) of the Companies Act 1985, which provides that the subscribers of a company's memorandum are deemed to have agreed to become members of the company, applies to a commonhold association: CLRA 2002, Sch 3, para 15.

[48]   See **3.53**.

of the association. A developer is the person who makes an application for registration of the freehold estate in the commonhold land. Thus, the subscribers or subscriber to the memorandum and the developer are the only possible members of a commonhold association until the end of the transitional period. They are also the only members who may resign by notice in writing.[49] No doubt it will be standard practice for the subscribers to resign on activation of the commonhold. At any time after the registration of the first unit-holder, the developer may choose to resign, but he is unlikely to do so while the development continues. His resignation will normally occur on the sale of the last unit. Unfortunately, Sch 3 to the CLRA 2002 only provides that a member of a commonhold association *may*[50] resign. It does not require the resignation at any particular time. If such resignation is not offered, there seems to be no provision in the Act or in the regulations that requires the subscribers or developers to cease membership.[51] The provision that members of commonhold association cease to be members when they cease to be unit-holders would not assist in this respect, because the subscribers or the developer will not or may not ever be a unit-holder. Therefore, they cannot cease to be a unit-holder.

4.25 After *activation of the commonhold* and termination of the transitional period,[52] membership of the association, previously restricted to subscribers and the developer, extends to new unit-holders. A person is automatically entitled to be entered in the register of members on becoming the unit-holder of a commonhold unit in relation to which the commonhold association exercises functions. This may take place when the unit becomes commonhold land by first registration with unit-holders[53] or will otherwise occur on the first sale or transfer of a unit.[54] A person may not become a member of the commonhold association in any other way.[55] As we have already seen, the commonhold association will be under a duty to enter a new unit-holder as a member of the company on pain of financial sanction.

4.26 A commonhold association may not be a member of itself.[56] This provision could be seen as a natural and sensible consequence of limiting the

---

[49] CLRA 2002, Sch 3, para 13.

[50] My emphasis.

[51] CLRA 2002, Sch 3, para 12. If, however, a developer is not seen to have membership in his own right, but becomes a member as unit-holder of the unsold units after the first sale, then this provision would apply when the last unit is sold, requiring him to cease to be a member.

[52] Ie when a person other than the applicant for registration becomes entitled to be registered as the proprietor of the freehold estate in one or more, but not all, of the commonhold units.

[53] Under CLRA 2002, s 9.

[54] Ibid, Sch 3, para 7.

[55] Ibid, Sch 3, para 10. Therefore a person cannot become a member by agreement and s 22(2) of the Companies Act 1985 does not apply: CLRA 2002, Sch 3, para 15(2).

[56] Ibid, Sch 3, para 9. Companies Act 1985, s 23, relating to holding companies, cannot be relevant and does not apply: CLRA 2002, Sch 3, para 15(2).

membership of the commonhold association to the unit-holders and then maintaining the separation of interests between the individual unit-holders as members on the one hand and the collective totality of the members acting through the medium of the association on the other. However, it may be the product of suggestions at the time of the final consultation that to allow the commonhold association to own units would open the way to assist in unscrupulous persons gaining control of a development.[57]

Joint unit-holders

4.27   Where there are joint unit-holders, as commonly will be the case, it will not be possible for both or all of those unit-holders to be registered as members of the commonhold association. This provision seems to be in furtherance of the principle, already noted, of one member, one vote. There can only be one vote per unit. To avoid joint unit-holders disagreeing on the way their vote is to be exercised, the CLRA 2002 adopts what may be seen as a rather draconian provision – only one of any two or more persons who are joint unit-holders can be registered as the member of the commonhold association.

4.28   Joint unit-holders, therefore, must nominate one of themselves to be entered in the register of members in the commonhold association. A nomination is made in writing to the commonhold association and must be made within a prescribed period.[58] If no nomination is received by the association before the end of this period, then the person whose name appears first in the proprietorship register as registered proprietor of the unit is entitled to be entered in the register of the members of the association.[59] This provision is administratively convenient in that, unless nomination is made, the secretary of the commonhold association will have a clear guidance as to which person is to be entered as the member of the association.[60] Moreover, it avoids the possibility of a unit not having a member entered in the register because of disagreement between joint owners. It is always open for joint unit-holders to make a fresh nomination, in which case the nominated person is entered in place of the existing member.[61] There remains

---

[57]   See *Commonhold and Leasehold Reform, Draft Bill and Consultation Paper*, Cm 4843, August 2000, p 88, s 3.2. Whether preventing a commonhold association being a member of itself will really hinder one person determined to buy up commonhold units and obtain voting control may be doubted. Indeed, para 4.8 of the current draft memorandum of association specifically permits an association to acquire the freehold estate in any commonhold unit, but Sch 3, para 9 would appear to deny membership rights in such circumstances.

[58]   CLRA 2002, Sch 3, para 8(2) and (3).

[59]   Ibid, Sch 3, para 8(4). If, for any reason, the registration of the unit has not been completed, there could be uncertainty.

[60]   The secretary will need to know for, as noted, he may be liable to a fine for failing to enter a member in the register of members in due time.

[61]   CLRA 2002, Sch 3, para 8(6).

considerable room for dispute between joint unit-holders as to which person is to exercise the rights as member of the commonhold association. A solicitor or other legal adviser on a proposed purchase of a commonhold unit will always have to discuss with the clients which of the joint unit-holders is to be the member of the association.

4.29 If the joint unit-holders cannot agree among themselves, then the matter can only be resolved by application of any joint unit-holder to the court.[62] A court may order that a joint unit-holder is entitled to be entered in the register of members in place of a person who would be entitled to be registered by virtue of the 'first name' default provision. Quite what principles the court would apply to decide a dispute between joint unit-holders where each had an equal share or right to the unit is a question to which there is no obvious answer. There is no statutory guidance. It is likely that good reason would have to be shown for the court to replace an existing member. Thus, the court is likely to replace a joint unit-holder who no longer resides in the commonhold unit with a joint unit-holder who remains in occupation.

4.30 Membership rights arise only when the commonhold association registers the person as a member in pursuance of its statutory duty.[63] They do not arise on entitlement to be entered in the register.[64]

4.31 It is not possible, as we have seen, for a member to resign.[65] Ownership of a commonhold unit will always, of necessity, carry membership of the commonhold association. Thus, it is provided that a member of a commonhold association ceases to be a member of the association on ceasing to be a unit-holder or joint unit-holder of a commonhold unit in relation to the relevant association.[66] Rights and liabilities acquired or incurred by a former member while a unit-holder or joint unit-holder are not affected by termination of membership of the association.[67]

MEETINGS OF THE ASSOCIATION

4.32 The regulation of the meetings of the commonhold association will be a matter for the articles of association of the company. The intention is that there should be detailed provision in the draft standard articles to be promulgated by regulation. At the time of writing, there is only a draft,

---

[62] CLRA 2002, Sch 3, para 8(5).

[63] Companies Act 1985, s 352.

[64] CLRA 2002, Sch 3, para 11.

[65] Other than a person who was an original member of the association as subscriber or developer: CLRA 2002, Sch 3, para 13.

[66] Ibid, Sch 3, para 12(a).

[67] Ibid, Sch 3, para 12(b).

published to assist members of Parliament as they considered the Bill.[68] The draft, which is set out in an Appendix, covers the following issues:[69]

- general meetings;
- notice of general meetings;
- proceedings at such meetings; and
- votes of members, including the appointment of proxies.

4.33 There is still work to be done on the detail of the standard articles of association, so it is not thought helpful at this stage to analyse the draft provisions in detail. The issues which could cause difficulty include:

- the percentage of the quorum for meetings. It is currently suggested at 20%.[70] This seems rather low, allowing a vote by just 11% of members to decide issues by majority of those present. But to set the quorum too high could hamper day to day business; and
- the appointment of proxies. Experience in other jurisdictions suggests that there may have to be a limit on how many proxies a single individual can garner. Control of a large number of proxy votes (perhaps secured from owners of units which are held as investment properties and let) could hand effective control of the association to a single individual.

OFFICERS OF THE COMPANY

4.34 The commonhold association will need to have directors and a secretary. This is of course a standard corporate requirement and there are no special provisions in the CLRA 2002 to make a commonhold association different in this respect from any other company limited by guarantee. The Act does impose duties on the directors of a commonhold association as a body but, except as expressly provided, the duties of a director of the commonhold association will be similar to that of any corporate body. However, much more detailed provision relating to the qualification, appointment, and removal of the association's directors is made in the standard articles of association of any commonhold association.

4.35 Details of these matters as they relate to a functioning commonhold are considered later.[71] However, there are special provisions relating to the

---

[68] The draft was published on 8 October 2001; the draft form in the Appendix was updated on 24 January 2002.

[69] In cls 7–41.

[70] Clause 17 of the draft standard articles of association.

[71] See Chapter 10.

officers of the company prior to the registration of the commonhold and during any transitional period.[72]

The initial directors and company secretary

4.36   The initial directors and secretary of the company will be those persons named in the documentation delivered to the Registrar of Companies on incorporation.[73] These directors may remain in office until the first annual general meeting of the company after the end of the transitional period. At that meeting, all directors, other than any developer's directors, will retire from office.[74] Since the first annual general meeting may take place a considerable period of time after the formation of the company, those first directors will probably be the ones giving certification on registration of the commonhold. It is therefore suggested that these initial directors should be persons actively involved in the establishment of the commonhold.[75]

Developer's directors

4.37   Under the standard articles of association, the developer of a commonhold has the right to appoint and remove directors of the commonhold association, if the CCS confers that right on a developer.[76] In a new development, such a right is likely to be standard. In such a case, the developer is permitted to appoint a maximum of two directors during the transitional period, these directors being in addition to any appointed by the subscriber or subscribers to the memorandum of association.[77] There is a right to remove or replace any of the developer's directors appointed in this way.[78]

4.38   After the end of the transitional period, the developer continues to be entitled to appoint directors for as long as he is the unit-holder of more than one-quarter of the total number of units in the commonhold.[79] In such situations, the developer is entitled to appoint a total of one-quarter, or the nearest whole number exceeding one-quarter, of the maximum number of directors of the commonhold association and is also, once again, entitled to remove or replace any director so appointed.

---

[72]   For a transitional period, see **3.53**.

[73]   See Companies Act 1985, s 10(2).

[74]   Draft standard memorandum of association, cl 45.

[75]   It may not be essential for the directors appointed on incorporation to be actively involved as the subscriber members could appoint new directors, but since it appears essential for the subscribers to the memorandum to be actively involved, it seems sensible for the first directors to be involved also.

[76]   Draft standard memorandum of association, cl 44.

[77]   Ibid, cl 44.1

[78]   This is effected by notice in writing and takes effect on receipt at the association's registered office or on action by the Secretary from the date specified in the notice: ibid, cl 44.4.

[79]   Ibid, cl 44.2.

4.39 The ability to appoint directors is an important right given to a developer. It enables a degree of control of the commonhold association after the first units in the development are sold. After the first annual general meeting after the end of the transitional period, the developer cannot have automatic or total control of the commonhold association. The developer will not have control of meetings of the company. Although he will, effectively, be the unit-holder of all unsold units, he will have only a single vote in the meetings of the commonhold association during the period when the development is being marketed and the units progressively sold.

4.40 A director need not be a member of the commonhold association and there must always be a minimum number of two directors.[80] The normal maximum number of directors will be as determined by ordinary resolution of the commonhold association, but if there is no such resolution the maximum number is six.

Duties of directors

4.41 The duties of directors and other officers of the association are considered more fully in the context of the rules and regulations applying to management and running of a constituent commonhold community.[81] It is worthwhile noting, however, that the initial directors and the developer's directors of a commonhold association are subject to the general statutory duty contained in the CLRA 2002.[82] This duty requires the directors to exercise their powers so as to permit or facilitate, as far as possible, the exercise by each unit-holder of his rights and the enjoyment by each unit-holder of the freehold estate in the unit. This duty will be particularly important in the running and establishment of the commonhold in the period between the end of any transitional period (when the first unit is sold) and the termination of the office of any developer's directors.

---

[80] Draft standard memorandum of association, cls 42 and 43.

[81] See Chapter 10.

[82] CLRA 2002, s 34.

CHAPTER 5

THE COMMONHOLD COMMUNITY STATEMENT

THE CONCEPT

Definition

5.1   The statutory definition merely states that a commonhold community statement (CCS) is a document which makes provision in relation to specified land for the rights and duties of the commonhold association and the rights and duties of the unit-holders.[1] This simple and straightforward definition hardly does justice to what is in fact the central document of the whole commonhold community. The registered title to the estate in commonhold land, at first registration, will show the extent of the land forming the community and how it is divided between the commonhold units and the common parts. The commonhold association is a corporate personality holding title to the common parts. It provides a mechanism for the members of the community, through membership of the association, to have an equal say in community affairs. However, it is the CCS, drafted for a particular commonhold community, that will command the closest attention of any would-be buyer of a commonhold unit. In regulating the rights and duties of the community, it will be this document to which first reference will be made in the event of any need to resolve the extent of relevant powers and duties and to assist in resolving disputes and difficulties. Indeed, it is the plans that will be attached to the statement that are the basis of the registered titles and the division of the community into its constituent parts.

A local law for the community

5.2   Each unit-holder has a separate freehold title to his commonhold unit. As registered proprietors of such units, unit-holders will, in principle, have the same rights, duties and benefits as other any other registered freehold owners. However, the CCS will be the source of a new local law that will transform a

---

[1]   CLRA 2002, s 31(1).

unit-holder's position.[2] It will set out the details of how the community is to be run. The person entitled to a commonhold unit will have rights and duties, benefits and limitations that will have a considerable impact on the enjoyment of the freehold estate in the land. Unlike any other freeholder, the unit-holder, by virtue of the title to that unit, will be obliged by the CCS to expend funds. This may involve paying money to the commonhold association for the repair and maintenance of the common parts; or towards the benefit of building up a reserve fund; or to undertake works of repair and maintenance to the unit itself. There may be an obligation to grant access, perhaps to other unit-holders and certainly to the commonhold association, and to give notices on the happening of certain events. A whole range of restrictions may apply to unit-holders by virtue of the CCS. Commonhold unit owners may be limited in the nature of works and alterations that can be undertaken in relation to the unit. As well as specified restrictions on the way the unit is used,[3] behaviour that causes nuisance or annoyance to others within the community and certain other specified behaviour may be prohibited.

5.3   Lastly, but certainly not least, the CCS will contain the miscellaneous rules formulated for that particular community. If experience in overseas jurisdictions is a guide, then there will be regulation of, or restrictions on, the keeping of pets and other animals, the placing of TV aerials and satellite dishes and the playing of children in the common parts. Regulations may be made on such detailed matters such as the hanging out of washing, the placing of window boxes and the display of signs in windows. These issues may generate disagreement between unit-holders with divergent approaches to community life. Yet all these duties and restrictions will, in applying equally to all the other unit-holders, exist for the benefit of the community as a whole. They will be subject to change and modification if the community so wishes. A buyer into the community will be aware of the exact content of this local law, embodied in the CCS, when considering the purchase and, after the purchase is completed, will always be able to promote or participate in proposed changes to that statement.

5.4   An analogy can be drawn between the preparation of the CCS for a new commonhold and the preparation of a draft lease for a new development of flats by way of 99- or 999-year leases. As with a draft lease, the CCS must be ready for the first sale. It also achieves not dissimilar functions in delineating the property transferred on the sale of the flat and regulating the rights of the parties. A commonhold, however, with the CCS, has a number of distinct advantages. Instead of two documents for each flat, a lease and a counterpart,

---

[2]   CLRA 2002, s 31(3) gives the authority for a CCS to impose duties either on a commonhold association or on a unit owner and s 31(5) contains a range of examples, widely defined and not an exclusive or exhaustive list, of the duties which may be imposed.

[3]   One of the few specified restrictions relating to a commonhold unit which may have a counterpart in standard freehold titles in the form of restrictive covenants.

there is the single CCS. Immediately, in a block of 50 flats, 100 long documents are reduced to one. There is no risk, as with leases, of different provisions applying to each flat. The delineation of the common parts from the individual flats is on one set of plans and not spread among 50 such sets. There is a prescribed procedure for changing the CCS, which is straightforward when compared to the tortuous procedure for changing the terms of defective flat leases.[4] Finally, instead of forcing the duties and responsibilities into the straightjacket of a landlord and tenant relationship, the CCS is the document regulating a freehold community.

THE STATUTORY PROVISIONS

Form

5.5   Despite its central importance, there is remarkably little in the statute itself relating to the commonhold community statement. It must be a document which provides for all the land within the commonhold[5] and be in the prescribed form with a definitive plan.

An initial requirement

5.6   As we have seen, the CLRA 2002 provides that land can be commonhold land only if there is a CCS making provision for the rights and duties of the parties.[6] Moreover, that statement is one of the documents that must be delivered to the Registrar on any application for registration of land as commonhold land.[7] However, apart from requiring the statement to be in a final and definitive form at the outset of the establishment of a commonhold, the Act then does little more than provide an enabling framework for the drafting and production of a CCS.

The enabling framework

5.7   In just three sections,[8] the CLRA 2002 provides the necessary framework for the drafting of a CCS for any particular proposed commonhold land. Thus, it provides that the CCS must be in the prescribed form[9] and it contains the necessary power to make regulations about the

---

[4]   Landlord and Tenant Act 1987, Part IV, as amended by the Housing Act 1988 and the Leasehold Reform Housing and Urban Development Act 1993, gives either party to a long lease of a flat the right to apply for an order varying the terms of the lease. The CLRA 2002 varies the grounds and transfers jurisdiction from the court to a leasehold valuation tribunal – see ss 162–163.

[5]   CLRA 2002, s 57(2). There will be a single CCS even if the commonhold consists of two or more parcels of land.

[6]   Ibid, s 1(1)(c).

[7]   Ibid, Sch 1, and see **3.24**.

[8]   Ibid, ss 31–33.

[9]   Ibid, s 31(2).

provisions of the content of that statement.[10] The Act ensures that regulations from time to time will provide for a standard form for all statements, although the exact wording of the relevant section[11] would not satisfy the exponents of plain English drafting:

> 'The regulations may permit, require or prohibit the inclusion in a statement of—
>
> (a) specified provision, or
> (b) provision of a specified kind, for a specified purpose or about a specified matter.'

The first such draft regulations do, indeed, provide such a standard form.[12]

5.8   The ability of the CCS to impose duties either on the commonhold association or on the unit-holder, and for the allocation of decision-making within the management of a commonhold, is defined in extensive terms.[13] The power is given to impose duties either on the commonhold association or on a unit-holder.[14] The duties are specifically defined to include duties to pay money; to undertake works; to grant access;[15] to give notice; and to indemnify the commonhold association or a unit-holder in respect of costs arising from the breach of a statutory requirement.[16] The restrictions that may be imposed are referred to in the statute as 'duties to refrain from' doing something. These naturally include what in another context would be known as a restrictive covenant, namely, a duty to refrain from using the whole or part of a commonhold unit for a specified purpose or for anything other than a specified purpose.[17] However, the restrictions may also extend to imposing a duty to refrain from entering into transactions of a specified kind in relation to a commonhold unit,[18] from undertaking works (including alterations) of any specified kind, from causing nuisance or annoyance or from behaving in

---

[10]   CLRA 2002, s 32(1).

[11]   Ibid, s 32(2).

[12]   The drafts of these regulations were provided during the parliamentary passage of the legislation because of the importance of the contents in assisting parliamentary scrutiny of the Bill.

[13]   CLRA 2002, s 31(3)–(5).

[14]   Ibid, s 31(3)(a) and (b).

[15]   The reference to granting access would appear to refer primarily to a duty on a unit-holder to give the commonhold association power of access, no doubt for specified purposes and at specified times, to commonhold units. However, it would not appear to be so limited and could, it is submitted, extend to imposing a duty on a unit-holder to grant access to another or other unit-holders.

[16]   CLRA 2002, s 31(5)(a)–(d) and (j).

[17]   Ibid, s 31(5)(f). The wording of this sub-section would suggest that it does not extend to requiring the unit-holder to use the unit in a particular way. But the breadth of ss 14 and 31 generally suggests that a CCS could impose a positive obligation or duty to use a unit in a defined manner.

[18]   CLRA 2002, s 31(5)(e); this will apply particularly in relation to powers of leasing the commonhold unit, a topic more fully discussed at **6.17–6.27**.

specified ways.[19] To ensure fairness within the community and, in particular, to prevent any disadvantage to prompt payers, any duty to pay money contained in the CCS can include provision for payment of interest in the case of late payment.[20] Duties conferred by a CCS either on a commonhold association or a unit-holder shall not require any other formality.[21] This ensures that a statement does not seek to discourage the exercise of rights or the performance of duties by the imposition of any extra formalities. For the avoidance of doubt, it is also specifically provided that a CCS may not provide for the transfer or loss of an interest in land on the occurrence or non-occurrence of a specified event.[22] This provision is undoubtedly intended to ensure that nothing equivalent to a forfeiture of a lease can be introduced through the CCS by the back door.[23]

5.9 There is the overriding rule that all provisions within a CCS are subject not only to the primary legislation, but also to secondary legislation and the memorandum or articles of the commonhold association. A provision in a statement is of no effect to the extent that it is prohibited, or is inconsistent with, the CLRA 2002; or is inconsistent with anything treated as included in the statement by regulation; or is inconsistent with the memorandum or articles of association of the commonhold association.[24]

AMENDMENT

5.10 A commonhold community statement is a document regulating an ongoing and changing community. Consequently, the CLRA 2002 provides that the regulations[25] must require a CCS to make provision about how it can be amended.[26] This will be achieved by requiring any statement to be treated as including prescribed provision for amendment if none is actually included.[27] Any amendment which involves changing the size or extent of a commonhold unit or involving additions to common parts is subject to special statutory provisions,[28] but otherwise amendments will be in accordance with the

---

[19] CLRA 2002, s 31(5)(g), (h) and (i).

[20] Ibid, s 31(6).

[21] Ibid, s 31(7).

[22] Ibid, s 31(8).

[23] It may be thought unlikely that this would have ever been possible, since a commonhold unit is freehold land, but is a useful safeguard to ensure that some form of contingent or determinable estate or interest cannot be created in the CCS.

[24] CLRA 2002, s 31(9).

[25] Made under s 32.

[26] Ibid, s 33(1)

[27] Ibid, ss 33(2) and 32(3)(a).

[28] Ibid, ss 23, 24 and 30; and **6.35** and **7.14**.

procedure set out in the statement itself.[29] That procedure must also meet the requirements of the regulations (not yet made).

5.11 An amendment of a CCS will have no effect until registered.[30] Application for registration of an amended CCS is made by the commonhold association and must be accompanied by a certificate given by the directors that the amendment satisfies the statutory requirements.[31] If the amendment redefines the extent of a commonhold unit, then the application must be accompanied by the necessary consents[32] or by order of the court dispensing with consent.[33] Similarly, consents must accompany the application if the extent of the common parts is changed.[34] The Registrar then arranges for the amended CCS to be kept in his custody and referred to in the register in place of the previous version of the statement, making any consequential amendments that he thinks appropriate.[35]

DRAFTING A COMMONHOLD COMMUNITY STATEMENT

5.12 A glance at the standard form CCS provided by the regulations[36] rapidly reveals that the person drafting the statement must provide a lot of material. The statutory model is not dissimilar in this respect to an office precedent for a long residential lease. Just as that precedent will provide the starting point for a draftsman (by suggesting what ought to be included), so also the statutory model of CCS gives guidance on what should be included. The difference is that the majority of the standard 'Rules of the Commonhold Association' set out in the CCS[37] are mandatory. Only those provisions printed in italics are optional. These are provided by way of illustration only and may be adopted if relevant to the community being established. The first parts of the statement, Parts I–III, are a mere template for the draftsman to complete.

---

[29]   It is likely that the regulations will permit a CCS to make its own provision for its amendment within the statutory parameters – see CLRA 2002, s 32(3)(b).

[30]   Ibid, s 33(3).

[31]   Ibid, s 33(4) and (5).

[32]   These will be consent of the unit-holder in writing prior to the amendment being made and a similar consent from the registered proprietor of any charge over the unit – see CLRA 2002, ss 23(1) and 24(2).

[33]   Ibid, s 33(6).

[34]   Ibid, s 33(7). The consent required is that of the registered proprietor of the added land under s 30(2), although regulations may enable the court to dispense with consent in specified circumstances.

[35]   Ibid, s 33(4) and (8).

[36]   The draft available at the time of writing, which represents 'work in progress', is printed in Appendix 2.

[37]   In CLRA 2002, Part 4.

Factual background

5.13 The first part of a CCS will be a straightforward description of the totality of the land. This may comprise a brief description in words, but in a usual case the *address* of the commonhold will be sufficient since the plan attached (and, eventually, the registered title) will show the extent of the community and the estate in commonhold land. The title number of the freehold estate in commonhold land and the date of registration of the freehold estate in commonhold land will not appear.[38]

5.14 The commonhold association, which of course must be established before the CCS can be finalised, will provide the next set of factual details. The CCS will set out the name of the commonhold association, its registered number,[39] its date of incorporation and its registered office at the time of the completion of the CCS.

5.15 Finally, the name (and company registration number, if applicable) of the applicant for registration will be stated.[40] This information will be important if the applicant is a developer reserving developer's rights in the CCS.

Definition of the commonhold

5.16 Part II of the CCS will be centred on the *plan or plans* of the commonhold.[41] They must together show each commonhold unit, the common parts and any limited use areas and be attached to the statement. In the event of an inconsistency between any of the descriptions and the plans, the plans will prevail. Alongside the plans, the verbal description will begin by stating the *type of commonhold* (ie whether it is to be residential only, commercial only or mixed-use).

5.17 The division of the commonhold into units, common parts and (in some cases, limited use areas) will be articulated. The total number of *commonhold units* must be stated and listed, and each unit identified by reference to the plans. For each unit, there will need to be a description, a distinctive address and a description of any excluded structures, fittings, apparatus or appurtenances. A residential unit will be specifically identified as such as some rules of the commonhold only apply to residential units. Most importantly, in every case, the relevant percentage or percentages allocated to the unit for the purposes of payment of the commonhold assessment and levies in respect of

---

[38] Neither the title number nor the date of registration can be known when the CCS is prepared in readiness for registration of the commonhold.

[39] At the Companies Registry.

[40] It is not clear from the draft if this will always have to be included or only in those cases where there is a developer.

[41] The draftsman will be able to choose whether to have a single plan or more than one. In any event, the scale and detail of the plans will probably have to conform to regulations.

reserve payments must be fixed at this point.[42] Even the first buyer of a unit will have the assurance that the percentage allocated to the unit being purchased is constrained and defined within an overall conception of the total number of units and the total percentage, which must add up to one hundred.[43]

5.18   A buyer of a unit will be able to identify from the CCS the nature of the *common parts*. Although it may include a description of the common parts, it may be sufficient to show these only on the plans, as the common parts will necessarily consist of those parts of the commonhold not forming part of any unit.[44] However, any area of the common parts designated as *limited use areas* must be specifically identified and described with a description of the area, a statement of the classes of persons who may use each such area and the kind of use to which the area may be put. Such limited use areas might include balconies to certain flats or gardens set aside for specific unit-holders.

5.19   If a *legal mortgage* of the common part later exists,[45] this will be included only on the charges register of the title to the common parts.

Development rights

5.20   The rights of a developer of a commonhold are discussed later.[46] Where there is a developer, then the CCS must include a statement of the rights claimed by the developer. These may include:

– the right to add land to the commonhold;
– the right to remove land from the commonhold;
– the right, if any, to redefine the commonhold units; and
– the right to complete works.

5.21   Any of these rights, if stated, must show the land to which they relate. They will have a termination date, the date on which they will expire if unexercised.

5.22   Similarly, the extent and effect of development business, the rights to market the commonhold units and the rights to appoint and remove directors of the commonhold association[47] must be set out in the CCS, where relevant.

---

[42]   For the purposes of CLRA 2002, ss 37 and 38. See further **10.21–10.32**.

[43]   Ibid, s 38(2)(a).

[44]   The current draft does not suggest a separate description of the common parts.

[45]   This will not be the case except where the procedures of CLRA 2002, s 29 have been followed.

[46]   See Chapter 8.

[47]   Known as developer's directors.

Other matters

5.23   If rights over commonhold units or the common parts exist at the time of its establishment, then these rights will appear on the registered titles in the usual way. These rights may include public rights, such as a public right of way or private rights which may be rights of drainage or private rights of way. The first suggested version of the CCS indicated that these would also be included in that document, but this has been deleted from the current draft.

5.24   Where the commonhold is being established with initial unit-holders,[48] usually by way of conversion from established leasehold titles in an existing development, then the persons who are the proposed initial unit-holders will be known. Originally, the CCS had to set out the list of these persons. Sensibly, this has been omitted from the current draft. A buyer will always be able to ascertain who the unit-holders are and an initial list would gradually become out of date.

Rules of the commonhold association

5.25   The final part of any CCS will be the Rules. The current version remains, at the time of writing, a working draft and further additions, changes and refinements are likely in the period before commonhold is implemented. It is not intended therefore to provide an analysis of the draft as it exists at present. The draft is printed in its latest form[49] and largely speaks for itself in any event. Some of its provisions, such as those relating to complaints, default procedures and enforcement are referred to elsewhere.[50] Some general points can be made at this stage.

–   Any set of rules in a CCS will consist partly of mandatory provisions, which will be drawn from the model form in the regulations, and partly of others, which will be drafted for the community in question.

–   A good number of the mandatory clauses repeat provisions of the CLRA 2002.

–   The model form shows optional provisions in italics by way of illustration, but there is a freedom to add to these suggested clauses provided always that the statutory framework is adhered to.

–   There is flexibility in the suggested clauses on use, repair and maintenance. It is necessary to make some provision on these matters. However, the choice, for example, of whether a unit is to be repaired entirely by the unit-holder or whether the exterior is to be the responsibility of the commonhold association, will depend primarily on

---

[48]   Under CLRA 2002, s 9 and with a statement giving a list of the proposed unit-holders.

[49]   See Appendix 2.

[50]   See **11.9**.

the nature of the development and to a lesser extent on the wishes of the developer.

Provision for termination

5.26   A CCS may make provision for the termination of the commonhold. The CLRA 2002 permits the CCS to make provision requiring a termination statement to make arrangements about the rights of unit-holders in the event of all the land ceasing to be commonhold land. These arrangements can be of a specified kind or may be determined in a specified manner.[51] It is unlikely to be common for a CCS to make express provision relating to its termination.[52] If, however, such provisions are contained in the statement, then the termination statement must comply with them.[53] The draft CCS suggests a possible approach. It states that any surplus on winding up be paid to or distributed among the members rateably in accordance with the percentages allocated to their commonhold unit in the CCS.[54] It will always be possible to add to the CCS, some years after the commonhold is first set up, provisions to take effect on termination.

---

[51]   CLRA 2002, s 47(2).

[52]   It may not be sensible as such provision could become inappropriate with the passage of time. In any event, the court has power to disapply all or part of the arrangements contained in the CCS – see CLRA 2002, s 47(4), and **12.14**.

[53]   Ibid, s 47(3). Termination of a commonhold is considered fully in Chapter 12

[54]   In cl 82 – see Appendix 2.

CHAPTER 6

THE COMMONHOLD UNIT AND UNIT-HOLDERS

DEFINITION OF A COMMONHOLD UNIT

6.1 Once the commonhold is activated,[1] there will be, necessarily, two or more commonhold units with different registered proprietors. A commonhold unit is defined as the unit specified in a commonhold community statement (CCS) in accordance with the Commonhold and Leasehold Reform Act 2002 (CLRA 2002),[2] a definition both practical and documentary.[3] It is for this reason that, at the outset, a CCS must specify at least two parcels of land as commonhold units and must define the extent of the units concerned.[4] We have already seen the necessity for such a statement to refer to a plan, set out the areas of the units and show exactly which parts of structures are included in the units and which are part of the common parts.[5] The prescribed precision in delineation of the commonhold unit in the CCS is a necessary consequence of defining the units in this way. It is clear that a unit need not be a building, but can be an undeveloped part of the commonhold, such as a car parking space or garden, and the unit need not contain all or any part of the building.[6] Within the area of the unit (as defined) any specified structures, fittings apparatus or appurtenances may be excluded from the unit, and the structures which delineate the unit may themselves be excluded from it.[7] In the case of a flat, for example, the unit may be defined so as to exclude the external walls of the building. It is possible to specify, if it

---

[1] The term used in this book to describe the moment when there is more than one unit-holder and the rights and duties conferred and imposed by the commonhold community statement come into force – see **3.63**.

[2] CLRA 2002, s 11(1).

[3] In other words, it depends entirely upon the provisions of the CCS drafted by the developer or freehold promoter of the commonhold.

[4] CLRA 2002, s 11(2).

[5] See **5.17**, and ibid, s 11(3)(a).

[6] Ibid, s 11(4). Indeed, a unit does not have to be marked out or delineated physically.

[7] Ibid, s 11(3)(b) and (c).

is desired, that all, or some, of the windows, air conditioning units or service pipes or conduits (or whatever) are excluded from the unit.[8]

6.2   Just as a commonhold itself can contain two or more parcels of land which need not be contiguous, so also a unit within the commonhold may refer to two or more areas of the commonhold community land – and again these need not be contiguous.[9] This will permit a flat and a parking space or garage to be defined within the CCS as a single unit. It will be a matter of choice whether such flats and garages are defined as a single unit or listed and delineated as entirely separate units within the commonhold. The advantage of a single unit of the two parcels of land will be greater simplicity in the allocation of the commonhold assessment and levies; but the alternative of keeping garages, car parking spaces and the like as separate units means that it will be possible to transfer them separately.[10] An additional motive for creating two (or more) separate units, rather than one, may be to give a unit-holder additional voting power in the commonhold association.[11]

THE UNIT-HOLDER

6.3   A unit-holder of a commonhold unit is the person entitled to be registered as the proprietor of the freehold estate in the unit.[12] Consequently, a unit-holder has full entitlement to the rights, and is subject to the duties, of unit-holder from the moment of the transfer of the unit. Any delay in completing the registration of the person entitled to the unit as proprietor is of no consequence.[13]

Joint unit-holders

6.4   As with any freehold estate in land, a commonhold unit can be held by two or more persons as joint unit-holders.[14] The CLRA 2002 provides for joint unit-holders of a commonhold unit wherever two or more persons are

---

[8]   By excluding such items, they become part of the common parts and so subject to repair and maintenance by the commonhold association, not the unit-holder.

[9]   CLRA 2002, s 11(3)(d).

[10]   This may or may not be an advantage. It might be thought unhelpful to permit the transfer of a commonhold parking space or garage unit to a person who does not reside in the commonhold community (for example). Section 39 of the New South Wales Strata Schemes (Freehold Development) Act 1996 includes garages in a definition of a 'utility lot' and restrictions can be imposed by local councils to prevent use of the garage other than by an owner. It is likely the CCS could equally provide that units such as garages are not to be used except by a resident within the commonhold.

[11]   See the discussion at **4.16–4.20**.

[12]   CLRA 2002, s 12.

[13]   Ibid, proviso.

[14]   The maximum number of joint unit-holders will be four (Trustee Act 1925, s 34(2)) with the unit-holders holding the legal estate in the commonhold unit as joint tenants at law upon a trust of land in the usual way.

entitled to be registered as proprietors of the freehold estate in the unit.[15] Consequently, all the references in the statute to a unit-holder include a reference to the joint unit-holders together.[16] Certain specified sections provide that reference to a unit-holder is not only a reference to the joint unit-holders together but also a reference to each joint unit-holder individually.[17] Rights and responsibilities on unit-holders are therefore either joint or joint and individual and the position is clear for any particular reference to a unit-holder in the CLRA 2002. Generally, references to joint responsibility occur where all joint holders need to act together or be seen as one person, such as in relation to transfer of the unit or consent to changes.[18] The concept of individual rights and responsibility, in addition to the joint right or liability, arises primarily in relation to the obligations contained in the CCS and in respect of co-operation with the developer.[19]

Membership of the commonhold association

6.5 As soon as a person is entitled to be registered as the proprietor of a freehold estate in a commonhold unit, that person is entitled to become a member of the commonhold association.[20] Although the unit-holder is entitled to the rights and subject to the duties of unit-holders immediately on being entitled to register, he becomes a member of the commonhold association only when the company registers him in the Register of Members.[21] A unit-holder cannot avoid membership of the association. The commonhold association has a duty to complete the registration of the member and a unit-holder cannot resign as a member of the association.[22] As a consequence, the membership of the association consists of the persons who are entitled to be registered as freehold proprietors of commonhold units

---

[15] CLRA 2002, s 13(1). Once again, they become joint unit-holders on entitlement to be registered, whether or not they are in fact registered.

[16] Ibid, s 13(2) and (3).

[17] Ibid, s 13(3). All regulations are to make provision for the construction of the reference to unit-holder in the case of joint unit-holders by either stating that it is a reference to the joint unit-holder together alone or to each joint unit-holder and joint unit-holders together or by making some other provision: s 13(4). The regulations themselves can amend the detailed provisions of the meaning of the reference to a unit-holder within s 13(2) and (3): s 13(5). Regulations may provide for the correct construction of references to a unit-holder in any other statute, a CCS, the memorandum or articles of association or, indeed, any other document: s 13(6).

[18] Thus the duty to notify the association of a transfer of the unit (ibid, s 15(3)) is a joint responsibility. The requirement of consent of the unit-holder to an amendment of the CCS (s 23(1)(b)) is also a reference to all the unit-holders jointly.

[19] For example, the rights and duties of the unit-holders (ibid, s 31(1)(b)) as provided in the CCS is a reference to unit-holders both jointly and individually. Likewise, the duty to co-operate with a developer (s 58(3)(a)) is a duty owed both jointly and individually by each joint unit-holder.

[20] Ibid, Sch 3, para 7; either on transfer of the unit or on the unit becoming commonhold land by registration under s 9.

[21] Ibid, Sch 3, para 11, and see the discussion at **4.21**.

[22] Ibid, Sch 3, para 13.

in the commonhold as defined in the CCS, and may consist of no other persons.[23]

6.6   Only one person out of the joint unit-holders may become a member of the commonhold association. There are provisions to ensure that the commonhold association will either register as a member the person nominated by the joint unit-holders in writing to the association or, in default of nomination, the person whose name appears first in the proprietorship register.[24]

TRANSFERS OF THE UNIT

Free alienability

6.7   A commonhold unit will be transferred by registered land transfer in the same way as the transfer of any other freehold property.[25] Just as it is not possible to restrict the transfer of the freehold estate in land,[26] nor may the transfer of the freehold estate in a unit in commonhold land be restricted. It is specifically provided that a CCS may not prevent or restrict the transfer[27] of a commonhold unit.[28] Similarly, the CCS cannot prevent or restrict the creation, grant or transfer by unit-holder of an interest[29] in the whole or part of his unit or restrict in any way a charge over the unit.[30] These specific provisions ensure that there can be no possibility of imposing restrictions, such as those often found in long leases, relating to the assignment of the lease or the creation of

---

[23]   Except for the subscriber members and the developer when the commonhold association is first established who, exceptionally, are permitted to resign – see CLRA 2002, Sch 3, paras 5, 6, 10 and 13 and **4.24**.

[24]   Ibid, Sch 3, para 8(4). There might be a potential problem for the secretary of the commonhold association where joint unit-holders are entitled to be registered but for one reason or another the registration is not complete, yet the time for registration of unit-holder in the register of members of the company is about to expire or has already expired. In those circumstances, in the absence of either a nomination or registration, it would seem that the secretary of the commonhold association would not know the name of the person who should be entered as the member of the association. See also the discussion in **4.28**.

[25]   It is not yet clear whether special forms of transfer for commonhold units, separate from those for standard freehold, are to be prescribed.

[26]   Except through the medium of a trust.

[27]   A reference to the transfer of a commonhold unit is a reference to the transfer of a unit-holder's freehold estate in a unit to another person whether or not for consideration, whether or not subject to any reservation or other terms and whether or not by operation of law: CLRA 2002, s 15(1).

[28]   Ibid, s 15(2). In Part 1 of the Act, a reference to the transfer of a commonhold unit means a reference to the transfer of the freehold estate in a unit to any other person whether or not it is for consideration, whether or not it is subject to any reservation or other terms and whether or not it is not by operation of law: s 15(1).

[29]   Interest in this context does not include a charge or an interest which arises by virtue of a charge: s 20(6).

[30]   Ibid, s 20(1). But the statute specifically provides for restrictions on leasing (see **6.17**), so the freedom of the unit-holder is limited to that extent – see s 15(2).

charges. The only obligation that is similar to that in the long leasehold situation is the requirement for any new unit-holder, following a transfer, to notify the commonhold association accordingly.[31] There is power for regulations to prescribe the form and manner of the notice of such a transfer, to prescribe the time within which notice is to be given or to make provision about the effect of failure to give notice which may include a provision requiring the payment of money.[32]

Restriction on the creation of prescribed interests

6.8 The general principle, namely that preventing or restricting the creation grant or transfer by a unit-holder of an interest in the whole or part of his unit, is subject to one important exception. It is not possible to create an interest *of a prescribed kind*[33] in the whole or part of a commonhold unit unless the commonhold association is party to the creation of the interest or consents in writing to its creation.[34] The Bill as drafted made reference to *an interest other than a term of years absolute.* The aim was to limit the creation of legal interests such as easements and profits or other interests that might cause a nuisance to other unit-holders except with the approval of the commonhold association.[35] However, it was pointed out that the original wording could have extended[36] to interests created behind a trust of land or to interests arising by way of constructive trust.[37] The amendment was duly made to ensure that the necessity for the consent of the association did not extend beyond those matters that could affect other unit-holders. Regulations will now prescribe the interests to which the clause applies. The creation of easements and profits, or any other prescibed interest, over a unit will require the consent of the association and there will be consultation on whether other specific interests should be prescribed as requiring consents. Any instrument or agreement purporting to create an interest without the required consent of the commonhold association will be of no effect.[38]

6.9 Obtaining the consent of the association to the creation of a prescribed interest may not be easy. The consent can only be provided by a resolution to

---

[31] CLRA 2002, s 15(3).

[32] Ibid, s 15(4).

[33] The author's italics.

[34] CLRA 2002, s 20(3).

[35] See HC Deb, Vol 381, col 677 (Mr Michael Wills).

[36] The use of the phrase 'in' the unit, rather than 'of' or 'over' the unit, might have suggested that the requirement of consent would have extended to the creation of interests behind a trust of land.

[37] It would be very strange if consent of the commonhold association had been required for a unit-holder to place the unit in trust for his family, for example. By their very nature, it would be unlikely that consent could be sought for any interests arising under a constructive trust, nor could the commonhold association be a party to their creation. The same argument could be made in relation to interests arising by estoppel.

[38] CLRA 2002, s 20(5).

take the action to become party to the creation of the interest, so a meeting of the association will have to be called after due notice. When the resolution is proposed at the meeting, at least 75% of those who vote on the resolution must vote in favour.[39] This consent procedure also applies where consent is sought for the creation of an interest in part only of a commonhold unit.[40]

Liability of unit-holder for the time being

6.10   One of the essential objectives of a commonhold is that a departing unit-holder should not incur future rights and duties relating to the commonhold and a new unit-holder should take over all those rights and duties. The CLRA 2002 therefore provides that a right or duty, whether conferred or imposed by a CCS or by the Act, shall affect a new unit-holder in the same way as it affected the former unit-holder.[41] In this way, the common-law rule in *Austerberry v Oldham Corporation*[42] is abrogated within the commonhold. The rights and liabilities relating to the unit pass to the new unit-holder. As a corollary, a former unit-holder cannot incur a liability or acquire a right under or by virtue of the CCS.[43] Liabilities incurred before the transfer are not affected.[44] To ensure that there is no possibility of getting round these basic principles, it is further provided that the freedom of a former unit-holder from future liabilities may not be disapplied or varied by any agreement.[45]

6.11   It should be noted that the new unit-holder acquires the rights and incurs the liabilities immediately on transfer of the unit and the former unit-holder can no longer incur a liability nor acquire a right from the same date. This effect is achieved by the relevant definitions of *former unit-holder* and *new unit-holder*. These are defined, respectively, to mean a person from whom a commonhold unit has been transferred or is transferred, or to whom the unit is transferred, whether or not the person has become the registered proprietor of the unit.[46]

6.12   Upon ceasing to be a unit-holder or a joint unit-holder for a commonhold unit, the person concerned ceases to be a member of the commonhold association, again without prejudice to any rights or liabilities

---

[39]   CLRA 2002, s 20(4). The majority rule seems to look to the number of voting members even where, after a call for a poll, one or more members have the right to exercise more than one vote – see **10.14**.

[40]   Ibid, s 21(4), and **6.30**.

[41]   Ibid, s 16(1).

[42]   (1885) 29 Ch D 750; and see the discussion in **1.11**.

[43]   CLRA 2002, s 16(2)(a).

[44]   Ibid, s 16(3)(b).

[45]   Ibid, s 16(3)(a). Similarly, when the consent of a commonhold association is required to the creation of an interest in the unit, such consent cannot provide for a former unit-holder to acquire rights or incur liabilities: s 16(2)(b).

[46]   Ibid, s 16(4).

acquired or incurred while he was a unit-holder and member of the commonhold association.[47]

6.13 The aim of these provisions overall is to ensure that the current unit-holder is always the person with the full range of benefits under the CLRA 2002 and the CCS and is subject to all the obligations of a unit-holder relating to the unit that is held. More particularly, they mean that no one else can have a greater interest in the unit than the unit-holder. No contract, transfer or other action can bind a unit-holder beyond the date of the transfer of a unit, which the unit-holder is permitted to sell or give away at any time. Equally, after transfer, a former unit-holder can gain no benefit or right from the community once he has ceased to be a member of the commonhold association and an owner within the community.

RULES AND RESTRICTIONS NOT APPLICABLE TO OTHER FREEHOLDS

6.14 Although a commonhold unit is part of the freehold estate in commonhold land and is a defined freehold section of that commonhold community, nevertheless there are many rules and restrictions arising from the nature of the community title which are not applicable to other freeholds. A selling point for commonhold units will be the fact that they are freehold titles, but the reality is different. There is the necessity (which will probably be understood begrudgingly) to pay regular commonhold assessments and levies by way of establishing reserve funds. However, the commonholder will find that the unit is subject to much greater restrictions than could ever be the case in a standard freehold.

Use and maintenance

6.15 Any freehold title may be subject to provisions relating to the use of that land.[48] A commonhold unit, however, *must* be subject to provisions regulating its use. A CCS must make this provision.[49] In many circumstances, this requirement will be met by stating that the unit is designated as a residential unit (or for purposes ancillary to such residential use) or for mixed use, or that the use is restricted to commercial industrial or retail purposes.[50] However, more specific and detailed provision regulating use would seem to be possible. For example, the provision within a community designed as homes for retired people within warden-controlled accommodation could

---

[47] CLRA 2002, Sch 3, para 12.

[48] By virtue of the imposition of restrictive covenants.

[49] CLRA 2002, s 14(1).

[50] Part II of the current draft of the standard CCS provides for a description of the type of unit (whether residential only, commercial only or mixed use). Clause 16 of the rules of the association sets out a compulsory designation of use whenever a commonhold includes any residential units.

make provision not only regulating the use as residential, but also requiring that those purchasing the units do so for the purpose only of permitting residence by persons who exceed a particular age.[51]

6.16   The CCS must go further than merely regulating the use of a unit. Unlike any other freehold land (where positive covenants and duties in respect of insurance repair and maintenance cannot be imposed so as to bind successors in title), a CCS must make provision imposing duties in respect of these responsibilities in relation to each commonhold unit.[52] In other words, someone must have the obligation to insure the unit[53] and to be responsible for repair and maintenance. Those duties do not have to be imposed on the unit-holder and may be a responsibility of either the unit-holder or the commonhold association.[54] What is important is that the developer of a commonhold community should decide how these responsibilities are to be divided. It will be usual in the case of a block of flats that the responsibility to insure and maintain the external structure (which will be defined as part of the common parts) will belong to the commonhold association. Internal repairs, maintenance and decoration of a flat unit would normally be the responsibility of the unit owner. Where, however, the units are detached houses, all the responsibilities for insurance and repair can be allocated to the unit owner. There is no reason why the responsibilities in the relation to the unit cannot be divided between the commonhold association and the unit-holder, as appropriate to each individual situation.

Restrictions on leasing of units

Rationale of the restrictions on residential units

6.17   One of the more controversial aspects of the CLRA 2002 relates to the restrictions on the ability of a residential unit owner to lease the commonhold unit. It is not possible to create a term of years absolute in a residential commonhold unit unless the term satisfies the prescribed conditions and regulations.[55] The conditions may relate to the length of the term, the circumstances in which it is granted or any other matter.[56]

---

[51]   Such restrictions are currently commonly found in long leases of units designed for the elderly with a resident warden on site. However, transfers of such units could not be restricted to persons of a certain age.

[52]   CLRA 2002, s 14(2). 'Repair' is not defined by the CLRA 2002 but a reference to maintaining property includes a reference to decorating it and to putting it in a sound condition: s 69(2)(b).

[53]   A reference to a duty to insure includes a reference to a duty to use the proceeds of insurance for the purpose of rebuilding or reinstating: CLRA 2002, s 69(2)(a).

[54]   Ibid, s 14(3).

[55]   Ibid, s 17(1); the power to make regulations is contained in s 19.

[56]   Ibid, s 17(2).

6.18 The rationale of restrictions on leasing appears to be two-fold. The justifiable reason is to avoid the creation within the commonhold of long leases at low rents. Commonhold is designed as the future way to develop residential homes and flats that are purchased at a premium rather than let at market rent. It would not have been sensible to permit unrestricted long leases at low rents of commonhold units in any event, as the unit owner would then be left with no real interest in the community. Long leases at low rent of commonhold units make no sense. If this were the only rationale, it may have been sufficient to impose only a modest restriction; for example, that the leasing of a commonhold unit should be at the best rent obtainable without the demand for a premium or a fine.[57] Such a requirement for any lease to be at a market rent would, in effect, have ensured that longer leases were not in general a desirable proposition, but it would have permitted a unit owner who, for example, wished to work abroad for a long period of time to lease the property for as long as he wished. There would have been no undue restriction on those persons who wished to invest in a commonhold unit and let it for an income return.

6.19 An additional reason, less justifiable, was articulated for leasing restrictions, namely the idea that the unit-holder, who is the member of the commonhold association, should normally reside in the unit and have an interest in the commonhold community as a resident.[58] The belief, apparently, was that a commonhold is likely to be better managed in such circumstances. However, the idea of commonholds being less viable when primarily occupied by tenants involves a failure to see this new form of landholding being used other than as a simple replacement for long leasehold. In other jurisdictions, it is quite common for strata title units to be developed primarily for rent and for purchase by investors. The management of such units is undertaken not by the members themselves (on an unpaid basis) but by professional agents who market their expertise in running such developments. A key cultural change in England and Wales will be for property managers (who currently largely work on behalf of those who own reversions to residential leases) to see the opportunity to market their services to commonhold associations. Members of associations assume general oversight of management through the general meeting, but professional directors can implement the commonhold's policies and manage it on an efficient and smooth basis on behalf of the residents. Outside investors purchasing commonhold units for rent will almost certainly prefer professional management.

---

[57] A concept already well established by virtue of s 54(2) of the Law of Property Act 1925.

[58] Thus the consultation paper referred to the need for unit-holders to 'have an incentive to take an interest in the doings of the association and to take part in the setting of budgets'. In seeking consultation on the maximum length of the let there was 'a need to balance the proper expectations of a unit-holder to be able to take a foreign posting for their job and to return to their unit in due course'.

The proposed residential leasing restrictions

6.20   The settled policy of imposing restrictions on a leasing of commonhold units that are designed for residential use generated considerable debate in Parliament.[59] The initial intention was to have a very tight limitation on the number of years that could be granted.[60] The intentions now are somewhat less restrictive and the announced policy is that the regulations will prescribe a maximum term of 7 years.[61] Given, however, that the conditions with which a lease of a residential unit must comply are contained in regulations, there is always the prospect of more restrictive control being imposed. However, it will also be possible to relax the length of a permitted tenancy if the current concerns about leasing residential commonhold units are later found to be misplaced.

6.21   However, the decision to determine the maximum length of residential lease at 7 years, even if a compromise, is sensible in the light of the Land Registration Act 2002 and is unlikely to be changed in the foreseeable future. Once that Act is in force,[62] all leases for terms in excess of 7 years will be registrable with a separate title. Investors in commonhold units who intend to let them at market rents would, therefore, be reluctant to grant terms longer than 7 years. It is much more likely that any leases will be assured shorthold tenancies.[63]

6.22   'Residential', for the purposes of the leasing restrictions, means a unit used either for residential purposes within the commonhold community statement or for residential and other incidental purposes.[64]

Leasing of non-residential units

6.23   The leasing of commonhold units which are not residential as defined may be restricted if the CCS so provides. The width of this provision[65] suggests that it may even be possible to impose a restriction preventing the creation of some types of lease. This might be appropriate in the case of some units, such as car parking spaces ancillary to the commercial units, where it may be important to ensure that the person having the benefit of these units is not otherwise a stranger to the community. Leases of such units might only be permitted if they were to other unit-holders within the community. It would

---

[59]   In the debates on both the Bill introduced in 2000 as well as the subsequent Bill of June 2001 which became the Act.

[60]   The proposed limit was originally 3 years.

[61]   Regulations 'will provide for a seven-year maximum lease, but it will be renewable without limit. It could not be sold at a premium' – per Michael Wills, Standing Committee D, 15 January 2002, p 31.

[62]   This is likely to be in the autumn of 2003, but certainly before Part I of the CLRA 2002 is in force.

[63]   When the term expires, they may continue on a periodic basis or fresh tenancies can be negotiated.

[64]   CLRA 2002, s 17(5).

[65]   Ibid, s 18.

also seem entirely possible and appropriate to impose relevant restrictions on the nature of the leases of retail or other commercial units. Such restrictions will need to be carefully defined to ensure they are acceptable in the market and do not in practice negate or prevent the use of such units for the defined purposes.

Can the Commonhold Community Statement further restrict residential leasing?

6.24 A possible concern is the relationship of s 18 of the CLRA 2002 to s 17. Since it is provided that an instrument or agreement which creates a term of years in a commonhold unit *which is not residential*[66] shall have effect subject to any provision in the CCS, the question arises whether the CCS can also make any separate provision for leases of residential units? The failure to specify that this is acceptable could suggest that such leases need only satisfy the prescribed conditions.[67] It is to be hoped that the prescribed conditions include a similar rule to that contained in s 18 for leases of non-residential units, permitting the CCS to provide greater restrictions on some units (such as residential car parking spaces) where desired.

Regulatory powers

6.25 The regulations relating to leasing may be widely drawn. Thus, they may modify a rule of law about leasehold estates, whether derived from common law or from an enactment, in its application to the term of years in a commonhold unit.[68] The regulations are not confined to imposing the promised restrictions on residential units. They may impose obligations on the tenant of any commonhold unit or enable a CCS to impose obligations on that tenant.[69] The purpose is to ensure that any tenant of a commonhold unit is subject to the obligations relating to that unit. Thus, the regulations may (in particular) require a tenant to make payments to the commonhold association or to a unit-holder, in discharge of payments which are due from the unit-holder in accordance with the CCS.[70] Similarly, provision can be made for the amount of payments made by the tenant to be set against sums owed by the tenant, whether these are due to the unit-holder or to some other person, or for the amount of payments to be recoverable from the unit-holder or another tenant of the unit.[71] Different provisions for different descriptions of

---

[66]   My emphasis.

[67]   As provided by CLRA 2002, s 17.

[68]   Ibid, s 19(4).

[69]   Ibid, s 19(1). A tenant for this purpose includes a person with matrimonial home rights: s 61(a).

[70]   Or, indeed, for those which are due in accordance with the CCS to be made by another tenant of the unit – see s 19(2).

[71]   Ibid, s 19(3).

commonhold land or commonhold unit can thus be made by virtue of the regulations.[72]

Leases in contravention are void

6.26   If an instrument or agreement purports to create a term of years of a residential commonhold unit in contravention of the regulations in force, then it is of no effect.[73] To ensure that there is no disadvantage to a person who is granted a lease that is void by virtue of the CLRA 2002, it is provided that any party to the instrument or agreement can apply to the court for an order.[74] That order may provide for the lease or other instrument or agreement to have effect as if it provided for the creation of term of years of a specified kind or it may provide for the return of payment of money or make such other provision the court thinks appropriate.[75] It is likely that the exercise of the court's discretion under this provision would normally be directed to amending the lease or agreement to ensure it meets the prescribed conditions.

Leases for lives and perpetually renewable leases

6.27   A lease for life, or a perpetually renewable lease, will be subject, in the case of residential units, to the prescribed conditions and, in the case of a commonhold unit which is not residential, to any provision of the CCS. This is achieved by consequential amendments to earlier statutory provisions. So a grant of a perpetually renewable lease, which is converted into a term of 2,000 years,[76] will be of no effect if (as is almost certain) it does not satisfy the conditions prescribed by regulation in the case of a residential unit or is contrary to the provisions of the CCS in any other case.[77] The validity of a lease for life or lives, or terminable on marriage, of a commonhold unit, which takes effect as a grant of a term of 90 years, is likewise treated as if it was indeed a 90-year term.[78] So it will be of no effect if it is a lease of a residential unit and subject to the CCS in other cases.

6.28   Lawful tenants of commonhold units will need to be aware that obligations may arise not only by virtue of the terms of the lease or tenancy agreement that they sign, but also as a consequence of the provisions in the CCS or of the regulations made under the CLRA 2002.

---

[72]   CLRA 2002, s 19(5).

[73]   Ibid, s 17(3). This will also apply to an attempt to grant a lease for life of a residential commonhold unit – see Sch 5, para 3, which adds sub-sections (7) and (8) to Law of Property Act 1925, s 149.

[74]   Ibid, s 17(4).

[75]   Ibid, s 17(4)(a)–(c).

[76]   Or, if a sub-lease, one day less than the superior term.

[77]   CLRA 2002, Sch 5, para 1, which amends Law of Property Act 1922, Sch 15, para 5.

[78]   Ibid, Sch 5, para 3, adding subsections (7) and (8) to Law of Property Act 1925, s 149.

Maintaining the integrity of the commonhold

6.29   A commonhold unit is defined by the CCS, a document that sets out the total number of units and assigns to each unit a percentage contribution to the costs of the community by way of commonhold assessment. The CLRA 2002 could not, therefore, have permitted a unit-holder an unfettered freedom to divide the unit into two, to change the size of the unit or to charge only part of it. But there may be circumstances where such changes are appropriate. The policy is to strike a balance between the interests of the unit-holder and the interests of the association. Thus, the unit-holder is permitted to let part of the unit, for example a bedroom, to a lodger, but transactions which involve changes to boundaries or to the total number of units are only possible as part of a comprehensive process. This involves obtaining the appropriate level of agreement from the community membership and amending the CCS.[79]

Interests in part of a unit

6.30   It is not possible create an interest in part only of a commonhold unit.[80] An instrument or agreement is of no effect to the extent that it purports to create such an interest.[81] This general principle preserves the integrity of the unit and the validity of the percentages of the commonhold assessment and levies chargeable to each unit.[82] By way of exception, there is a freedom to lease part of a unit. In a non-residential commonhold unit, the ability to create a term of years in part only of the unit will be unfettered, subject only to any limitation imposed by the CCS.[83] A letting of part of a residential unit will have to meet the same conditions as to the length of the term and other matters as are prescribed for any lease of a residential unit.[84]

6.31   Apart from permitted leases, only one other interest can be created in part only of the unit. The transfer of the freehold estate in part only of a unit is possible where the commonhold association consents in writing to the

---

[79]   The principle is that such changes can only be made with the consent of the commonhold association and alongside a consequent amendment to the CCS – see the explanation of the Commons amendments on this issue at HL Deb, Vol 633, cols 688–691 (15 April 2002).

[80]   CLRA 2002, s 21(1).

[81]   Ibid, s 21(3).

[82]   The integrity of a commonhold has led to the modification of certain powers. Thus, trustees of land cannot exercise their powers to partition trust land so as to divide or charge part of a unit (CLRA 2002, Sch 5, para 8, amending Trusts of Land and Appointment of Trustees Act 1996, s 7). A mortgagee's power of sale under Law of Property Act 1925, s 101 is amended by being made subject to CLRA 2002, s 21 so that a disposition of a part unit is not possible: CLRA 2002, Sch 5, para 2.

[83]   CLRA 2002, s 21(2)(b) and s 18.

[84]   Ibid, s 21(2)(a) and (6) and s 17(2) and (4). Regulations may modify the application of the provisions of the Act relating to either the unit-holder or the tenant where part of a unit is held under a lease: s 21(7). This is to permit wrinkles in day-to-day operation to be ironed out: Standing Committee D, 15 January 2002, p 36.

transfer.[85] Such consent can only be provided after a resolution to give it is passed, so a meeting of the association will have to be called after due notice. When the resolution is proposed at the meeting, at least 75% of those who vote on the resolution must vote in favour.[86] Since the registration of a transfer of part necessarily requires an amendment of the CCS at the same time, the integrity of the commonhold community is maintained. This is reinforced by the express provision that the part of the commonhold unit so transferred with consent becomes a new commonhold unit.[87] It may alternatively become part of an existing unit if, when seeking the consent of the association, the request for consent specifies the unit to which the part will be transferred.[88]

6.32   The general prohibition on an interest in part of a unit might cause difficulty where land becomes commonhold land or, particularly, is added to a commonhold unit. If immediately before such addition there is an interest in the land which cannot be created in part of the unit, then that interest is extinguished to the extent that it could not be created.[89]

Mortgages and charges

6.33   The basic rule is that a CCS cannot prevent or restrict the creation, grant or transfer by a unit-holder of a charge over his unit.[90] The commonholder will be free to sell and to raise money on the security of the unit in the same way as the owner of a standard freehold.[91] In other respects, however, restrictions on charging flow from the nature of commonhold itself. Thus, it is not possible to create a charge over part only of an interest in a commonhold unit.[92] An instrument or agreement attempting to create such an interest is of no effect to the extent that it contravenes this rule.[93] The underlying principle is that the unit-holder has the usual freedom of a freehold registered proprietor to create mortgages and charges over his title by way of

---

[85]   CLRA 2002, s 21(2)(c).

[86]   Ibid, s 20(4), as applied by s 21(8).

[87]   Ibid, s 21(9)(a). Regulations may make provision, or require a community statement to make provision, about the registration of units so created: s 21(10).

[88]   Ibid, s 21(9)(b). An example would occur if one unit owner wished to transfer a garage, defined as part of the unit, to another unit-holder.

[89]   Ibid, s 21(4) and (5). There is no provision, as in the case of s 10, for any compensation to be payable to the holder of the interest.

[90]   Ibid, s 20(1); see **6.7**.

[91]   However, a mortgagor of a commonhold unit will be subject to an additional implied covenant when a unit is mortgaged with either full or limited title guarantee. By virtue of Law of Property (Miscellaneous Provisions) Act 1994, s 5(3A), inserted by CLRA 2002, Sch 5, para 7, a mortgagor covenants fully and promptly to observe and perform all the obligations under the CCS imposed on him as unit-holder or joint unit-holder.

[92]   CLRA 2002, s 22(1). A unit as such cannot be charged; it is the unit-holder's interest in the unit that is charged.

[93]   Ibid, s 22(2).

security interest, but such charges must be of the whole unit concerned.[94] If the mortgagee or chargee wishes to realise its security then it will be able to secure a sale of the whole of the commonhold unit. A charge of part only would have created a significant problem in realising the security.

6.34 Once again, if immediately before land is added to a commonhold unit, there is a charge over the land which would become a charge over part of the unit, then that charge is extinguished to the extent that it could not be so created.[95]

Consents required for changing the size of a commonhold unit

6.35 An amendment to the CCS which redefines the extent of a commonhold unit needs the consent of both parties. A redefinition of the extent of a unit by the CCS, which will be taken by the association in general meeting, cannot be made unless the unit-holder consents in writing before the amendment is made.[96] Similarly, a redefinition of a unit over which there is a registered charge cannot be made unless the registered proprietor of the charge consents in writing before the amendment is made, thus preserving the chargee's rights.[97] In either case, regulations may enable a court to dispense with the requirement of consent on the application of the commonhold association in circumstances prescribed in those regulations.[98] Since there cannot be a charge over part of a unit, the charge in relation to land taken out of the charged unit is automatically extinguished and, where land is added, the charge is extended to cover it.[99]

---

[94] Where the unit consists of two or more parcels of land, which need not be contiguous, then it will not be possible to charge part only even if the unit would appear to be physically severable. Such a consideration may militate against two or more parcels of land within a commonhold being a single unit.

[95] CLRA 2002, s 22(3) and (4). There is again no provision for any compensation to be payable to the chargee, but this should not normally cause difficulty since adding land will trigger an amendment of the CCS, which cannot be made without the consent of the registered proprietor of the charge: s 24.

[96] Ibid, s 23(1). The example postulated in the published explanatory notes is where the commonhold association wishes to demolish a block of garages and the garages are designated as parts of units. In such a case, the consent of every unit owner with a garage would be needed in advance.

[97] Ibid, s 24(1) and (2).

[98] Ibid, ss 23(2) and 24(3). It is likely that the circumstances will be limited and will not extend generally to allowing a court to override a unit-holder's wishes.

[99] Ibid, s 24(4) and (5). Regulations may be made to require notice to be given to the Land Registrar and requiring the Registrar to register changes so arising: s 24(6).

CHAPTER 7

COMMON PARTS AND LIMITED USE AREAS

COMMON PARTS

Definition

7.1   The common parts of a commonhold community comprise the land and structures that are part of the land registered as freehold estate in commonhold land but are not part of land designated as part of a commonhold unit. The definition is therefore a negative one. 'Common parts' in relation to a commonhold means every part of the commonhold which is not for the time being a commonhold unit.[1] Reference must therefore be made to the commonhold community statement (CCS) to ascertain the exact extent of the common parts. After subtracting the land and structures defined as commonhold units the remainder of the land registered as an estate in commonhold land by definition comprises the common parts of the community.

Ownership of the common parts

7.2   The common parts of a commonhold community will be vested in the commonhold association.[2] The association is entitled to be registered as the proprietor of the freehold estate in the common parts as soon as the commonhold is activated.[3] In practice, all access ways used in common by owners of commonhold units, such as halls, stairways, lifts, pathways and roads, will be part of the common parts. Communal facilities, such as gardens, play areas, laundry facilities, rubbish storage areas, swimming pools, tennis courts and so forth, will be common parts.[4] The external structures of buildings containing more than one commonhold unit are likely to be defined

---

[1]   In accordance with the CCS: CLRA 2002, s 25(1).

[2]   This will occur as soon as there are two or more persons entitled to be registered as proprietors of commonhold units: ss 7(3)(a) and (b) and 9(3)(a) and (d), and **3.63**.

[3]   Ie as soon as a person other than the applicant for registration of the freehold becomes entitled to be registered as a proprietor of the freehold estate in one or more, but not all, of the commonhold units – see ss 7(3) and 9(3). Registration of the commonhold association as proprietor of the freehold estate in the common parts does not require any application.

[4]   Unless designated as limited use areas – see **7.4**.

as part of the common parts and under the ownership of the commonhold association. An office for use by the association, or even a flat for a caretaker, may be designated as common parts.[5]

7.3   In some situations, there may be a choice whether to designate certain facilities as part of the common parts generally, as limited use areas within the common parts or as part of a commonhold unit. For example, a car park could be divided in such a way as to make specified parking places within it part of designated commonhold units.[6] However, this may involve greater difficulty in maintenance and upkeep of the car park. It will usually be far better either to designate each parking space as a limited use area for a particular unit or merely to vest the car park in the commonhold association as part of the common parts generally of the community. Provision may then be made in the CCS for the allocation of car parking spaces to particular units.

LIMITED USE AREAS

7.4   Specified sections of the common parts may be designated as limited use areas by a CCS, which may restrict the classes of person who may use them and the kind of use to which they may be put.[7] The purpose of providing for limited use areas is to vest them in the commonhold association as part of the common parts, and thereby subject to regulation of use and repair and maintenance by the commonhold association, while permitting them to be used by one or more commonhold unit-holders only. A classic example would be a balcony to a flat. The balcony is likely to be an integral part of the external structure of the building. As such, it may be more sensible to provide that its repair and maintenance should be the responsibility of the commonhold association, rather than of the particular unit-holder. By designating the balcony as a limited use area for the use of a particular unit-holder only, maintenance by the commonhold association is achieved but use of the balcony is confined to the unit-holder concerned.[8]

7.5   The CCS may make provisions which have effect only in relation to a specific limited use area or may make different provisions for different limited use areas.[9] This ensures the maximum flexibility possible. A limited use area

---

[5]   It may be better to provide for a caretaker's flat to be a unit vested in the association. If the flat is later no longer required, it could then more easily be sold.

[6]   Either as a separate unit or as part of a unit.

[7]   CLRA 2002, s 25(2).

[8]   The same approach may be appropriate for some garden areas (perhaps where some, but not all, unit-holders are to hang out washing), car parking spaces, even garages, rather than defining them as parts of commonhold units.

[9]   CLRA 2002, s 25(3). Limited use areas are to be identified, where appropriate, in Part II of the draft standard CCS. Clause 21 of the draft rules of the commonhold association makes optional provision for limited use areas.

such as a balcony, although repairable by the commonhold association, could be subject to cleaning responsibilities or even painting by the unit-holder. Where certain unit-holders have the enjoyment of limited use areas to the exclusion of others, it will be important that the percentage allocation of the commonhold assessment reflects the benefit of the limited use area to those who have the use of them. A limited use area is otherwise subject to repair and maintenance by the community as a whole through the commonhold association.

USE AND MAINTENANCE

7.6   Just as a commonhold unit-holder must be under an obligation relating to use and maintenance, it is also a requirement that a CCS must make provision for the use, repair and maintenance of the common parts. Therefore, there must be provision in the CCS regulating the use of the common parts, requiring the association to insure, repair and maintain them.[10] In this way, the purchaser of a commonhold unit can be assured that the association will be required to maintain full insurance,[11] to keep the common parts in good repair and maintain them to an appropriate standard for the benefit of the whole community.

7.7   The draft standard CCS accordingly makes provision for the use of the common parts by all unit-holders, with alternative wording, to include unit-holders who have let or parted with possession if desired, provided for selection by the developer.[12] As regards repair and maintenance, the suggested standard wording is that the commonhold association shall be responsible for repair and maintenance in accordance with specifications and standards which may be set by the Board of Directors and published to unit-holders from time to time.[13]

7.8   Additionally, the standard CCS provides[14] a series of miscellaneous provisions, some of which relate to the common parts. For example, no unit-holder is to do anything, or leave or permit to be left goods, rubbish or any other object, which obstructs or hinders lawful access to any part of the commonhold.[15] The commonhold association is responsible for regular cleaning of the common parts.[16] In the words of the explanatory notes to the

---

[10]   CLRA 2002, s 26. For the statutory definition of 'duty to insure' and 'duty to maintain', see s 69(2).

[11]   And will, no doubt, wish to inspect the policy before purchase.

[12]   Fourth draft of the CCS, cl 20.

[13]   Ibid, cl 29.

[14]   In section H, Miscellaneous Rules.

[15]   Draft CCS, cl 56.

[16]   Ibid, cl 59.

CLRA 2002, the CCS must set out the rules and regulations for corporate living.

DEALINGS

Transactions

7.9 It is specifically provided that nothing in a CCS is to prevent or restrict the transfer by the commonhold association of its freehold estate in any part of the common parts.[17] Therefore a commonhold association is free to take advantage of a development opportunity and perhaps sell part of its garden for development and for the benefit of the members of the association.[18] Similarly, the CCS cannot prevent or restrict the creation of an interest[19] in any part of the common parts.[20] Thus, the association is enabled to create rights of access, drainage or other easements over the common parts of a commonhold community in favour of adjoining landowners. It may grant a lease of a portion of the common parts, where appropriate. The association is thus granted considerable flexibility by the CLRA 2002. Decisions to sell off part of the common parts or create interests, such as leases or easements, over them do not appear to require unanimity.[21] In comparable legislation, unanimous resolutions are required.[22] This could be a source of conflict and the wording of the Act suggests that attempts in a CCS to require wider support within the community for such action would not be permissible.

Charges and mortgages

7.10 There are, however, special provisions related to charges. The general rule is that it is not possible to create a charge over the common parts and the freedom to create an interest over the common parts does not include the creation of a charge or an interest that arises by virtue of a charge.[23] An instrument or agreement that purports to create a charge over common parts shall be of no effect.[24] The issue of charges was the subject both of

---

[17]   CLRA 2002, s 27(1)(a).

[18]   But it appears that it may be difficult for an association to distribute any profits from such a sale – see **4.16**.

[19]   'Interest' in this context does not include a charge or an interest which arises by virtue of a charge: CLRA 2002, s 27(2), and see **7.10**.

[20]   Ibid, s 27(1)(b).

[21]   Compare s 29, which provides that a legal charge of any part of the common parts can (exceptionally) be created after a unanimous resolution of the commonhold association before the mortgage is created.

[22]   Compare the position in New South Wales under the Strata Schemes (Freehold Development) Act 1973, s 26 and Ilkin, *Strata Schemes and Community Schemes Management and the Law* (3rd edn, 1998), at [210].

[23]   CLRA 2002, ss 27(2) and 28(1).

[24]   Ibid, s 28(2).

considerable consultation prior to the enactment of the CLRA 2002 and of some debate and discussion during the passage of the Bill through Parliament. The earlier Commonhold Bills[25] simply made the creation of a charge over the common parts invalid. Such a rule protects the land vested in the commonhold association from being taken in execution of judgment or the security of a charge being realised by an enforced sale. After the consultation, the general rule was maintained in both the 2000 Commonhold Bill and in the CLRA 2002. The primary concern must be the protection of the integrity of the common parts for the benefit of the community.

7.11 The consequence of the general rule is that when a commonhold association is registered as the proprietor of common parts, a charge that relates wholly or partly to the common parts is extinguished to the extent that it relates to the common parts.[26] This means that persons who hold charges or mortgages over the new freehold estate in commonhold land[27] will need to ensure that the security in the unsold commonhold units is sufficient to cover the loans made to the developer. This important section permits the unencumbered registration of the commonhold association to all the common parts and restricts the existing charges to the unsold commonhold units.[28] It will operate frequently as it is likely that most developers will have a charge over the estate in commonhold land before the sale of the first unit.

7.12 Similarly, if additions are made to the common parts,[29] any charge which relates wholly or partly to the land added to the commonhold is also extinguished by virtue of the CLRA 2002; again only to the extent that it relates to the land added to the common parts.[30]

An exception for permitted legal mortgages

7.13 An exception is permitted to the general rule against the creation of mortgages or charges over the common parts. A legal mortgage is allowed if its creation is approved by a resolution of the commonhold association passed unanimously before the mortgage is created.[31] This limited exception enables the commonhold association to raise money on the security of the common

---

[25] In 1990 (cl 5(2)) and 1996 (cl 2(2)).

[26] CLRA 2002, s 28(3). Registration occurs by virtue of either s 7 or s 9 – see **3.20**.

[27] After registration as an estate in commonhold land, but before the first unit sale. See **3.49–3.52** for a full discussion.

[28] It is not yet clear how the Registrar will show registered charges after the association is registered with title to the common parts; but whether shown on a single title, or in relation to the title to each unsold unit, the lender's charge will apply only to the unsold units after registration of the association to the title to the common parts.

[29] Under CLRA 2002, s 30, following an amendment to a CCS.

[30] Ibid, s 28(4).

[31] Ibid, s 29(1) and (2). A legal mortgage has the meaning given to it by s 205(1)(xvi) of the Law of Property Act 1925: CLRA 2002, s 29(3).

parts where it is appropriate to do so and where no dissent is voiced.[32] However, the association will have to convince each member, voting in general meeting,[33] of the wisdom of raising money on the security of part of the common parts of the association. Lenders are likely to be very wary of lending money on legal mortgage because of the difficulties of realising the security. Loans to the commonhold association may well take the form of unsecured loans without the need for proprietary security if the lenders are satisfied that the income stream from the commonhold assessment is sufficient to service the loan.

Additions to the common parts

7.14   A CCS can be amended to make additions to the common parts by redefining the land previously designated as part of a unit.[34] Where it is desired to add land to the common parts, there are certain conditions to be satisfied.

7.15   If it is desired to convert that which is currently part of a commonhold unit and add it to the common parts, then the amendment must specify the land which forms part of the unit and provide for it to be added to the common parts.[35] Such amendment may not be made unless the registered proprietor of any charge over the added land consents in writing before the amendment to the CCS is made.[36] There is power for regulations to enable a court, on the application of a commonhold association, to dispense with the requirement for consent in specified circumstances.[37]

7.16   The purpose of such a provision would appear to relate primarily to the time before the developer has sold all the units. There may be a change to reduce the number of units or to alter the details. In such a situation, the lender, perhaps financing the development, will have the security of only the unsold units. The security could be compromised unless the lender's consent were required. However, there may be situations in an established commonhold when all parties wish to make adjustments and move a unit, or part of a unit, into the common parts.

7.17   It is axiomatic that the unit-holder will also have to consent to the transfer of part of the unit to the common parts, as this will have the effect of

---

[32]   In practice, it is likely anyway that any lender would be concerned to see that only severable sections of the common parts are subject to the mortgage. There is not much security value in staircases.

[33]   A resolution is passed unanimously for this purpose if every member who casts a vote votes in favour. Every member must be given an opportunity to vote by post, proxy or in some other manner in accordance with the CCS – see CLRA 2002, s 36, and **10.13**.

[34]   For amendments generally to the CCS, see **5.10**.

[35]   CLRA 2002, s 30(1).

[36]   Ibid, s 30(2). This is vital because the effect of adding the land is to extinguish the charge over the added land – see **7.11**.

[37]   Ibid, s 30(3).

redefining the extent of a unit.[38] A freehold title – which is what the unit-holder has – cannot be altered without the consent of the registered proprietor.

7.18 Where such an amendment is made, it takes effect, as always, only on registration of the amendment to the CCS.[39] Once the amended CCS is registered and filed with the Land Registrar, then the commonhold association is entitled to be registered as the proprietor of the freehold estate in the added land. The registration of the added land will be made without a formal application from the commonhold association.[40]

---

[38] The amendment is therefore also subject to s 23 which requires the unit-holder's consent in writing – see **6.35**.

[39] By virtue of CLRA 2002, s 33.

[40] Ibid, s 30(4).

CHAPTER 8

DEVELOPMENT RIGHTS

CONCEPT AND PURPOSE

Concept

8.1 Development rights are designed to enable a person or company creating a commonhold from scratch, either by way of new build or by way of conversion of existing premises, to have certain additional powers and rights until the development is complete. These powers give the developer greater freedom to develop the site and market the sale of units after the establishment of the commonhold and the sale of the first unit, but before completion of the sale of the last unit. Development rights seek to balance the competing interests of developer and the initial unit-holders. On the one hand, the purchasers of the first commonhold units to be completed and offered for sale need some protection against alteration of the conception or facilities of a commonhold from that presented to them when they purchased. On the other hand, the commercial developer must be able to react reasonably to commercial pressures during construction.

8.2 Consequently, the development rights enable a builder to retain a degree of commercial freedom. A developer will be able to complete the sale of one or more units while certain aspects of the common parts are yet to be completed. Rights may be reserved to add further land to the commonhold if a development is successful; similarly, there is the option of retaining rights to remove land from the commonhold or, indeed, even to change the exact size and nature of unsold commonhold units.

Contained in commonhold community statement

8.3 A developer[1] can insert into the commonhold community statement (CCS) certain defined development rights. Since the CCS must be filed when the commonhold is first registered, which by definition must be before the completion of the sale of the first unit, any purchaser of a commonhold unit will know the exact nature of the rights reserved. Development rights, by their nature, will be of limited duration. They will end, at the very least, when the developer ceases to have a freehold estate in any part of the commonhold –

---

[1] This is a widely defined concept – see **8.6**.

that will occur when the last unit is sold. Development rights are to be of limited duration and the time limit will be stated in the CCS. The rights may be passed on to a successor in title of the developer who purchases all or part of the commonhold, but only within the limits set out in the legislation.

Rights subject to regulation

8.4   The provisions of the CLRA 2002 relating to development rights are essentially enabling. The statutory provisions on the topic are brief and not illuminating. The key regulations which will flesh out the details and set out the limits to the development rights that may be granted have yet to be made.[2] However, one limitation arises by the very nature of commonhold. Development rights can only apply to the particular commonhold land as defined in the CCS in which the development rights are reserved. Each developer must set out the desired rights in that CCS prior to registration. There is no mechanism for creating or amending them at a later date.[3]

8.5   In theory, development rights should mean that developing by way of long leases is not more attractive to a developer than commonhold, since the same commercial freedom can be maintained through the reservation of development rights. Yet that theory may not be true in practice. The principal difference is that, for a commonhold, those rights must be clearly set out in advance and in writing in the CCS. Developers may well see this as a limiting factor. However, a first purchaser of a commonhold unit will be better off than his counterpart who may purchase by way of a grant of a new residential long lease on a very similar development. A purchaser of such a lease is at risk of future and probably unforeseen changes by the developer to the rest of the development, except where protection is secured by the lease or by contract. The purchaser of a commonhold unit will be able to understand exactly what development rights have been conferred and make the necessary enquiries of the vendor to seek reassurance or elucidation of any concerns that may be raised as a result of such rights.

Meaning of developer

8.6   The definition of 'developer' is a wide one. A developer is a person who makes an application to register a freehold estate in land as a freehold estate in commonhold land.[4] This means that any person registering commonhold land may, if he wishes, reserve development rights. It is highly unlikely, however, that development rights will be either relevant or needed when the freeholder is a company controlled by existing long leaseholders who are making the

---

[2]   Under CLRA 2002, ss 32 and 58(4) and (5).

[3]   Although it is possible that they could be added by a later amendment of the CCS by a resolution of the commonhold association – see **5.10**.

[4]   CLRA 2002, s 58(1); the definition is by reference to s 2 and therefore refers to any registered freeholder.

registration as part of the conversion process from long leases to commonhold. In all other cases, it is likely that development rights will be reserved as a matter of course within the CCS drafted prior to the first registration.[5] There may be joint developers, just as there may be an application for a registration of a commonhold by joint applicants, each of whom is the registered freeholder of part of the land to which the application relates.[6] Indeed, the CLRA 2002 envisages that a single developer may transfer part of the freehold estate in the commonhold to another person who will take over some of the development rights.[7] It is likely, therefore, that standard practice will develop, with extensive development rights being reserved in a CCS. Provision may be made for the sharing of those rights between two or more developers.

Transfer of development rights

8.7 Development rights may be passed to successors in title to the freehold estate in the whole or part of the commonhold, except where there is a transfer of the freehold estate in a single commonhold unit.[8] The greatest freedom occurs during the transitional period.[9] If the developer transfers the freehold estate in the whole of the commonhold to another person, that successor in title will be treated as the developer in relation to any matter arising after the transfer.[10] Similarly, in relation to a transfer of part in the transitional period, the successor in title will be treated as the developer in relation to any matter arising after the transfer which also affects the estate transferred.[11]

8.8 Where there is no transitional period or where the transfer occurs after the transitional period has expired, a successor in title either to the whole or to part of the commonhold can only be treated as a developer if the transfer is expressed to be inclusive of the development rights.[12] The successor to the freehold estate in the whole or part of the commonhold is then treated as the developer for the purpose of any matter which arises after the transfer and affects the estate transferred.[13] However, a person who is an outsider to the

---

[5] For the contents and drafting of a CCS, see **5.12–5.26**.

[6] CLRA 2002, s 57(3). Regulations may make provision about an application made jointly by two or more persons, each of whom is the registered freeholder of part of the land to which the application relates.

[7] Ibid, s 59(3).

[8] Ibid, s 59(3)(a), proviso.

[9] For transitional periods, see **3.53**.

[10] CLRA 2002, s 59(1). By definition, during the transitional period there are no unit-holders and the common parts are not vested in the commonhold association.

[11] Ibid, s 59(2).

[12] Ibid, s 59(3)(b).

[13] Ibid, s 59(3).

development, not holding a freehold estate in any part of the commonhold, can never exercise development rights.[14]

DEVELOPMENT RIGHTS AND DEVELOPMENT BUSINESS

Self-granted rights

8.9   The essence of development rights is that, within the statutory and regulatory limits permitted, the rights are those that the developer drafts and grants to himself by including them in the CCS. Such rights are therefore likely to be widely defined by a commercial developer to give the maximum commercial freedom permitted by law.[15] Since the developer controls the drafting and creation of the CCS for the proposed commonhold, they can be described and understood as essentially self-conferred rights. A crucial limitation is that they must be fixed at the outset in the CCS, before registration of the commonhold land occurs. There is no provision for development rights to be granted or extended at a later date. Any such attempt would have to be (if at all) by the standard method for amending the CCS[16] and, as such, would require the consent of any existing unit-holders. It is likely that such unit-holders would resist the creation of new development rights or, at least, make it very difficult, except when it would be in their interests to agree.

Two types of development right

8.10   The CLRA 2002 describes development rights[17] as those conferred by the CCS and either (first) permitting a developer to undertake development business or (secondly) facilitating the undertaking of development business.[18] This close association between development rights and the permitting or facilitating of development business may impose a significant restriction on the developer's freedom in the creation of those rights. Development business is exhaustively defined by the Act,[19] and rights which do not clearly permit or facilitate the undertaking of the business as so defined may well not qualify as development rights.

---

[14]   CLRA 2002, s 59(4). A developer must continue as a registered proprietor of at least one commonhold unit and must once have been the registered proprietor of the freehold estate in more than one of the units.

[15]   The CLRA 2002 provides that regulations, yet to be made, may regulate and restrict the exercise of rights conferred by the CCS, so what is drafted must accord with those regulations – see s 58(4)(a) and (5).

[16]   See **5.10**.

[17]   It is not a definition and is not included in the index of defined expressions in CLRA 2002, s 70.

[18]   CLRA 2002, s 58(2).

[19]   In Sch 4 – see **8.13**.

8.11 It is expressly provided that a CCS may include provision requiring either the commonhold association or a unit-holder to co-operate with the developer for specified purposes connected with development business.[20] Such a provision also may also set out the effect of breach of the requirement to co-operate.[21] The developer will not be able to interfere with the unit-holder's freehold interest in the commonhold unit, nor his ability to transfer it.[22] Thus, it is likely that the term or condition imposed for failure to co-operate may be either the imposition of a financial penalty or (more likely) the provision of certain consents on behalf of the unco-operative unit-holder or association. In relation to a commonhold association, the term or condition could perhaps relate to additional powers granted to the developer's directors to ensure the co-operation of the association. In relation to a unit-holder, it might be possible for the developer to provide for the consent of an unco-operative unit-holder to be overridden.

8.12 The exercise of development rights conferred by the CCS may also be made subject to terms and conditions. Although developers may wish their development rights to be as wide as possible, they may find it sensible to set out the terms and conditions on which they are to be exercised clearly and fairly enough to satisfy the legal advisers to the purchasers of the first commonhold units.[23] Once again, the CCS may make provision about the effect of any breach of such terms or conditions.[24]

Development business

8.13 The CLRA 2002 sets out the matters which may be considered development business for the creation of development rights.[25]

Addition and removal of land from a commonhold

8.14 The most important matters to qualify are those giving the power to vary the extent of the commonhold. Development business includes the power for a developer either to add land to a commonhold or to remove land from it.[26] Without this right, the exact extent of a commonhold and the exact number and extent of commonhold units and the common parts would be fixed at the outset. The units are necessarily delineated at the very creation of the commonhold by virtue of the plan attached to the CCS, defining the

---

[20] CLRA 2002, s 58(3)(a).

[21] Ibid, s 58(3)(c).

[22] See **6.7**.

[23] CLRA 2002, s 57(3)(b).

[24] Ibid, s 58(3)(c).

[25] These are set out in Sch 4 to the Act, which sets out the matters which are development business for the purposes of s 58.

[26] Ibid, Sch 4, paras 4 and 5.

extent of each unit.[27] The right to add or remove land may need to be related to the provisions relating to the percentage contributions of each unit to the commonhold assessment and so forth. Without provision to add or remove land, it would not be possible to respond to commercial pressures.

8.15   The CLRA 2002 does not make it clear whether the power to add and remove land and to amend a CCS includes the right to add to the number of units planned or to reduce them. It is submitted that the right must exist because the reference in Sch 4 is to 'land', not just to 'common parts'. Moreover, the provision would otherwise make little commercial sense. A particular commonhold may prove to be exceptionally popular and the developer may wish to use adjoining land to build additional units to add to the commonhold so that the same facilities can be granted to those additional units. Conversely, it may be that a particular commonhold development is not as commercially profitable as thought and the developer may wish to reduce the number of units and develop the removed land in an alternative way.

8.16   The addition or removal of land may be a fairly straightforward matter if all the developer wishes to do is to reduce the common parts, perhaps, for example, by reducing the extent of communal garden land. However, where the addition or removal of land involves substantial variation to the essential features of the commonhold, such as the number of units, a major amendment to the CCS will be required.[28] Not only will there be a new plan, but there may have to be a change to the rights and duties of existing unit-holders, particularly in relation to the commonhold assessment and levy percentages for the units concerned.

8.17   What is certain is that the right to add or remove land to a commonhold will have to be carefully drafted. There may have to be terms and conditions which protect the interests of any existing unit-holders. It is likely that regulations yet to be made under the CLRA 2002[29] will define and restrict the nature of this right in the interests of consumer protection.

Redefinition of units and amendment of commonhold community statement

8.18   The addition or removal of land may necessitate the redefinition of units or the amendment of the CCS. However, such a power to amend the CCS and redefine the extent of community units is specifically defined as development business quite independently of whether addition or removal of land from the commonhold is involved. This is likely to be the most

---

[27]   See **5.16**.

[28]   Amendment to a CCS is included separately as development business in CLRA 2002, Sch 4, para 6, even though any addition to, or removal of land from, a commonhold necessitates an amendment to the CCS.

[29]   By virtue of CLRA 2002, s 58(4) and (5) and subject to regulations under s 32.

important aspect of development business in practice. It may be very likely that commercial pressures will lead to a wish to redefine the extent of proposed units as yet unsold or unbuilt. A developer may wish to make one unit larger at the expense of another; to combine two units set out in the CCS into one at the request of a proposed purchaser; or to create (say) four smaller units instead of the three larger ones initially envisaged in the CCS when it was drafted. Consequently, every developer is almost certain to reserve the right to make amendments to the CCS and to permit amendments to redefine the extent of units.[30]

8.19 Once again, the exact terms and conditions on which these rights may be exercised will be of concern to any purchaser of a unit in an uncompleted development. In many cases, the amendments may be relatively minor and may not harm the interests of existing unit-holders. In other cases, the amendments may have a significant financial impact. Thus, the intention by a builder to create more intensive development, perhaps by doubling the number of remaining units, could be significantly disadvantageous to existing unit-holders. Alterations will need to be made by proper and fair amendments to the CCS, which ensure financial parity between all unit-holders. The issues may not be just matters of finance, as any amendment which redefines the nature of the duties and rights of unit-holders may also have an impact on the position of existing unit-holders.

8.20 It should be noted that the express right to reserve the ability to redefine the extent of a commonhold unit is not stated to be limited to unsold units. However, it must be so confined. Alteration to units already sold to unit-holders cannot meaningfully be described as development business and such changes would need the consent of the unit-holder and any mortgagee of the unit.[31]

Works

8.21 By their very nature, new build commonholds, or commonholds which involve conversion of existing premises, will require development rights to be reserved in relation to uncompleted works. Any developer is likely to wish to be able to sell units as soon as they are ready for occupation even if other units remain uncompleted and even if some of the expected facilities on the common parts are not yet structurally complete. Consequently, the definition of development business includes the completion or execution of works on the commonhold, on land which may be added to a commonhold or on land which has been removed from a commonhold.[32] This will permit a developer to complete the remaining units and to defer the completion of works on the

---

[30] An amendment to redefine the extent of a commonhold unit is specifically mentioned as one amendment which may be made.

[31] By virtue of CLRA 2002, ss 23 and 24.

[32] Ibid, Sch 4, para 2.

common parts and unsold units until later. The right to execute works will be especially vital in relation to the land designated as common parts, since such land will be vested in the community association once the first unit is sold.[33]

8.22   Although the concept of phasing a development, which appeared in earlier Commonhold Bills,[34] makes no appearance in the CLRA 2002, it is likely that the standard provisions relating to development business for uncompleted works will involve an element of phasing. Purchasers of units will be anxious to ensure that the completion of the shared facilities such as car parks and gardens is not left entirely until the sale of the last unit. Consequently, legal advisers to purchasers are likely to wish to see developers phase the completion of the common parts as units are progressively sold. The co-operation of unit-holders[35] in the completion of these works is obviously an important aspect of the reservation of the rights.

Marketing

8.23   Less contentious as development business is the reservation of rights in relation to transactions in commonhold units and for advertising and other activities designed to promote transactions in the commonhold units.[36] These development rights are less likely to be of real concern to purchasers of units. The reservation of rights of access to 'show homes' or the advertising for sale of units is not likely to be contentious. Similarly, the reservation of advertising rights by way of hoardings placed on the common parts or even on walls of the building containing units which have been sold would be expected by the purchaser of a unit in any commercial new development.

Commonhold association

8.24   The final aspect of development business is the appointment and removal of directors of a commonhold association.[37] This particular right is expressly limited by the memorandum and articles of the commonhold association[38] and therefore relates primarily to the appointment of the developer's directors, a matter which has already been considered.[39] The use of developer's directors will be crucial to allow a developer to maintain a significant voice within the commonhold association while the sale of the units is in progress.

---

[33]   The developer will need complete freedom to execute works on those common parts and to have access across the common parts to work on the unsold units, which remain vested in the developer.

[34]   For example, the 1996 Commonhold Bill, cls 10 and 11.

[35]   Which may be required by CLRA 2002, s 58 – see **8.11**.

[36]   CLRA 2002, Sch 4, para 3.

[37]   Ibid, Sch 4, para 7.

[38]   Ibid, s 58(4)(b).

[39]   See **4.37**.

Control by regulations

8.25 There will be significant regulatory control of the exercise of development rights. This is specifically authorised by the CLRA 2002.[40] These regulations may be specifically directed to regulating or restricting the rights, but control may also be exercised by the more general regulatory power [41] to make provision about the content of a CCS. The nature of this regulatory control is not yet clear as, at the time of writing, no drafts have been published.

TERMINATION OF DEVELOPMENT RIGHTS

8.26 Development rights may terminate in a number of ways. They may be expressly surrendered; they may be time-limited and expire by effluxion of time; or they may become effectively otiose by completion of the development and the termination of the developer's interest in the commonhold.

Termination by surrender

8.27 A developer may expressly surrender the development rights by sending a notice to the Registrar. The notice does not have to be in any particular form. On receipt of the notice, which is kept in the custody of the Registrar, the Registrar arranges for a reference to the termination of the development rights to be made in the register of the commonhold land.[42] The right ceases to be exercisable from the time when the notice is so registered and the commonhold association is to be informed by the Registrar as soon as reasonably practicable.[43]

Effluxion of time

8.28 Development rights will be time-limited so as to expire on the sale of the last unit and by the date that appears in the CCS, but it may be necessary to add a further, 'long-stop' time limit. This may be necessary to ensure that a developer does not retain rights for a prolonged period of time by keeping at least one commonhold unit long after the rest have been sold or transferred. It would be inimical to the concept of a commonhold for development rights

---

[40] CLRA 2002, s 58(4)(a) and (5).

[41] Under s 32(1).

[42] Ibid, s 58(6)(a).

[43] Ibid, s 58(6)(b) and (c).

to continue beyond the time when they have a commercial *raison d'être*.[44] The draft CCS provides for specific expiry dates for all the rights reserved.[45]

Expiry by completion of the development

8.29   In many cases, development rights, by reason of their formulation, will be exhausted once certain works have been completed. In any event, development rights will come to an end when the developer sells the last unit. Thus, it is provided that a person shall not be treated as the developer in relation to commonhold land for any purpose unless he is, or has been at a particular time, the registered proprietor of the freehold estate in more than one of the commonhold units, and remains the registered proprietor of the freehold estate in at least one of the commonhold units. This provision means that a developer cannot simply be someone who purchases a single unit; it is also clear that he must, at least, have been the registered proprietor of more than one unit, and must remain the registered proprietor of at least one unit at all times.[46] Therefore, on the sale of the last unit, development rights must cease.

Transfer of development rights

8.30   Within prescribed limits, a developer may transfer the development rights to another person. The restrictions on the ability to transfer these rights differ depending on whether the transfer takes place during the transitional period or whether it occurs at a later date.

Within the transitional period

8.31   If a developer transfers the freehold estate in the whole of the commonhold to another person during the transitional period, then the successor in title is to be treated as developer in relation to any matter arising out of the transfer.[47] Thus, prior to the sale of the first unit and before the commonhold is activated, there is complete freedom for a developer to transfer the development rights to a successor in title, together with the freehold estate in commonhold land.

8.32   Moreover, a developer can transfer part of the commonhold to another person during the transitional period. In such a case, the successor in title is treated as the developer only for matters which arise after the transfer and which affect the estate transferred.[48] This provision permits the developer of a

---

[44]   Otherwise a developer could retain one unit for use as a home or office with the benefit of the original development rights.

[45]   In the fourth draft, Part III.

[46]   CLRA 2002, s 58(4).

[47]   Ibid, s 58(1).

[48]   Ibid, s 58(2).

proposed commonhold to share the development with another person or company, perhaps by dividing the development between them. Once again, the freedom to transfer the development rights is relatively unrestricted where the transfer occurs before the sale of the first commonhold unit.

When the commonhold is activated

8.33 If a transfer of the freehold estate in all or part of the commonhold occurs after a transitional period or in any case where there is no transitional period,[49] then there will no automatic transfer of development rights. If a developer transfers the freehold estate in the whole of his remaining interest in the commonhold or part of it,[50] then development rights are transferred only if the transfer expressly states that these rights are to be included. In such a case, the successor in title is treated as the developer for the purpose of matters arising after the transfer and affecting the estate transferred.[51] It should be stressed that it is only possible to transfer development rights in such a case where the transfer is of more than a single commonhold unit.

8.34 Except during a transitional period, a person is not to be treated as the developer in relation to any commonhold land for any purpose unless he is, or has been at a particular time, the registered proprietor of the freehold estate in more than one of the commonhold units. Additionally, and importantly, a person is not to be treated as the developer unless he continues as the registered proprietor of the freehold estate in at least one commonhold unit.[52]

IMPORTANCE OF DEVELOPMENT RIGHTS

8.35 The importance of development rights to the success of commonhold cannot be underestimated. If a developer considers that there are practical and financial advantages to continuing with long leasehold, he is likely to continue to do so.

8.36 Much will therefore depend on the detail of the regulations to come. However, there are concerns arising from the way the CLRA 2002 has provided for development rights. The matters that constitute development business are listed exhaustively and may not be extensive enough. For example, in a large development at present, the developer retains absolute control over the whole estate, except those parts where long leases have been granted of houses, flats or units. The main services to the estate, whether roads, pipes, sewers or cables, are provided by that developer. If an adjoining

---

[49] In either case, there will be a CCS in force and at least one other person other than the developer will be the freehold registered proprietor of one or more of the commonhold units.

[50] Other than by transfer of the freehold estate in a single commonhold unit.

[51] CLRA 2002, s 58(3).

[52] Ibid, s 58(4).

house builder finds that he needs to use or join into the services so constructed, he can negotiate a deal. The developer will secure a substantial payment for the sale of those rights. In a commonhold, the services will already be vested in the commonhold association, preventing the developer from benefiting.

8.37   There is a possibility that would enable a developer to retain maximum freedom during construction. An area of the common parts could be excluded from the commonhold at the outset. The developer would contract with each person who has purchased a unit to transfer and add to the commonhold those areas of the common parts initially excluded once the final unit is sold. This may not be feasible or necessary for a block of flats but may be useful where the estate is larger and consists of free-standing units.

CHAPTER 9

BUYING A COMMONHOLD UNIT

GUIDING PRINCIPLES

9.1 Until the Land Registry Rules and forms are available, and especially until all the necessary regulations have been promulgated, it is possible only to suggest some general principles which will apply when acting for a buyer of a unit.

A freehold transfer

9.2 Commonhold aims to establish a form of community title in which freehold units can be bought and sold and dealt with in the same way as any standard freehold title. Consequently, the sale and purchase of a commonhold unit will be subject to standard conveyancing searches, procedures and practices, particularly those relating to the mortgage of such units, local searches and standard enquiries before contract, and requisitions on title. However, it is possible that special forms of transfer will be prescribed by regulations and that those special forms of transfer will mark out commonhold as essentially different in key ways from the usual freehold transfer situation.

The registered title

9.3 One distinguishing feature of a commonhold unit title will be documentation which will accompany the office copy entries of the title concerned. The Registrar will have in his custody the prescribed details of the commonhold association, the details of the registered freeholder of each of the other commonhold units as well as those of the vendor, a copy of the commonhold community statement (CCS) and a copy of the memorandum and articles of association.[1] These details will be referred to in the register. There may also be additional documentation kept in the custody of the Registrar and referred to in the register if it has been submitted when the land was first registered as a commonhold.

9.4 These documents mean that the examination and advice on a commonhold title will not be dissimilar to the exercise conducted in respect of

---

[1] CLRA 2002, s 5.

a long leasehold title. Instead of, as now, examining and advising on the provisions of the lease and seeking details of the freehold reversionary title, a conveyancer will instead have to peruse and advise on the local law contained in the CCS and make the necessary enquiries as to the form, conduct and current financial position relating to the commonhold association.[2]

The state of the commonhold development

9.5   The conveyancing practice on the transfer of a commonhold unit will depend on the state of the commonhold development. The easiest position will be in the case of an established commonhold where development is complete. Additional work will be required where the transfer of the unit is from the developer, or from a unit-holder in a development that is not yet complete and is still in the course of construction. This will be necessary to protect the client and, particularly, to advise the client in connection with any developer's rights reserved.[3] The most difficult conveyancing will occur when a client wishes to make a contractual commitment to purchase a unit which is not yet structurally complete in a development where registration of the commonhold has not yet occurred.[4] Indeed, the construction of the commonhold may not have even started, but in the case where there is high demand for a particular housing complex, a client may wish to be first in the queue and secure a place in the planned community. In such circumstances, which may be referred to as 'purchasing off the plan',[5] there will be a special concern to ensure that the interests of the client are fully protected between contract and the completion of the purchase when the unit is eventually structurally complete.

MATTERS OF CONCERN TO ALL BUYERS

Investigation of title

9.6   A buyer of a commonhold unit will be supplied with the office copies of the title to the unit being sold. The usual office copy entries of the title will be accompanied by the documents referred to in the register. These must include the prescribed details of the commonhold association, the prescribed details of the freeholder of each commonhold unit, a copy of the CCS, and a copy of the memorandum and articles of association of the commonhold association.

---

[2]   A copy of the insurance policy in force, minutes of association meetings, and details of any community disputes are examples of information which will be commonly sought.

[3]   See Chapter 8.

[4]   It is argued at **3.6** that developers will want, in the interests of flexibility, to delay registration for as long as possible.

[5]   This is the term used in New South Wales, Australia.

Commonhold association

9.7 Whenever there is an existing commonhold title there must be, by definition, a functioning commonhold association. This association will be the registered proprietor of the common parts.[6] The proposed buyer will be able to see from the plans attached to the CCS the extent of the common parts. It is likely that a buyer will ask to see (if it is not supplied) a copy of the title of the commonhold association to the common parts. The registered title should be checked to ensure it conforms with the plan on the CCS.

9.8 The memorandum and articles of the commonhold association should be checked to ensure that they conform with the statutory requirements as to form and content.[7] A particular concern will be the powers of the association and of any features that deviate from the standard form set out in the regulations.

9.9 Of necessity, the commonhold association will be a private company limited by guarantee and will specify £1 as the amount required as the member's guarantee.[8] It is likely that a commonhold association will have largely, if not completely, adopted the standard form in the regulations.[9] To the extent that any provision is not contained in the standard form, the adviser will need to ensure that it is not inconsistent with the regulations.

9.10 The membership of the commonhold association should be noted with particular care to check, in the case of a recently established commonhold, that the developers and subscribers to the original memorandum have ceased to be members and have resigned.[10]

Commonhold community statement

9.11 As the local law relating to the community, the CCS will need to be carefully analysed and its main features explained to the potential buyer. The form and contents of the CCS will need to comply with the statutory and regulatory requirements.[11] But a CCS is not only a regulatory document setting out the rules and principles of the community; it is also a form of consumer protection for a buyer – hence its importance.

9.12 Consequently, the first step will be to check the plan of the unit and ensure that the plan in the statement conforms to that in the title. The CCS

---

[6] Unless this is a transfer of the very first commonhold unit to be sold, in which case the commonhold association will become registered proprietor of the common parts on completion of the sale of the first unit – see CLRA 2002, s 7(3) and **3.63**. The association becomes fully functioning only after the first transfer of a unit is complete.

[7] Contained in CLRA 2002, s 34 and Sch 3; see Chapter 4.

[8] In pursuance of s 2(4) of the Companies Act 1985 – see CLRA 2002, s 34(1)(b).

[9] For the draft CCS available at the time of writing, see Appendix 2.

[10] See CLRA 2002, Sch 3, para 13; and also see **4.24**.

[11] Ibid, s 31, and regulations made under s 32 – details to come.

must contain regulations as to the use of the unit being purchased. The usual regulation will refer to use as residential or for retail, industrial or commercial purposes.

9.13 Where the unit consists of more than one piece of land, such as a flat and a car parking space or garage, greater care will be required. This is also the case if there are special limited use areas.[12] The adviser will not only be concerned with a limited use area for the benefit of the unit being purchased (such as a balcony) but will also need to be aware of the impact of limited use areas granted to other units within the commonhold and to check the assessments and levies in relation to such areas.

9.14 Advice will need to be given on the way in which the CCS regulates the running of the community including the repair and insurance obligations for the common parts. The miscellaneous rules may contain provisions on the keeping of pets, television aerials, washing facilities, and so forth, which may impact on the residential use and lifestyle of the occupier.

The unit being purchased

9.15 The CCS will contain the details of how the unit being purchased is to be repaired, maintained and insured. Depending on the nature of the commonhold, these matters may be the responsibility of the unit-holder or they may be the responsibility of the commonhold association. In the case of a flat, it is highly likely that the insurance of the whole building will be the responsibility of the commonhold association, in which case the adviser will need to see the insurance policy and check that the sum insured meets any lenders' requirements. It is also likely that, in most cases, interior repair and maintenance and decoration responsibilities for the unit will fall on the unit-holder. This will naturally lead to enquiries, if needed, about the date such responsibilities will next fall due and confirmation that the responsibilities have been met up to date. External repair responsibilities are likely to be the responsibility of the commonhold association, except in the case of a detached unit such as a house.

9.16 Particular attention will be directed to the details in the commonhold statement relating to the community assessment and any levies and the provisions for reserve funds. The percentage required in relation to the unit being purchased towards the community assessment will be stated. A check will be made to ensure that the percentages add up to 100%, and an analysis may need to be done in respect of the assessment as a whole to give the purchaser client some assurance that the assessment in relation to the unit being purchased is fair in relation to the commonhold as a whole.

---

12   For limited use areas, see **7.4**.

Common parts and available facilities

9.17   One feature of the sale of commonhold units will be the availability of the communal facilities. The existence, for example, of a swimming pool for the use of a community may be a highly advantageous feature that will increase the cost and desirability of the units when they are sold. Consequently, the exact nature of the facilities and services made available to the community and the nature of the common parts will be as important to a buyer as the assessment of the unit itself. A buyer will want to know if any mortgage or lease of any portion of the common parts has been validly created.

9.18   A buyer will have a keen interest in the state of repair of the common parts, such as car parking areas, and the arrangements made for the upkeep of gardens and amenity areas. The cost of providing any expensive luxury facilities such as a swimming pool or warden service will be reflected in the annual commonhold assessment in respect of each unit. An adviser will need to find out these details to advise the client of what may be expected after the purchase.

Details of management

9.19   A buyer of a unit will wish to know the names and details of the directors and the secretary[13] of the association. A comparison between the details of the directors and those of the membership of the association will quickly reveal whether the directors are residents or owners of units within the community or whether external directors have been appointed. If an agency has been appointed to run the association, details will be needed if these are not supplied with the purchase documents.

9.20   It will be standard practice to require details of the management of and accounts for the association over a number of recent years. The minutes of the first annual general meeting will remain useful for some time to come, and the minutes of subsequent annual meetings and any special meetings will reveal to a buyer the history of the development of the association. The minutes will also be useful for a buyer to gain some understanding of how harmonious the community is in its business and personal relationships. A particular requirement will be details of the annual accounts of the association, together with a copy of the most recent annual return to the Registrar of Companies.[14] Together, these should give a picture of the financial position, with details of the reserve funds established and the amounts set aside for future expenditure. With a well-established commonhold, there should be

---

[13]   Notice of the transfer will have to be given to the secretary – see CLRA 2002, s 15(3) which imposes a duty on a new unit-holder to notify the association of the transfer.

[14]   This will ensure that the commonhold association has not been struck off for failing to file returns.

made available any reserve study[15] or other survey undertaken by the commonhold association. This will be a useful document, alongside any lender's survey, and will enable an assessment to be made of the quality of repair and maintenance of the common parts and the external structures if they are the responsibility of the association.

9.21 In recently established commonholds, developer's directors may still hold office and their powers will need careful analysis.[16]

Assessments in relation to the unit being purchased

9.22 Unlike the assignment of a long leasehold interest in a flat, it may seem less necessary for a buyer to ensure that the outgoing unit-holder selling the unit has fully satisfied the obligations of a unit-holder in relation to the unit. In particular, unlike a leasehold, the obligations of a defaulting unit-holder do not directly pass to a subsequent buyer of the unit.[17] There is and can be no forfeiture of a commonhold unit. However, it is submitted that it is in every buyer's interest to ensure that the community association confirms to the buyer's legal advisers that the seller is fully paid up with contributions to reserve funds and in respect of the assessment relating to the unit. This is because any shortfall that cannot be recovered may not fall directly on the buyer but will certainly fall on the community as a whole of which the buyer becomes part.[18] It will therefore be in the buyer's best interest to seek assurances as to the obligations being fully met and, if there are outstanding arrears, to ensure that they are paid off from purchase moneys at completion.[19] There are undoubted conveyancing difficulties in the event of a sale of a unit with outstanding debts due from the seller, and these issues are more fully explored later.[20]

---

[15] See clause 31 of the draft standard community statement in Appendix 2. The original intention was to require a 'reserve study' of the assets of the association to estimate the remaining life of these assets and the cost of maintaining and replacing them. A quinquennial survey of the commonhold to inform the association as it planned for future maintenance was suggested, but this is now considered too prescriptive and a reserve study may now be required only every ten years.

[16] See **9.35–9.37**.

[17] Unless it is possible in law, and provided by the CCS, that such an obligation should pass to a transferee. See the discussion at **11.2.6**. A seller is never liable for liabilities arising after completion of the transfer – see CLRA 2002, s 16(2), and **6.10**.

[18] Whether a buyer of a unit would be liable as a member of a community for unpaid and irrecoverable debts of a defaulting member incurred before the purchase is a moot point. See the discussion at **11.2.5**.

[19] However, if a buyer is not liable for the seller's unpaid commonhold assessment and levies, the buyer may not have the right to insist on the discharge of the debts from the purchase moneys. There may need to be a contractual clause to this effect. Discharge could be demanded if the commonhold association has obtained a charging order on the unit.

[20] At **10.33**, in connection with the management of a commonhold, and at **11.18–11.26**, where remedies are discussed.

Treatment of contributions to reserve funds on sale of a unit

9.23   Reserve funds are best seen as a method of fairly apportioning the eventual costs of major repair, rebuilding or refurbishment of buildings forming the common parts between all unit-holders, including those who have been members but have transferred the unit before the works are done. In the period prior to the works being done, the owners for the time being have had the benefit of the facilities and contributed to their wear and tear. Consequently, the buyer of a unit ought not to make any payment in respect of the contributions to the reserve fund or funds made by the seller unless, at least, the seller can demonstrate that contributions have been made at too generous a rate. However, this issue is a matter for bargaining between parties when a sale of a unit is negotiated and it will not be invalid for a seller to successfully seek some reimbursement from the buyer in respect of reserve fund contributions.

Enquiries to be made

9.24   The assessment of the conveyancing documents will give rise to a whole raft of enquires appropriate to the particular case in question. However, there will be a number of standard enquiries that a buyer will need to make prior to contract. Thus, a buyer will be supplied with a copy of the CCS on the title. A standard enquiry should involve confirmation that no amendment as yet unregistered has been made to the CCS.[21] Similarly, it will be of significant impact if there are plans to add land to the commonhold or delete land from it, or to make amendments to other units within the commonhold. A standard enquiry should establish whether such amendments have been made but not yet registered, and whether proposed amendments have been put for consideration by the association.[22]

9.25   A buyer will not be concerned directly with the arrears of other unit-holders within the community. However, on becoming a member of that community, any unit-holder will have a vested interest in ensuring that fellow members of the community regularly meet their assessments and levies and co-operate to make the community a pleasant place to live (or work). It is therefore likely that it will be standard practice to enquire of the community association whether there are outstanding debts from unit-holders within the community.[23] The existence of defaulters may make it more difficult to sell other units within the community and therefore make it more likely that the association will be zealous in ensuring that defaulters are not allowed to stay in default for long periods of time.

---

[21]   For amendments, see **5.10**.

[22]   For adding or deleting land, see **6.35**, **7.14** and **10.35**.

[23]   But such enquiries may raise privacy or data protection issues, especially in relation to a proposed buyer who is, at the time the question is put, a stranger to the community.

Joint owners

9.26   Where it is intended to purchase a property in joint names it will be necessary for the adviser to discuss with the proposed joint unit-holders which of them should be the member of the commonhold association. Only one such person can be the member.[24] If the joint owners can agree between themselves, then it will be appropriate to make a nomination of the member of the association and prepare this for dispatch to the secretary of the commonhold association as soon as possible after completion.[25] The association must receive the nomination before the end of the prescribed period.

9.27   If no nomination is made, then it will be the duty of the secretary of the association to enter as a member the person whose name appears first in the proprietorship register of the unit in question.[26] Consequently, where the proposed joint unit-holders cannot agree who is to be the member, a problem arises for the adviser. Deciding which name comes first in the proprietorship register will determine who becomes the member of the association. The issue will therefore have to be resolved before completion. A later nomination could be made to change the person who is the member of the association.[27]

9.28   In a particularly difficult case, it may be necessary for joint unit-holders to enter into an agreement between themselves. An agreement might not only set out who is to be the member of the association but also regulate the way the joint unit-holder who is the member of the association votes in general meetings. In the case of more than two unit-holders, it might be possible to have a simple agreement that the person nominated as member acts on the majority views of the joint unit-holders.

Notice to the commonhold association

9.29   In any purchase, it will be necessary, following completion of the purchase, for the buyer or the buyer's adviser to notify the commonhold association of the transfer.[28] The form and manner of the notice and the time within which the notice is to be given may be prescribed by regulations which may also make provision, including provision requiring the payment of money, about the effect of failure to give notice.[29] It is to be noted that a person who is entitled to be entered in the register of members of a

---

[24]   This is the result of the 'principle of equality'. See CLRA 2002, Sch 3, para 8, and **4.16**. Some leasehold schemes only allow one joint long leaseholder to be a member of the residents' managing company.

[25]   Ibid, Sch 3, para 8(3).

[26]   Ibid, Sch 3, para 8(4).

[27]   But only with consent of the other joint unit-holders – see ibid, Sch 3, para 8(2).

[28]   Ibid, s 15(3).

[29]   Ibid, s 15(4).

commonhold association becomes a member only when the company registers him in pursuance of the statutory duty to register.[30]

MATTERS OF CONCERN FOR FIRST BUYERS OF UNITS

9.30 There will be additional work for legal advisers when acting for a first buyer of a unit in a new commonhold development when a commonhold is being developed and refurbished or existing buildings upgraded. In such cases, the following paragraphs assume that the commonhold has been registered[31] but that not all the units have yet been sold. A particular responsibility will fall on the solicitor for the first, or first few, buyers of units.

Concerns of the first buyer of the first unit

9.31 In the very first purchase of a unit in a registered commonhold, the buyer will find that the commonhold association has been registered and established and the CCS has been filed. The CCS will yet not be in force and the commonhold association will not be registered as the proprietor of the common parts. Only on the registration of the first unit-holder will there be more than two holders of commonhold units,[32] and that first transfer will enable the commonhold association to be registered as proprietor of the freehold estate in the common parts. Only at that point will the CCS come into force.[33]

9.32 The first buyer(s) will therefore be involved in seeing the community come into being and will have an important role in the first meeting(s) of the commonhold association.[34] Such a buyer's advisers will need to ensure that the registration of the commonhold has been completed correctly and there are no obvious errors requiring amendment.[35] The works on the commonhold may not yet be completed. It will therefore be necessary to make enquiry about the nature of any powers reserved for amending or changing the development as set out in the CCS.

Getting the commonhold association active and running

9.33 For all first buyers of units, it will be a concern to ensure that steps have been or are being taken properly to get the commonhold association

---

[30] Companies Act 1985, s 352; see CLRA 2002, Sch 3, para 11.

[31] Under CLRA 2002, s 2.

[32] The first buyer and the freeholder/developer.

[33] CLRA 2002, s 7(3).

[34] At least, in the first meetings of the association other than those called prior to the sale of the first unit and controlled by the developer.

[35] Under CLRA 2002, s 6.

functioning effectively. The first annual general meeting of the association is likely to take place fairly soon after the commonhold is activated by the sale of the first unit. A well-planned commonhold may well make detailed provision for the management of the association while the development proceeds. Indeed, a developer will have an obvious interest in ensuring that, while the development and marketing of the units takes place, the association is managed in an efficient way. It is therefore likely that many developments will put in place a managing agent who will take on the role, at least for the time being, of managing the community on behalf of the developer and incoming unit-holders together. This may be an efficient way of ensuring the duties of the association are carried out in the early stages and provide reassurance to buyers. For example, it will mean that there is a secretary in place to record the incoming membership of the community, to make arrangements for meetings and to deal with any difficulties in relationships between the developer and established unit-holders. Nevertheless, buyers will need to be aware that such agencies may be linked to developers. Some buyers may wish to become directors of the association jointly with any professional and the developer's own directors.

9.34   In any event, the buyer's advisers will need to know whether officers have been appointed, and on what terms, and to discuss with their client any concerns arising. If a developer has not put in place management arrangements, it is even possible that solicitors specialising in the conveyancing and establishment of commonholds might themselves offer to become remunerated directors of commonhold association and thereby secure some legal protection and advice for unit-holders until the development is complete.

Developer's rights

9.35   Unless the solicitor acting for a first buyer is purchasing the very last unit to be sold within a commonhold it is likely that new commonholds will not yet be physically complete and the freeholder/developer will remain the registered proprietor of any unsold units.

9.36   In such circumstances, it is likely that development rights will continue to exist.[36] These rights will relate to marketing the unsold units and may contain power to alter the terms and conditions of the CCS or even to add or delete land to the commonhold. An adviser will be careful to consider and explain the terms and conditions of any such development rights and powers and ensure that the client is protected in the way any changes could be made to the commonhold assessment levies or reserve funding provisions. The power of the developer's directors will or should be time-limited and should terminate as the units are progressively sold.[37] However, it will be necessary

---

[36]   See **8.9**.

[37]   See the provisions of the draft community statement set out in Appendix 2.

for careful advice to be given so that clients are aware of the nature of the development rights. A particular concern of a buyer will be to ensure that the development rights terminate and that there can be no possibility of a developer remaining with such rights by retaining a single unsold unit. Time-limitation of development rights is therefore an important safeguard.

9.37 There will be no need to ensure that the resignation of the developer's directors takes place at the appropriate time as this will happen automatically.[38] However, the resignation of the developer and any remaining subscribers to the memorandum as members of the association should be secured.

PURCHASING OFF THE PLAN

Concept

9.38 There may be circumstances in which clients wish to contract to purchase a commonhold unit where the commonhold is not yet registered as a freehold estate in commonhold land. Indeed, the commonhold may not actually exist except in the plans of a developer in a marketing office.

9.39 The reasons for early contractual arrangements are likely to be the result of both the desires of developers and the wishes of would-be buyers. In very popular proposed developments, there is likely to be market demand to secure units within the planned development. In current market conditions, it is already common for pre-sales of long leasehold or business units to take place. However, it is not only the buyers themselves who will seek to secure the prime units. A developer's cash-flow can be significantly assisted by the payment of early deposits. The commitment to purchase may also assist in funding arrangements.

9.40 Moreover, a developer may have good reasons to delay as long as possible registration of the commonhold under s 2 of the CLRA 2002.[39] By delaying, it will be easier to make detailed amendments to the development plans, whether to the number or size of the units, to the exact layout of the units, to the detailed nature of the facilities to be offered, or so forth. Once registered as a commonhold, the amendments to the CCS will become more formalistic and may be more difficult to secure. If it proves possible, a developer may even wish to avoid registration of the commonhold subject to s 7 of the CLRA 2002 and proceed instead with a later registration of the commonhold subject to s 9 of the Act.[40] At such registration, not all the

---

[38] By virtue of the (draft) articles of association, cl 44.6, when the developer ceases to be the unit-holder of more than one-quarter of the total number of units, any directors appointed by him cease to hold office immediately.

[39] As discussed at **3.6**.

[40] This possibility may be closed by regulations – see **3.6**, note 10.

unit-holders will be in place, but a number of unit-holders may have been signed up and be contractually committed to purchase the first units within the development. The flexibility this approach would give to a developer will be a matter of risk and concern to the proposed buyers. They will seek to obtain as much protection as possible within the contracts for such pre-sales. In other jurisdictions, such as New South Wales, Australia, it is now quite common to purchase off the plan, and detailed publications exist to assist buyers in such situations.[41]

Matters of contract

9.41 The completion of a purchase of a commonhold unit when a contract is entered into prior to registration of the commonhold cannot occur earlier than registration, whether subject to s 7 or s 9 of the CLRA 2002. A buyer will have paid a deposit but should be unwilling to pay more unless and until the unit is complete and ready for occupation, and the title can be registered. When entering into such a contract, the concerns will vary according to the circumstances but there are a number of key issues.

A draft commonhold community statement

9.42 A buyer off the plan will be concerned to see the draft CCS and ensure, as far as possible, that the details are fixed and satisfactory. The buyer should seek to place limits on the developer changing the statement except in ways that would be legitimate under developer's rights.[42] In particular, the number of units in the statement in terms of size and type will be a matter to be negotiated. A buyer will naturally be particularly concerned about the allocation of the commonhold assessment for the unit which it is planned to purchase.

Right to withdraw

9.43 One protection for a proposed buyer in such a situation is to seek an option to withdraw if certain key features are changed by the developer. For example, a reduction or increase in the number of units planned or a change to the type of units available could trigger the right to withdraw. Similarly, a change in the allocation of the percentage assessment or reserve levies might also be made the basis of a right to withdraw from the contract without penalty.

Registration

9.44 By definition in such a case, the commonhold is not yet registered. A prudent buyer will seek to have details of the draft registration documents,

---

[41]   See Michael Allen, *Buying off the Plan in NSW* (CCH Australia, 1999).

[42]   See **8.9**.

ensuring in particular that the consents for registration are in place.[43] The advisers to the buyer will need to satisfy themselves that securing registration of an estate in commonhold land should be straightforward.

---

[43] See CLRA 2002, s 3.

CHAPTER 10

OPERATION AND MANAGEMENT OF THE COMMONHOLD

BASIC PRINCIPLES

Control lies with the members as unit-holders

10.1 The commonhold will be managed through the medium of the commonhold association. The formation and constitution of the commonhold association, the principle of community equality of membership, the membership provisions generally and the appointment of the first directors have already been considered.[1] This chapter is concerned with the principles applicable to the operation of a functioning commonhold after registration of a person other than the developer as proprietor of the freehold estate in one or more of the commonhold units.

10.2 Prior to the registration of the commonhold land, the only members of the commonhold association are the subscriber or subscribers to the memorandum when the company was incorporated.[2] During this pre-commonhold period, the company will not have traded nor will it have incurred any liability that has not been discharged,[3] and the company will therefore have been effectively dormant. The first annual general meeting may not have occurred. It is likely in this period that the subscriber members and the persons appointed as the first directors will be nominees of the developer.[4]

First meeting of the company

10.3 If it has not already taken place, the first annual general meeting of the company is likely to take place shortly after the commonhold has been activated by registration of the first unit-holder other than the developer. At

---

[1] See **4.36**.

[2] CLRA 2002, Sch 3, para 5.

[3] Since on registration, the directors must so certify — CLRA 2002, Sch 1, para 7(d) and (e).

[4] Such persons might include the developer (and, if not, he may become a member – see **4.24**) or his solicitor or accountant. Perhaps the subscribers will be members of a property management company working with the developer. In a case where the commonhold is being formed from an existing leasehold community, it is likely that the subscriber members and directors will be existing leaseholders.

that time, the membership of the company will either consist of the first buyer or first few buyers of the first units to be completed and sold. In such a case, the developer will have title to the unsold units[5] but will not have effective control of the company in a general meeting. This is because he will be one member of the company with a single vote. However, he will have the additional right to appoint developer's directors[6] and will have almost certainly reserved development rights in the community statement.[7]

10.4 At the first annual meeting, the appointment of the directors originally put in place by the developer is likely to be confirmed, at least for the time being. One or more of the buyers may wish to be added as a director to represent the interests of those who have recently purchased into the community but, generally, if the developer has put in place management arrangements, they are likely to be acceptable for the time being.

10.5 Matters will be rather different where the registration is of an existing leasehold community converting to commonhold. It will be a matter for agreement among the unit-holders whether to run the community by electing directors from among their own number or whether to opt for professional management.

MEMBERSHIP AND MEETINGS

Membership

10.6 The statutory provisions as to membership have already been analysed.[8] Once the subscriber members and the director have resigned as members, only unit-holders may be admitted to membership of the association.[9] So the ultimate control of the affairs of the association is through the unit-holders in a general meeting of the association.

Meetings

10.7 The CLRA 2002 is virtually silent on the issue of meetings of members of the association. However, it is planned that detailed provision will be made in the articles of association for all commonholds. These standard provisions will provide the framework for the calling, frequency, conduct and procedures at meetings of the association.

---

[5]   The common parts will now be registered in the name of the commonhold association.

[6]   See **4.37**.

[7]   See Chapter 8.

[8]   See **4.16–4.31**.

[9]   CLRA 2002, Sch 3, paras 7 and 10. The register of members is therefore an important document, and both the Act (Sch 3, paras 11 and 14) and the draft articles of association (cl 6) reinforce the standard company law requirement and duty (Companies Act 1985, s 352) to maintain an up-to-date register of members.

10.8   Since the standard articles currently exist in draft form only, it is not appropriate to attempt a detailed analysis. But the main features are unlikely to change significantly. The following summary is based on the draft in existence at the time of writing.[10]

Types of meeting

10.9   The *annual general meeting* (AGM) may be supplemented by any number of *extraordinary general meetings* (EGMs). Such general meetings can either be called for by the directors or upon requisition of members. At least one EGM must be called to permit an interim review of the business and affairs of the association since the last AGM.

Notice

10.10   In the light of the statutory guide that voting provisions are satisfied only if every member is given the opportunity to vote,[11] the importance of the notice provisions, and due observance of them is obvious. The usual period of notice is 14 days, but this is increased to 21 days if there is to be a special resolution or a resolution to appoint a director. The notice requirements can be waived by agreement, but only by all members in the case of an AGM or by 95% of the membership in the case of an EGM, although accidental omission to give notice or non-receipt of notice shall not invalidate proceedings. Notices will have to contain the agenda, the texts of proposed resolutions and explanations of the motivation for them, as well as the time and place of the meeting.

Proceedings

10.11   Business can be transacted only if details of it are included in the notice, except amendments to ordinary resolutions. A quorum is needed for the transaction of business. The suggested level is 20%, and fears have been expressed that this might permit important matters such as amendments to the CCS to be authorised by only 11% of members, some of whom may be voting by proxy votes given to another member present in person. A balance is required to ensure that business is not hampered by difficulties in securing quorate meetings, but the current level does seem too low at 20%. Directors who are not members[12] are entitled to attend, speak and propose resolutions, but are not able to vote.

---

[10]   Clauses 7–30, set out in Appendix 1.

[11]   CLRA 2002, s 36(2) – see **10.12**.

[12]   This will always be the case when the members choose professional management.

Voting

10.12   The CLRA 2002 does set out a few key principles in relation to any provision of Part 1 of the Act which refers to the passing of a resolution by a commonhold association.[13] Such a voting provision is satisfied only if every member of the commonhold community is given an opportunity to vote in accordance with any relevant provision of the memorandum or articles of association or the commonhold community statement (CCS) of the association.[14] This section ensures that votes and resolutions of the commonhold association on these statutory matters will occur only if the opportunities given to members to vote are genuine. This provision would appear not only to catch the obvious attempt to sideline a member but also to cover failure to serve notice on members who later complain that they were not given the opportunity to be heard and to vote on a particular resolution because they did not know about it.[15] It is specifically provided that a vote is cast for the purposes of a voting provision whether it is cast in person, by proxy or by some other manner of casting the vote, provided that it is in accordance with the memorandum or articles of association or the CCS.[16]

10.13   Some sections of the CLRA 2002 require resolutions to be passed unanimously.[17] A unanimous vote on such matters is defined as one where every member who casts a vote votes in favour.[18] There is no requirement of any particular minimum number of votes for such unanimity,[19] and it would therefore appear that a resolution on such statutory matters may be passed unanimously by a minority of members provided that all those who do vote, vote in favour.

10.14   For other votes in a general meeting, the articles of association of the commonhold association will cater for voting matters. The current draft indicates the likely provisions.[20] Every member present (or, being a corporation present by a duly authorised representative) will have one vote,

---

[13]   CLRA 2002, s 36(1). The sections which refer to a resolution by a commonhold association are s 20(4) (resolutions to consent to the creation of prescribed interests over units or interests in part only of a unit), s 29 (resolution to permit a legal mortgage of common parts), s 41 (application to add land to the commonhold), and ss 43–45 (resolutions in respect of voluntary winding up).

[14]   Ibid, s 36(2).

[15]   It is suggested that the provision in cl 14 of the draft articles of association could not override the statutory requirement for these particular crucial votes.

[16]   CLRA 2002, s 36(3).

[17]   Ibid, s 29 (resolution to permit a legal mortgage of common parts) and s 41 (application to add land to the commonhold). The sections relating to resolutions in respect of voluntary winding up in ss 43 and 44 require 80% or 100% of the members of the association voting in favour rather than unanimity from those present.

[18]   Ibid, s 36(4). A unanimous vote in this context does not mean that every member eligible to vote has done so.

[19]   Subject to the need for a quorum to be present.

[20]   See cls 23–30 and 31–41 in Appendix 1.

regardless of the number of units held by that member. On a poll, however, which may be demanded by the chairman, or by at least five members having the right to vote, or by any member or members representing not less than one-tenth of the total voting rights, a member may have a vote for every commonhold unit in respect of which he is entitled to have his name entered in the register of members. Appointment of proxy votes must be in writing. A form of proxy appointment is provided.

DIRECTORS AND DIRECTORS' POWERS

Directors

10.15 The appointment of the first directors and their relationship to developers has already been discussed.[21] A director need not be a member of the association, and there needs to be minimum of two directors.[22] The members can decide by ordinary resolution what the maximum number of directors is to be.[23] If desired, all members can be directors in a small community. If no resolution is passed, the maximum number will be six. There are extensive planned rules as to the appointment and removal of directors.[24] Directors who were members when appointed cease to be directors if they cease to be members. Alternate directors can be appointed, but directors who are members can only appoint other members as their alternates.

10.16 Directors are not normally remunerated and the developer's directors cannot be remunerated at all. The responsibility for developer's directors' fees falls directly on the developer. However, the general meeting can resolve to consent to remuneration and will have to do so if directors wish to secure professional outside management. Members who are directors can also be remunerated with consent of the members in general meeting.[25]

The statutory duty to manage

10.17 The directors of a commonhold association will be subject to the duties and obligations imposed on all company directors, but are given particular rights and responsibilities as directors of a commonhold association. Members who assume the role as directors will therefore need to acquaint themselves with their responsibilities and be advised accordingly.

---

[21] See **4.36**.

[22] Although the minimum prescribed by Companies Act 1985, s 282(3) is one director, the draft standard articles of association, cl 43, provides for a minimum of two.

[23] Clauses 42 and 43 of the draft articles – see Appendix 1.

[24] See cls 44–58 of the draft articles. Developer's directors provisions are discussed at **4.37**.

[25] Clause 63.

The duty to facilitate the rights of unit-holders

10.18 A specific and overriding duty is imposed on the directors of a commonhold association. They are to exercise their powers so as to permit or facilitate as far as possible the exercise by each unit-holder of his rights and the enjoyment by each unit-holder of the freehold estate in the unit.[26] This overriding duty emphasises that the directors of the association are primarily there to serve the community, facilitate its smooth running and operation, and permit each unit-holder to enjoy the rights given by the CCS over the common parts. This duty arises whether the directors are some of the members elected to serve on behalf of the community or whether they are outside directors remunerated to undertake the task.

Duty to remedy failures by unit-holders

10.19 One of the main functions of the directors will be to ensure that all unit-holders observe their obligations towards the community as a whole and in relation to other unit-holders in particular. This secondary duty is a natural consequence of the overriding duty of facilitation even though it involves, ultimately, action against a defaulting unit-holder. The enjoyment of the freehold estate in every unit depends on the maintenance of the common parts, including the structures and the rights of access. These benefits must be paid for. Failures by one unit-holder may well inhibit the exercise of rights by others and their enjoyment of the freehold estate in the unit. It is therefore specifically provided that the directors shall, in particular, use any right, power or procedure available to them[27] to enforce the obligations of unit-holders. They must prevent, remedy or curtail failures on the part of a unit-holder to comply with a requirement or duty imposed by the CLRA 2002 or the CCS.[28]

The right of inaction

10.20 The CLRA 2002, recognising that a duty to remedy *all* failures by unit-holders, however trivial, could be a recipe for one member demanding inappropriate and heavy-handed action by the directors, allows the directors a right of inaction. The Act expresses the importance of the directors bearing in mind the need for harmonious relationships between all unit-holders. It is therefore specifically provided that, by way of exception to the duty to remedy

---

[26] CLRA 2002, s 35(1). A unit-holder in this context includes a tenant of a unit and those with matrimonial home rights – ibid, ss 35(4) and 61(b).

[27] Ie those remedies conferred or created by s 37 of the CLRA 2002 authorising regulations for enforcement and compensation.

[28] CLRA 2002, s 35(2). The remedies available and the resolution of disputes between the commonhold association and any particular unit-holder, and between individual unit-holders, is considered in Chapter 11.

failures,[29] the directors need not take action if they reasonably think that inaction is in the best interests of establishing or maintaining those harmonious relationships. The directors are permitted to decide not to take action only if they reasonably think that inaction will not cause any unit-holder (other than the defaulter) significant loss or significant disruption.[30] It is feared that this well-meaning provision could be the subject of litigation to establish the exact parameters of the right to take no action against defaulters.

Commonhold assessment

10.21 One of the fundamental and ongoing duties of the directors of the commonhold association will be the financial management of the community. They will need to maintain the income stream by way of the commonhold assessment on the unit-holders[31] to ensure that the day-to-day expenses of providing the community services and the regular maintenance and decoration of the fabric of the common parts is ensured.

10.22 They will be assisted in this task by the provisions of the CCS. The community statement of each commonhold must, first, make provision requiring the directors of the commonhold to make an annual estimate of the income required to be raised from unit-holders to meet the expenses of the association.[32] The directors will therefore be required to produce an annual budget which, no doubt, will be presented at the annual general meeting of the association. This estimate will set out the income required for payment of regular expenses, for example utility services such as gas, electricity, water and rates in respect of the common parts, and the cost of upkeep of the grounds. It will normally include contingencies for day-to-day repairs and maintenance of buildings comprising the common parts, such as replacing light bulbs, dealing with burst pipes and the myriad of other costs which will affect the community in question. Secondly, the community statement must enable the directors to deal with the need to raise additional income. They must be permitted to make estimates from time to time of the income required in addition to the annual estimate.[33] If, therefore, the annual estimate proves to be inadequate to meet the needs of the community during a 12-month period, the directors will be able to issue additional estimates and so raise additional income during the year.

---

[29] The exceptional nature of the right of inaction is shown by the statutory 'But ...'. It is a curious feature of this statute that subsections begin with 'And' and 'But'. No member of Parliament was concerned that traditional standards of grammar were not being maintained.

[30] CLRA 2002, s 35(3)(a).

[31] And, in some cases, tenants. The term 'commonhold assessment' is the name chosen instead of 'service charge' although it only appears as the heading to CLRA 2002, s 38, and is not in the text of the statute.

[32] CLRA 2002, s 38(1)(a).

[33] Ibid, s 38(1)(b).

10.23   The income so raised by assessments on the unit-holders will be according to the percentage of the overall cost allocated to each unit. A community statement must make provision specifying the percentage of the assessment allocated to each unit, and the percentages when totalled together must amount in aggregate to one hundred.[34] This ensures that there will be no income shortfall but it also makes clear that there cannot be a profit element by raising more than 100% of the amount required. A particular unit need not be subject to an assessment levy. This is specifically permitted by the CLRA 2002,[35] and enables a community to be designed with open units such as garden spaces that do not themselves attract an assessment. It would be appropriate to take advantage of this provision only where the unit in question obtains no benefits whatsoever from the services provided by the community at the cost of the community. Thus, an open car parking space may be a separate unit but some assessment in relation to that car parking space may well be appropriate to cover the associated costs related to the provision of car parking for the residents who benefit from this provision.[36]

10.24   The assessment will be raised by the directors of the commonhold association serving notices on the unit-holders specifying the payments required to be made by them. The CCS must require the notices to state the date on which each payment is due.[37] It will always impose on each unit-holder the requirement to pay the percentage of the estimate allocated to the unit in question.[38] The current draft CCS contains this requirement which is stated as a duty to pay on the due date specified in the notice.[39]

10.25   It is likely that each unit-holder will have the opportunity to comment on the estimates as these will usually be presented for approval by the members in advance at either the annual general meeting or some other general meeting of the community association.[40] Not unnaturally, the amount of the assessment may be a contentious issue among the members of the association who may have different perceptions of the level of service that is properly required under the CCS relevant to the community in question. Members may need to take the opportunity presented by meetings of the association to air their views on the assessment proposed. Unlike long leaseholders, who can take the issue of reasonableness of a service charge to a

---

[34]   CLRA 2002, s 38(1)(c), (2)(a).

[35]   Ibid, s 38(2)(b).

[36]   Car parking spaces, and indeed garages, can be treated as part of a single unit, or designated as separate units. Alternatively, they could be part of the common parts, especially where every resident has a space, and therefore repairable by the association. They might be then designated as limited use areas, one for each unit. See further **7.4**.

[37]   CLRA 2002, s 38(1)(e).

[38]   Ibid, s 38(1)(d).

[39]   Clause 35 of the draft CCS – see Appendix 2.

[40]   In this context, it is proposed that members will have the right, on reasonable notice, to inspect books, minutes, documents or accounting records of the association: draft articles of association, cl 83.

leasehold valuation tribunal,[41] unit-holders within a commonhold will not be able to challenge the commonhold assessment by any analogous procedure. If a unit-holder is dissatisfied, the remedy lies in convincing a majority of fellow members of the community of the need for action and taking up the matter in general meeting.[42]

Reserve funds

10.26 One of the weaknesses of the leasehold system in many leasehold developments is that the provisions for long-term maintenance of the fabric of the common parts integral to the community in question have been inadequate. Very often, where such reserve funds exist, they have been under the control of an outside landlord, and decisions on the level of reserve funding (if any) and the way those reserve funds are expended have often been beyond the control of the leaseholders.

10.27 One of the more attractive features of commonhold therefore is the provision made for reserve funds by the CLRA 2002. Although the Act provides that regulations *may*[43] require a commonhold community to make provision for reserve funding, it is highly likely that such regulations will so provide and reserve funds will be a standard feature of every commonhold community.

10.28 Regulations[44] may impose on the directors of the commonhold association a duty to establish and maintain one or more reserve funds to finance the repair and maintenance of the common parts.[45] When a community statement provides that the responsibility for repair and maintenance of commonhold units is imposed on the commonhold association rather than unit-holders, then again regulations may require the directors to establish similar reserve funds for the repair and maintenance of those units.[46] Whether or nor there is a single reserve fund for repair and maintenance, or more than one, will depend in part on the detailed regulations yet to be made but also on the nature of the commonhold in question. A single reserve fund may well be appropriate for the most straightforward

---

[41] The statutory regime in Landlord and Tenant Act 1985, ss 18–21, applicable to dwellings, is centred on consultation and reasonableness. The regime was enacted in response to abuse by 'outside' landlords but applies equally where the landlord is a resident-controlled management company. It is undoubtedly the case that a single leaseholder or a minority of leaseholders who have lost the argument in a general meeting of the residents' management company, often then use the statutory procedures to argue the case again.

[42] Resolutions could either seek a reduction in the amount of the assessment or seek removal of the directors who proposed the amount of the assessment.

[43] CLRA 2002, s 39(1); my emphasis.

[44] Made under CLRA 2002, s 32.

[45] Ibid, s 39(1)(a).

[46] Ibid, s 39(1)(b). If the responsibility is imposed on unit-holders, reserve funds would obviously not be appropriate.

situations where each commonhold unit receives similar benefits from the community as a whole and it is therefore appropriate and convenient that each unit-holder should contribute to the one common reserve fund. Where, however, a commonhold provides that certain services or benefits are made available only to some unit-holders it may be sensible to have separate reserve funds for the long-term replacement and major repair work to those parts of the community that provide services to some unit-holders alone.

10.29 By way of example, one potentially difficult issue will be the question of the provision of a reserve fund for long-term replacement and major repair work to lifts within a building containing a large number of residential flats. Unit-holders on the ground floor may consider that it is proper that only those unit-holders making use of the lift on the upper floors should contribute to the reserve fund. Indeed, similar issues may arise in relation to the day-to-day maintenance of lifts. It is probably, however, much better for these sorts of services to be maintained by the community as a whole rather than have the complexity and difficulty of a reserve fund which is contributed to unequally and according to use.

10.30 Where the CCS does so provide for the establishment of one or more reserve funds then there must be additional provision in the statement setting out how this is to be achieved. The provisions are not dissimilar to those relating to the commonhold assessment. Thus the directors of the commonhold association must be required or enabled to set a levy from time to time for contributions to the reserve fund.[47] The statement must specify the percentage of any levy which is to be allocated to each unit and once again the percentages allocated to the units must amount in aggregate to one hundred, and the statement may specify a nil percentage allocation in relation to a unit.[48] The provisions relating to the levy also mirror those relating to the assessment in that the statement must make provision requiring the directors to serve notices in advance specifying the payments to be made and setting out the date on which levies are due.[49] There will be a specific requirement in the statement requiring the unit-holder to make the payments in respect of the levy made.[50]

Protection of reserve funds

10.31 It is provided that the assets of reserve funds established and maintained by a commonhold association are protected against judgment creditors. The funds are not to be used for the purpose of enforcement of any

---

[47]   CLRA 2002, s 39(2)(a).

[48]   Ibid, ss 39(2)(b) and (3). A nil percentage allocation will be especially appropriate where the unit in question derives no benefit from the facility in respect of which the reserve fund applies.

[49]   Ibid, s 39(2)(d).

[50]   Ibid, s 39(2)(c). See cls 32 and 33 of the draft CCS in Appendix 2.

debt except a judgment debt referable to a reserve fund activity.[51] A reserve fund activity is an activity which in accordance with the CCS can or may be financed from the fund established and maintained by virtue of the CLRA 2002.[52] The combination of this statutory provision and the CCS itself will ensure that the reserve funds are used only for the purposes for which the funds are established.

10.32 The Act gives some guidance as to when the reserve fund can be taken in satisfaction of a judgment debt referable to a reserve fund activity. It is specifically provided that reserve funds may be taken in execution or they may be made the subject of a charging order[53] if the debt relates to the reserve fund activity. Additionally, the assets may be used to pay interest payable on such judgment debt.[54]

Enforcement of unpaid assessments and levies

10.33 The issue of disputes between the commonhold association and unit-holders and the enforcement of obligations is dealt with in the next chapter. However, a potential practical difficulty is that there is no provision in the CLRA 2002 granting the commonhold association a charge on the commonhold unit for unpaid debt that would rank in priority to other creditors. There was considerable argument during the passage of the legislation through Parliament on this issue. Opposition parties argued that there was a need for a draconian remedy against a unit-holder who does not or will not pay assessments and levies due. The fear is that other members of the community will have to contribute extra sums temporarily to cover defaulting unit-holders while the commonhold association pursues standard remedies for recovery of the debts due.[55] It was considered by such critics that the charging order process was slow and expensive and gave no priority to the association in priority to other creditors of the defaulting unit-holder.[56] This issue is analysed more fully in the discussion on remedies.[57]

10.34 It is to be regretted that it was not possible to persuade the Government of the arguments in favour of some protection for the commonhold association against a recalcitrant unit-holder. There was an

---

[51] CLRA 2002, s 39(4). The protection of reserve funds ceases if a court makes a winding-up order in respect of the association or if the association passes a voluntary winding-up resolution: ibid, s 56(a) and (b), and see **12.33**. Protection also ceases when land ceases to be commonhold land by order of the court: ibid, s 56(c).

[52] Ibid, s 39(5)(a).

[53] Under s 1 of the Charging Orders Act 1979.

[54] CLRA 2002, s 39(5)(b) and (c).

[55] If a defaulting unit-holder avoids payment, perhaps after selling the unit and moving away, and cannot be found, then the sums may have to be found permanently by the remaining unit-holders.

[56] See for example Lord Goodheart, HL Deb, Vol 627, col 505.

[57] See **11.18–11.24**.

obvious desire to avoid any statutory provision for commonhold equivalent to forfeiture, and this is an understandable sentiment. However, it would have been better to allow an association to hold a first charge over a commonhold unit for unpaid debts of the unit-holder in priority to all other charges.[58] A convenient way of doing this would be for the statute to have permitted a CCS to provide that unpaid but validly made assessments and levies should from time to time be a first charge on the commonhold unit on any transfer or sale of the unit. In this way, the commonhold association could be assured of recovering unpaid sums in due course. As it is, the commonhold association must make do with the standard recovery remedies available to any creditor of a debtor who has a freehold property and use the standard debt-collecting machinery for this purpose.[59]

ENLARGEMENT OF THE COMMUNITY

10.35   There are two ways that a commonhold, once established, may be enlarged. The first of these mechanisms is through the application of development rights. One of the rights a developer may reserve to himself is the ability to add land to the commonhold.[60] Enlargement of a commonhold by means of development rights has already been discussed.[61] The other method of enlarging the commonhold is after resolution of the commonhold association under CLRA 2002, s 41.

Circumstances where enlargement may apply

10.36   There are a number of circumstances where the enlargement provisions may apply. A developer may simply wish to enlarge a commonhold of which he is the proprietor after first registration but during the transitional period. A developer may agree with a commonhold association that he will develop adjoining land and add it to the commonhold. It may be that a commonhold, once established with unit-holders, has the opportunity to purchase and develop through the commonhold association adjoining land either to add to the common parts of the commonhold or to construct additional units. It is possible that a neighbouring leasehold development could conveniently be amalgamated with the existing commonhold community rather than become a separate commonhold.

---

[58]   This is effectively the position in long leaseholds since a mortgagee of a long residential lease needs to discharge any unpaid rent, and service charges reserved as rent, to realise its security. So it is unlikely that lenders would be adverse to lending on commonhold units just because of the existence of such a first charge.

[59]   See **11.24** for a discussion of these remedies.

[60]   CLRA 2002, Sch 4, para 4.

[61]   See **8.14**.

Process of enlargement

10.37   Any enlargement can occur only where an application is made to the Registrar[62] where the commonhold association for the purposes of the application already exercises functions in relation to commonhold land.[63] Such an application is known as an application to add land, and the land to which the application relates will be referred to as the added land.[64] An application to add land cannot be submitted unless it is approved in advance by resolution of the commonhold association.[65] The resolution, which must be passed before the application to add the land is made, must be unanimous.[66]

Documentation required

10.38   All applications to add land will require the following documentation:

- any relevant consents;[67]
- an application[68] for registration of an amended CCS, which will need to make provision for both the existing commonhold and the added land;[69]
- a certificate given by the directors of the commonhold association that the application to add land satisfies all the statutory requirements, namely that there has been a prior unanimous resolution of the commonhold association and that none of the land to be added is land which may not be commonhold.[70]

Enlargement with existing unit-holders on land to be added

10.39   The application to add land may be subject to CLRA 2002, s 9.[71] This will apply only if the added land includes additional units to be added to the existing units within the commonhold, and the application to register the added land includes a statement requesting s 9 to apply to the units on the added land. It would therefore be relevant in the situation where the added

---

[62]   Under CLRA 2002, s 2, by the freeholder of the land it is sought to add to the commonhold.

[63]   Ibid, s 41(1). The phrase 'exercising functions' merely indicates that a commonhold association has been incorporated in respect of defined land that constitutes and is registered as an estate in commonhold land but excludes the land which it is intended to add – see s 1(1) and (2) .

[64]   Ibid, s 41(2).

[65]   Ibid, s 41(3) and (4)(a).

[66]   Ibid, s 41(4). Unanimity, in this context, means every member who casts a vote voting in favour: ibid, s 36(4).

[67]   As required by CLRA 2002, Sch 1, para 6 and s 41(5)(a). If the consents which are required are not obtainable then the only alternative will be to obtain either an order of the court dispensing with the requirement for the consent or for consent to be deemed to be given. For a fuller discussion of these possibilities, see **3.40**.

[68]   Under CLRA 2002, s 33 – see **5.10**. The application is by the commonhold association.

[69]   Ibid, s 41(5)(b).

[70]   By virtue of CLRA 2002, Sch 2 – see s 41(5)(c).

[71]   See **3.21**.

land is an existing building with owners of the would-be units in place. An example would be where a commonhold exists consisting of flats in (say) three former converted terraced houses and the long leaseholders in flats in an adjoining converted house in the same terrace agree to join the existing commonhold. On registration of the added land, the existing, and amended, community statement applies to the added land immediately[72] and any leases over the added land are extinguished.[73]

Enlargement with added units but no existing unit-holders

10.40   An application to register additional land subject to CLRA 2002, s 7 will be more usual.[74] It will apply in a variety of situations, but the common feature will be an intention to form further commonhold units on the added land (and the amended community statement will so provide), although the application will not identify any new unit-holders.[75] The more straightforward situation will be where title to the land to be added is vested in the developer of a commonhold which has already registered but where a transitional period applies.[76] In such a case, the added land will remain registered in the name of the applicant developer. The CCS will not be in force in relation to the added land (or any part of the commonhold land).[77] The developer and the subscriber members will be the only members of the commonhold association and thus have control of it for the purposes of the necessary resolution to add the land. Thereafter, the position will be the same as any registration subject to s 7. The enlarged commonhold will be activated only when a person other than the commonhold association becomes entitled to be registered as the proprietor of the freehold estate in one or more but not all of the new commonhold units. Any lease which exists over the added land will be extinguished at that point in the same way as occurs in relation to any application for registration of a commonhold.[78]

10.41   If the commonhold to which the land is to be added is already activated, that is, there is more than one unit-holder, then the enlargement process applies differently although the application to add land with more units remains subject to CLRA 2002, s 7. The application will be made by the registered freeholder of the land to be added.[79] This may be the existing

---

[72]   CLRA 2002, s 9(3)(e) applies but only to the rights and duties in the CCS as they affect the added land – see s 41(6)(b).

[73]   The references to the commonhold land in CLRA 2002, s 9(3)(f) in such a case relate only to the added land – see s 41(6)(a). For extinguishment of leases, and the compensation provisions, see **3.65**.

[74]   For a discussion of the effect of s 7, see **3.20**.

[75]   Ie there will be no statement accompanying the application requesting that CLRA 2002, s 9 applies.

[76]   See **3.53**.

[77]   See CLRA 2002, s 41(6). The references to commonhold land in s 7(2)(a) are treated as references to the added land.

[78]   See **3.65–3.71** for a full discussion.

[79]   CLRA 2002, s 2(1).

commonhold association or it may be a developer acting with the agreement of the commonhold association or by virtue of a reserved development right.[80] On registration of the added land, the applicant (whether developer or commonhold association) continues to be the registered proprietor of all the added land, and the rights and duties conferred and imposed by the CCS do not come into force so far as they affect the added land.[81] When, after registration of the added land, a unit comprising part of the added land is transferred, then the commonhold association is entitled to be registered as proprietor of the freehold estate in the common parts of the added land, without further application, and the amended CCS comes into force.[82] Any lease of any part of the added land will be extinguished.[83]

Enlargement by adding only to the common parts

10.42   There is special provision if the added land is merely to become part of the common parts of an existing commonhold and it is not intended to add any more units. In such a case, the application can proceed without CLRA 2002, s 7 applying to the application to add the land.[84] On registration of the added land, the commonhold association is entitled to be registered (if it is not already so registered)[85] as the proprietor of the freehold estate in the added land.[86] The rights and duties conferred by the CCS shall, insofar as they affect the added land, come into force on registration.[87]

Enlargement by building upwards

10.43   The most obvious example of vertical enlargement is where the commonhold association wishes to develop an existing building by extending upwards and either constructing units in the roof space or building new units on the roof. This will be a development opportunity from which the existing members of the commonhold association will be able to benefit. The enlargement provisions would appear to apply to this situation as land is being added to the commonhold.

---

[80]   If the registered freeholder of the land to be added is not the commonhold association, co-operation is essential since the application to add land needs both the unanimous approval of the association and a completed application to amend the CCS.

[81]   CLRA 2002, s 7(2), as amended in relation to added land by s 41(6).

[82]   In relation to the added land, but the amendments thereafter will apply to the whole enlarged commonhold. See CLRA 2002, s 7(3), amended as it relates to an application to add land by s 41(6).

[83]   Ibid, ss 7(4) and 41(6)(a).

[84]   Ibid, s 41(7)(a).

[85]   It is almost certain that the commonhold association will be the applicant to register the added land and therefore already the freehold registered proprietor. However, the title will need amending to bring the added land within the commonhold.

[86]   CLRA 2002, s 41(7)(b); such registration of the commonhold association will be made by the Registrar without an application being made – see s 41(7)(c).

[87]   Ibid, s 41(7)(d).

CHAPTER 11

DISPUTE RESOLUTION

INTRODUCTION

Importance of effective procedures

11.1 Resolution of disputes within a residential community, whether it is a commonhold, or some other sort of association or a group of long leasehold residents is undoubtedly a critical process. It is trite but true that no form of land holding, be it commonhold, strata title, condominium, or leasehold, will of itself encourage individuals within a community to live in harmonious relationships. Sadly, there will always be situations where, perhaps, a few individuals behave unreasonably and others refuse or are unable to pay financial contributions. Inevitably, there may also be a clash of cultures or living styles where attitudes to noise, children and pets, let alone repairs, decorations and the colour of paint, differ. Alternative views and approaches can be reasonably held but may result in disagreement and the need for resolution of the differences. What is needed is an internal framework in which disputes and genuine disagreements can be dealt with sensibly and an external process to deal with intractable problems which provides for final resolution and disposition of the issues as simply, as economically and as quickly as possible.

Possible dispute resolution processes not adopted

11.2 There are a number of possible approaches that could have been taken in relation to the establishment of dispute resolution processes within commonhold which have not been adopted.

No commonhold commissioner

11.3 It would have been possible to establish the office of a commonhold commissioner along the lines of the Australian model where a strata title commissioner is a public officer providing (inter alia) an inexpensive and straightforward mechanism for resolution of disputes between members of strata communities and their body corporate, or indeed between members themselves.[1] Attempts were made to introduce such a system for England and Wales by way of amendment as the legislation progressed through Parliament[2] but a dispute resolution system has never been a feature of any of the commonhold proposals. The proposed amendment was rejected by the Minister, and it was probably sensible to do so. To establish a commonhold commissioner, and a new disputes procedure, would be expensive and there would be relatively little work for the commissioner to do for some years, at least until commonhold was well established. Much more importantly, the Australian experience suggests that charging fees to resolve disputes does not cover the costs of the operation so the general taxpayer is funding a limited dispute resolution procedure for the benefit of a few.[3] There is also at least some evidence that having such a simple (and inexpensive) resolution procedure encourages relatively minor disputes to be pursued to final determination rather than resolved internally.

No jurisdiction for the residential tribunal service

11.4   An alternative approach to dispute resolution, which was urged on the Government by some interested parties, was to suggest that the residential tribunal service[4] should have a role in dispute resolution. Leasehold valuation tribunals have already built up considerable expertise in resolving disputes relating to forfeiture, service charges, trust funds, and the like, and could provide a ready-made source of tribunal arbiters to resolve disputes between the commonhold association and unit-holders. This idea would seem to have considerable attractions. The tribunals are established nationwide and could gradually absorb work as it developed in relation to commonholds. This suggestion, however, was not taken up and there is no specific allocation of jurisdiction to the tribunals. However, there is the ability to confer jurisdiction on a tribunal at a future date, since the power to confer jurisdiction on a court includes power to confer jurisdiction on a tribunal.[5]

11.5   It should also be noted that there is a significant lack of specific remedies for unit-holders which are available to leaseholders in analogous

---

[1]   The jurisdiction is essentially exclusive so that in New South Wales there is only a final appeal to the Supreme Court on a point of law. One similarity to the Commonhold and Leasehold Reform Act 2002 (CLRA 2002) is that mediation is also encouraged as the first step – see eg, Strata Schemes Management Act 1996 (NSW), s 125.

[2]   See HL Deb, Vol 627, cols 532–537. It was rejected on the grounds that a strata title commissioner had other duties; that such a scheme would be prohibitively expensive; and that the proposals in the Bill were sufficient.

[3]   The Australian systems demand resources from general taxation, although it may be argued that, in the long run, the cost is less under the Australian model given that disputes are resolved relatively easily without resort to expensive court procedures.

[4]   The new name for the cadre of persons sitting as rent assessment committees and leasehold valuation tribunals.

[5]   CLRA 2002, s 66(3). But there is no indication at present that assigning jurisdiction to hear disputes is contemplated.

situations. For example, a unit-holder cannot challenge the reasonableness of commonhold assessment or levies. The CLRA 2002 assumes that all members will have the opportunity to debate and agree the assessment and levies in a general meeting. This approach is to be welcomed. Sadly, the present provisions allowing leaseholders to challenge the reasonableness of service charge (which were designed as a remedy against outside landlords) are too often used by a minority who refuse to pay service charges set by a tenants' management company as landlord. Similarly, there is no requirement that the assessment and levies made by the association are held in trust for the members. In normal circumstances, this should not be a problem. The fund will be an asset of the commonhold association and wholly controlled by those paying the levies. The directors will be responsible to the members for the investment and use of the reserve fund and owe fiduciary duties to them and may indeed be members themselves.[6] However, there may be less protection for members against directors of the association who use the funds improperly.

Financial assistance and advice

11.6 Advice on how the new law and regulations affect unit-holders will be important, particularly when a dispute arises between a unit-holder and the commonhold association. Consequently, the Lord Chancellor is empowered to give financial assistance to a person in relation to provision by that person of general advice about an aspect of the law of commonhold land so far as it relates to residential matters.[7] This will permit the Leasehold Advisory Service (LEASE), or another person or body, to provide free advice about commonhold law. In particular, advice can be given on how disputes may be resolved.

COMMONHOLD DISPUTE RESOLUTION

The policy for dispute resolution

A fourfold approach

11.7 There is therefore no statutory system for the resolution of disputes. Instead of such a statutory system, the CLRA 2002 envisages a staged response. Although much will depend on regulations and rules to be introduced later, it is envisaged that the commonhold community statement (CCS) will set out an internal complaints procedure which members must first adopt. The dispute resolution procedures then involve an inter-relationship of

---

[6] These reasons were cited by the Minister when rejecting an amendment to the 2000 Bill which sought to require reserve funds to be held as trust accounts – see HL Deb, Vol 644, col 1118, 10 April 2002 (Lord Bach).

[7] CLRA 2002, s 62.

three approaches after any such internal procedures have been exhausted. There is specific provision for regulations to provide that a commonhold association shall be a member of an approved Ombudsman scheme. There is a general statutory duty on the directors of a commonhold association to have regard to the desirability of using arbitration, mediation or conciliation procedures (including referral under approved Ombudsman schemes), instead of legal proceedings.[8] Finally, the courts will have an overriding jurisdiction.

11.8   Dispute resolution will therefore centre on the amalgam of these approaches, at least for the time being. It is not envisaged that all will need to be used in a particular case. In some instances, the association may consider that it is vital to move to court action immediately the internal mechanisms are exhausted.[9] In other situations, a reference to an Ombudsman or to mediation may be preferable. Much of the details relating to both Ombudsman and arbitration, conciliation and mediation services is not dealt with in the CLRA 2002 itself but provisions are made for regulations before the Act comes into force. Until those regulations are available then, of necessity, the discussion of some aspects of dispute resolution must be generalised and tentative.

Internal procedures

11.9   The draft CCS indicates the probable nature of the internal complaints procedure to be prescribed.[10] There is to be a *Complaints Procedure*[11] that a unit-holder must follow before taking legal proceedings against another unit-holder or the commonhold association. This is envisaged as straightforward and informal, requiring that any complaint in relation to any possible breach of the articles of association or the Rules of the association must be notified in writing to the Board of Directors with full information as to the nature of the complaint. The directors are then obliged to take appropriate steps in an effort to resolve the matter. They must act in accordance with their duties under CLRA 2002, s 35 which include the duty to remedy a failure, the power of inaction in the interests of maintaining harmonious relationships and the desirability of using mediation and conciliation procedures rather than legal proceedings.[12] They may also take steps under the Default Procedure.

11.10   The *Default Procedure*[13] is the procedure to be followed by the commonhold association where the directors have reason to believe that there is breach by any person.[14] After an attempt to resolve the matter informally, a

---

8   CLRA 2002, s 35(3)(b).

9   For example, to secure payments of commonhold assessment from a defaulter who is selling a unit and leaving the community – see **11.24**.

10   See section F, cls 37–51, Appendix 2.

11   Clause 40.

12   See **10.20** and **11.16**.

13   Clauses 41–45.

14   'Any person' will usually be the unit-holder or a tenant of the unit-holder.

default notice may be issued specifying the breach and allowing a reasonable period for a response or a remedying of the breach. The default notice will contain a warning of the rights of the association and the right to refer the dispute to an Ombudsman or to take legal proceedings. Only after this procedure has been completed can other action be taken.

The commonhold Ombudsman

11.11   The idea of a commonhold Ombudsman was introduced during the passage of the legislation.[15] Regulations may provide that a commonhold association shall be a member of an approved ombudsman scheme.[16] Such a scheme is likely to be based on experience with the Housing Ombudsman who may well have joint functions in due course. The original intention had been to rely entirely on authorisation in the CLRA 2002 permitting the provision of arbitration, conciliation and mediation services. The main reason for expressly inserting the power to regulate for an Ombudsman scheme was the fear that the wording might not extend to permit the setting up of an approved ombudsman scheme.[17] So the commonhold Ombudsman scheme should be seen as one part of a wide range of alternative dispute resolution procedures to be provided for commonhold.

11.12   The Ombudsman scheme is designed to permit a unit-holder (or tenant)[18] to refer to the Ombudsman a dispute between the unit-holder or tenant and a commonhold association provided the association is a member of the scheme.[19] It also enables the commonhold association to make a similar reference to the Ombudsman of a dispute between the association and a unit-holder or tenant.[20] The CLRA 2002 does not specifically provide for the Ombudsman to deal with disputes between two unit-holders although it would be possible for this to be done since it is expressly provided that an approved ombudsman scheme may contain additional provisions to those set out.[21]

11.13   The approved ombudsman scheme, which will be approved by the Lord Chancellor, will require the Ombudsman to investigate and determine disputes referred to him.[22] A commonhold association which is a member of

---

[15]   During the passage of the 2000 Bill, at Report stage on 10 April 2001, see HL Deb, Vol 624, col 1123. This Bill was lost when the 2001 General Election was called.

[16]   Section 42(1).

[17]   See the explanation of the then Minister, Lord Bach, at HL Deb, Vol 624, col 1110.

[18]   By virtue of CLRA 2002, s 42(5), a reference to a unit-holder in relation to the Ombudsman scheme includes a reference to a tenant of a unit.

[19]   Ibid, s 42(2)(c). It is almost certain that the regulations will make it compulsory for all commonhold associations to be members of an approved ombudsman scheme.

[20]   Ibid, s 42(2)(d)

[21]   Ibid, s 42(3).

[22]   Ibid, s 42(2)(e).

the scheme will be required to co-operate with the Ombudsman in investigating or determining any dispute.[23] Although it is expressly provided that a commonhold association which is a member of the scheme is required to comply with any decision of the Ombudsman, including any decision requiring the payment of money,[24] it is not stated that a unit-holder who has referred a dispute to the Ombudsman or had a dispute between the unit-holder and the association referred by the association must comply with any decision. If the unit-holders are not required to be members, there is concern that the Ombudsman's decisions could be ignored by unit-holders. It may therefore be difficult to enforce rulings of the Ombudsman when the ruling is against the members rather than the association. A commonhold association will have to comply with all the regulations made by virtue of CLRA 2002, s 42. Any failure to comply will allow a unit-holder to apply to the High Court for an order requiring the directors of the association to ensure that the association complies with the regulations.[25]

11.14 More than one person can be appointed as Ombudsman under the scheme but such persons who are appointed must be approved by the Lord Chancellor.[26]

Arbitration, mediation or conciliation procedure

11.15 The policy of the CLRA 2002 is to direct that disputes arising within a commonhold, and the enforcement of rights and duties arising under a CCS, should be resolved by methods other than resort to the courts. There is relatively little within the Act on the detail of these issues, and much will depend on the regulations to come.

11.16 There is a general duty imposed on the directors of a commonhold association when faced with a failure on the part of a unit-holder to have regard to the desirability of using arbitration, mediation or conciliation procedures instead of legal proceedings wherever possible.[27] This general duty will be reinforced by the regulations when they are promulgated. It is specifically provided that the regulations may make provisions requiring the use of these specified forms of arbitration, mediation or conciliation before legal proceedings may be brought.[28]

---

23 CLRA 2002, s 42(2)(f).

24 Ibid, s 42(2)(g).

25 Ibid, s 42(4).

26 Ibid, s 42(2)(a) and (b).

27 Ibid, s 35(3)(b).

28 Ibid, s 37(2)(i).

Court proceedings

11.17 There is the recognition that court proceedings may be necessary, particularly for the enforcement of payment of assessment and levies through the normal debt collecting procedures. In principle, any disputes may be resolved by appropriate legal proceedings.[29] All references to 'the court' in Part 1 of the CLRA 2002 mean the High Court or a county court.[30] It is likely that court procedures will be possible immediately (or fairly soon) after completion of the Default Procedure. The exact details will be decided by the regulations to be made.

SECURING PAYMENTS FROM UNIT-HOLDERS

Importance of securing payment

11.18 A distinguishing feature of commonhold is the combination of a freehold estate in a unit with the obligation to make regular payments to the commonhold association for the upkeep of the common parts. These payments (as we have seen) are made by way of commonhold assessment or through levies.[31] The assessment covers the annual running costs and the day-to-day maintenance of the benefits that all members of the association enjoy.[32] The levies enable the association to build up one or more reserve funds. For example, the association can build up a reserve fund for replacement of a roof where it may have a life expectancy of 25 years. In this way, the long-term cost is equitably distributed among all members over the 25-year period and does not fall as a heavy burden on those members in place when the work is done.

11.19 Assessments and levies are for the overall benefit of the freehold unit-holders. In a standard freehold, the owner will pay for insurance and from time to time will have to undertake repair and maintenance of the property. Within a commonhold, as within a leasehold development subject to service charges, the unit-holder is liable for the payments at the time stated and as they fall due. A standard freeholder can allow a property to fall into disrepair. A commonhold will always be properly repaired and maintained.

11.20 A key concern therefore is the ability of the commonhold association to secure prompt and regular payment from all its members. This is important for maintaining cash-flow and fulfilling the association's liabilities. A

---

[29] The jurisdiction section of Part 1 of the CLRA 2002 is s 66. The limitation period for bringing an action for breach of a commonhold duty is six years: Limitation Act 1980, s 19A, inserted by CLRA 2002, Sch 5, para 4.

[30] Ibid, s 66(1). Jurisdiction is subject to provision made under s 1 of the Courts and Legal Services Act 1990 as regards allocation of business between the High Court and county courts: s 66(2).

[31] CLRA 2002, ss 38 and 39 – see **10.21** and **10.26**.

[32] The commonhold assessment is based on the annual estimate of the income required to be raised from unit-holders to meet the expenses of the association: CLRA 2002, s 38(1)(e).

commonhold association will usually have no significant assets that it can call on in the event of non-payment.[33] If one or more members cannot or will not pay then it may well fall to the remaining members to cover the shortfall for the time being. This opens up the prospect of community discontent whenever a dissident unit-holder withholds payments due on the unit.[34] This might be done for a variety of reasons, some more justifiable than others. However, in any event, it is vital that the commonhold association can act in the best interests of the majority and secure payment of commonhold assessment and levies by a simple, straightforward and reliable process. It is also important that sums adjudged due from a unit-holder are secure and the defaulting unit-holder does not have a way of avoiding payment.

No statutory provision

11.21 It is submitted that what should have been provided was for the commonhold association to have a statutory lien and first charge on each commonhold unit for the payment of commonhold assessments and levies as and when they fall due. Such a statutory charge arising from time to time would have taken priority to mortgages or other charges on the property. The ultimate sanction would then have been for the commonhold association to seek an order of sale of the property enabling recovery of the sums due – after exhaustion of the Default Procedure and all attempts at mediation. The existence of such a charge would mean that the association could be relaxed about operating the Default Procedure or subsequent mediation processes, knowing that sums properly due from defaulters were secured on the unit.

11.22 An alternative, less effective but perhaps a more acceptable course of action would have been to allow the commonhold association to have the ability to apply for such a lien or first charge to be imposed in a particular case. Notice of such an application could be given to mortgagees and chargees in the process but the association's charge, if granted, would take priority.[35]

11.23 Although the issue of recovery of sums due was raised in Parliament, the Government was resolute in declining to agree to this remedy.[36] The principal reason given was that this approach would be reintroducing forfeiture of leases into commonhold. It did not seem possible for the difference between forfeiture of a long lease and a statutory charge to secure payment of a commonhold assessment to be appreciated. Forfeiture of a lease ultimately deprives the leaseholder of what may be a substantial asset (subject

---

[33] Except income properly raised from the members, in addition to the annual estimate, for requirements including cash-flow needs – see CLRA 2002, s 38(1)(b).

[34] Even if the dissident unit-holder has a genuine grievance, the fact that the other unit-holders face the prospect of having to pay in lieu will do little for community harmony.

[35] The draft 1996 Commonhold Bill had a provision (in Sch 6, para 5) to permit a commonhold association to sell the commonhold unit to permit recovery of unpaid service charges.

[36] For example, in the Lords Committee stage, HL Deb, Vol 627, at col 505ff.

to relief from forfeiture). The purpose of a statutory first charge would be to encourage prompt payment and to secure the payment of sums properly due only if prolonged default occurs. There is no windfall gain as there is with forfeiture. Moreover, those sums due are integral to the commonhold scheme. The unit-holders (and the mortgagees) will have had and are getting the benefit of the insurance on the unit, of the upkeep and the use of the facilities that go with the unit, and the benefit of enhanced value of the unit as a consequence. The commonhold assessments and levies represent the cost of those benefits. Without them, the commonhold as a whole, and the units in particular, are less valuable in the market. Commonhold should have been seen as distinct from the leasehold it replaces. The threat of forfeiture of long residential leases is a draconian remedy, but it should have been recognised that behind that sledge-hammer is a nut that needs to be cracked. Forfeiture (for all its faults and abuses) does have the undeniable benefit of encouraging and ultimately securing payment of a service charge from those who benefit from the lease and refuse to pay, and in priority to mortgages and charges on the unit.

11.24   Since the CLRA 2002 makes no special provision, the commonhold association will be left with standard remedies for the recovery of debts. Obtaining money judgments will take time and incur further costs. The ultimate sanction will be a charging order on the unit, but such an order will not give priority over prior mortgages and charges registered. Nor will the obtaining of a charging order be a swift or inexpensive remedy. The dissident or awkward unit-holder cannot be easily brought to account. Indeed, the unit-holder may have sold or transferred the unit before a charging order can be obtained.

Position on sale or transfer

11.25   There is the prospect that a unit could be transferred to a buyer when outstanding assessments and levies remain outstanding in relation to the unit sold. The CLRA 2002 makes it clear that the former unit-holder is not liable in any way after the transfer, but is, naturally, still liable in relation to debts incurred before the transfer.[37] However, the CLRA 2002 is silent on the issue of whether a new unit-holder can be liable for existing overdue assessments. There is no rule or principle that would impose such liability generally, but in the light of the lack of a statutory prohibition, could the CCS provide for such a liability? The current draft is silent on the issue. If it were possible, it could become a common provision.[38] Without it, the commonhold association

---

[37]   CLRA 2002, s 16(2) and (3)(b), and see **6.10**.

[38]   One argument in favour is the possibility otherwise of deliberate transfers to avoid debts. Transfers of units cannot be restricted: CLRA 2002, s 15(2); and unit-holders may, of course, be corporate bodies. So an off-the-shelf company which was a unit-holder with indebtedness to the association and with no other assets could transfer a commonhold unit to another similar body controlled by the same individual.

would be left with the unenviable task of chasing payment from a person who is certainly unwilling to pay and who can, unless a charging order is obtained before the sale, walk away with the proceeds of sale of the unit. The best hope in such a situation is that the current practice of buyer's solicitors will continue. With leasehold units, it is standard conveyancing practice for the buyer to demand evidence that the rent and service charge is paid up to date. In a commonhold situation, the imperative for such a practice is very much less if the buyer is not liable for the outstanding sums due. If the buyer becomes liable, however, we can be sure that buyers of units will ensure that sellers discharge their outstanding liability from the proceeds of sale.[39]

11.26 It may, therefore, be possible for a CCS to be drafted to include a liability on a unit-holder for the time being for all arrears. Whether this is permissible may depend on the terms of the regulations yet to be made relating to the form of community statements. Even if possible, it is not a solution for recovery of debts where there is no sale in prospect. It is suggested that the inability to have a simple procedure to recover sums properly due from recalcitrant unit-holders is one of the biggest failings of the legislation in its present form. Given the clear policy articulated in Parliament against such a remedy, it is extremely doubtful whether regulations can be used to fill the gap.

REGULATORY POWERS

Enforcement and compensation

11.27 Apart from the use of the services of the Ombudsman, enforcement of rights and duties within the commonhold community and payment of compensation for failure to perform a duty is subject to control by regulations made by virtue of s 37 of the CLRA 2002. These regulations are likely to provide for the use, in many instances, of specified forms of arbitration, mediation or conciliation procedures before legal proceedings can be brought. They will also make regulations conferring jurisdiction on courts, which may be either the High Court or county courts.

---

[39] If debts are not carried over to the buyers of a commonhold unit, they might still be liable (proportionately with other members of the community) to make up a proportionate part of the loss where sums cannot be recovered from members of the community who have departed leaving debts. The problem is that *buyers* in such a situation could quite properly argue that the outstanding sums due from the seller of the unit purchased relate to a period before the purchase – when they were not members. Therefore, buyers may have little interest in ensuring that the debts to the commonhold association by way of outstanding assessment and levies are discharged to the community at completion of the sale if they incur no liability.

Scope of regulatory powers

11.28 The regulatory powers are wide.[40] The regulations may make provisions about the exercise or enforcement of a right or duty imposed or conferred by or by virtue of either the CCS or the memorandum or articles of a commonhold association or a statutory provision.[41] There is a long list of provisions that the regulations may, in particular, make in this regard.[42]

- *Compensation.* The regulations may make provisions requiring compensation to be paid. This may be appropriate where rights are exercised in specified cases or circumstances or when duties are not complied with.
- *Recovery of costs.* The regulations may enable recovery of costs where work has to be carried out for the purposes of enforcing a right or duty or where work is carried out in consequence of the failure to perform a duty.
- *Enforcement of duties by unit-holders.* The regulations may permit unit-holders to enforce duties imposed on either another unit-holder, on a commonhold association or on a tenant of any unit.
- *Enforcement of duties by the commonhold association.* Similarly, the regulations may permit enforcement of duties imposed on a unit-holder or tenant by the commonhold association.
- *Enforcement of duties by a tenant.*[43] A tenant of a unit may be empowered by the regulations to enforce duties imposed on a commonhold association, on a unit-holder or indeed on another tenant.
- *Enforcement of terms or conditions.* Regulations may permit the enforcement of terms and conditions to which a right is subject.

11.29 Provision about compensation shall include provision for determining the amount of compensation and provision for the payment of interest in the case of late payment.[44] It is specifically provided that such jurisdiction can be conferred on a court, and it is likely that it will be a court that makes such determination.

---

[40] As with all regulations under Part 1 of the CLRA 2002, they will be made by statutory instrument by the Lord Chancellor: s 64.

[41] Ibid, s 37(1). But regulations under this section are subject to any compulsory provision in the CCS required by regulations under s 32(5)(b) – s 37(4).

[42] The particular provisions which are listed in s 37(2) are not exhaustive but merely examples of provisions that may be made.

[43] 'Tenant', for the purpose of CLRA 2002, s 37, includes a person who has matrimonial home rights: ibid, s 61(c).

[44] Ibid, s 37(3).

RECTIFICATION OF DOCUMENTS

11.30   There is specific provision for rectification of documents at the suit of a unit-holder. The power to rectify the basic documents of a commonhold association is an additional power to the provisions relating to registration in error. It is likely that the power to rectify will be rarely used, but is most likely to be appropriate where a particular unit-holder is concerned that amendments to the memorandum or articles of association or amendments to the CCS which have been made by the commonhold association do not meet the current requirements either of the statute or of regulations made thereunder.

11.31   Consequently, it is provided that a unit-holder can apply to a court for a declaration that either the memorandum or articles or the CCS does not comply with legal requirements.[45] If the application is successful and a declaration is granted, the court has power to make any order which appears to it to be appropriate.[46] The most likely remedy is that the court will require a director or other specified officer of the commonhold association to take steps to alter or amend a document or to take other specified steps. Additionally or alternatively, a court can make an award of compensation to be paid by the commonhold association to a specified person, who may, of course, be the unit-holder who made the application. Such an award of compensation may be contingent upon the occurrence or non-occurrence of a specified event.[47]

11.32   An application must be made within time limits. This limit is either three months beginning with the day on which the applicant became a unit-holder (thus permitting an application by a unit-holder who is concerned with the documents being defective as they stand on his registration) or within three months of the commencement of the alleged failure to comply. The latter time-imit will be appropriate to changes to either the memorandum or articles or to the CCS which a unit-holder considers do not meet legal requirements. In any other case, an application can be made only with permission of the courts.[48]

11.33   It should be noted that the court does have power in an application under CLRA 2002, s 40 to make provision for the land to cease to be commonhold land.[49] This should certainly give a unit-holder cause to consider the position carefully before making the application. If an order is made in

---

[45]   Ie with regulations made under para 2(1) of Sch 3 to the CLRA 2002 about the form and content of the memorandum and articles of association or with any requirement for CCSs imposed by or by virtue of Part 1 of the Act. See s 40(1).

[46]   Ibid, s 40(2).

[47]   Ibid, s 40(3).

[48]   Ibid, s 40(4).

[49]   Ibid, s 40(3)(d).

this draconian way for the land to cease to be commonhold land then the provisions of the CLRA 2002 for termination of the commonhold by the court come into play.[50]

CHAPTER 12

TERMINATION OF A COMMONHOLD

BACKGROUND AND ISSUES

The need for voluntary termination provisions

12.1   There can be no doubt that there is a theoretical (if not very immediate) need for statutory provision to terminate a commonhold. In due course, a building housing a commonhold community (say) of a block of flats may become outmoded and beyond reasonable repair. A commonhold established in one vicinity may become less desirable as units to live in or use as work space. As property values change, a commonhold community may receive an advantageous offer from a developer who wishes to demolish and completely redevelop the site. None of these circumstances is likely to occur for many years after the establishment of a commonhold so the immediacy of the problem is not an issue. Indeed, in New South Wales and Singapore, strata title systems were established without any provision for termination of the strata title community. It was only after some decades of developing strata title in those jurisdictions that the legislature had to amend to provide for termination.[1] However, even a newly established commonhold might be destroyed by fire or other calamitous events may occur leading to a decision that it would be more advantageous to take the insurance monies for the benefit of the community and sell the site rather than reinstate the destroyed units.

12.2   It is therefore sensible to provide for termination at the outset even though it is unlikely that the termination provisions will be used very much for some years to come. Consequently, the Commonhold and Leasehold Reform Act 2002 (CLRA 2002) does include voluntary termination provisions permitting the unit-holders to have an effective mechanism for a collective sale of the commonhold land.

---

[1]   See, eg, the Singapore Land Titles (Strata) (Amendment) Act 1999 permitting a collective sale of a strata development.

The issue of insolvency

Early problems

12.3   A more contentious issue concerns the potential insolvency of a commonhold community. The early Commonhold Bills, in 1990 and 1996, envisaged that the commonhold association would be a new form of corporate body specially designed for managing and operating a commonhold community. This meant that the new corporate body that was envisaged was not covered by the Insolvency Act 1986 (IA 1986). Consequently, the 1990 Commonhold Bill, apparently at the insistence of the Department of Trade and Industry, contained a very large number of provisions applying the totality of the insolvency regime in the 1986 Act to the new corporate body which was to become the commonhold association.[2] A similar problem arose in 1996. This Bill still envisaged a separate corporate personality for the commonhold association and was also weighted down with provisions relating to insolvency.[3]

Limited or unlimited liability?

12.4   The experience in overseas jurisdictions suggests that strata title associations rarely become insolvent. However, their experience has to be treated with caution. For example, the unit-holders in a strata title in New South Wales do not enjoy immunity from liability for the debts of the owner's corporation – which does not have limited liability. There is therefore no real need for insolvency provisions. The unit-holders will have to pay and their personal assets are ultimately available to pay the corporation's debts.[4]

12.5   It can be argued that a commonhold association should not have had limited liability[5] and thus would never be subject to compulsory insolvency provisions and winding up. The commonhold association will only be trading and incurring obligations on behalf of the commonhold community as a whole. Its income stream is formed by the assessment and levies on the members of the community. So why should the members shelter behind limited liability? At the heart of this debate is an issue of principle. A standard freeholder, holding as an absolute owner or as a trustee of land, does not have the benefit of limited liability when contracting for repairs and maintenance to the freehold property. By way of analogy, the same could be argued for

---

2   The 1990 Commonhold Bill had 120 clauses and six long Schedules. Of these, 52 clauses and three Schedules were entirely devoted to insolvency. The Bill was then considerably larger than expected and the size of the Bill may well have been one factor in the decision not to introduce it into Parliament.

3   The 1996 Commonhold Bill contained only 14 clauses relating to insolvency but there were no less than five Schedules taking up 31 A4 pages on the issue.

4   See Ilkin, *Strata Schemes and Community Schemes Management and the Law* (3rd edn, 1998), at [305].

5   As a company limited by guarantee, it will have limited liability status – and the guarantee is a very nominal £1 – see **4.5.**

commonholders, the only difference being that they are a community of freeholders instead of a single person. On the other hand, for the CLRA 2002 to have permitted recourse direct to the members of the association would have drawn a clear and obvious distinction between commonholds on the one hand and leasehold developments on the other. Where long leaseholders control the freehold through a management company, they have the benefit of limited liability. The arguments are finely balanced but the CLRA 2002, in choosing the limited liability approach, then has had to deal with the difficulties of insolvency, especially to avoid members of the association taking undue advantage of the limited liability status of their association.

Restricted liability rejected

12.6 A form of restricted liability was the approach in the 1996 Bill[6] but this was criticised by commentators as a disincentive for people to buy into a commonhold. Different concerns have been raised now the alternative approach of standard limited liability has been adopted. At the instigation of the Law Society, the opposition put forward a new clause[7] to permit a judgment creditor of a commonhold association to apply to the court for an order enabling him to enforce payment of all or part of the debt against one or more unit-holders. The liability of such unit-holders would have been limited to the amount that the unit-holder would have been expected to have contributed by way of commonhold assessment or levy. This would have restored some form of restricted liability. The purpose behind the amendment was to enable contractors to recover debts from the association and its members more easily and without the necessity of putting the commonhold association into liquidation. The robust response of the Government was that contractors will not be worried about dealing with limited liability companies because they do so all the time.[8]

The need for insolvency provisions

12.7 In the event of the liabilities of the commonhold association exceeding its assets, even as a limited liability company, it has a simple remedy to move back into solvency by raising the level of the commonhold assessments on its members. However, there is at least one circumstance where it is important to have the sanction of a compulsory winding-up order available. A commonhold association, which of necessity is controlled by its members,

---

[6] The 1996 consultation document summarised the 1996 Bill as providing for an association which had unlimited liability to its creditors but with no personal liability on the unit-holders. The service charge mechanism was seen as the way liabilities of the association would normally be met, but in the event of the commonhold being wound up, each unit-holder would have been liable in a 'restricted' manner, namely up to his due proportion of the association's liabilities – see *Commonhold, Consultation Paper* (LCD, July 1996), pp 15–16.

[7] At Report stage.

[8] *Hansard*, Vol 381, col 642 (11 March 2002).

might deliberately choose, for whatever reason, not to pay outstanding debts and liabilities. The members and directors of the association might decide not to increase the association levy. Without the ultimate sanction of the threat of a winding-up order in circumstances where the association was deliberately starved of assets, it might be difficult for a judgment creditor to secure the funds that were due.

12.8 Consequently, the CLRA 2002 does provide for winding up. The compulsory winding up sections are founded on the standard IA 1986 provisions and run to no more than half a dozen short sections, and there is no need for detailed schedules to the legislation. This happy result is achieved at the cost of creating a commonhold association as a company limited by guarantee (which is therefore already covered by the IA 1986) rather than by creating a specially designed corporate personality. Whether this trade-off – losing a specially designed corporate body for the benefit of easy insolvency provisions – is an overall benefit is a matter for debate.

12.9 The CLRA 2002 assumes, without more, that a commonhold association can become insolvent. It permits the presentation of a petition for winding up under the IA 1986.[9] However, an ingenious solution is adopted to permit most commonhold associations effectively to survive winding up by provision for a successor association rising, phoenix-like, from the ashes of the old.

VOLUNTARY WINDING UP

Purpose and outline

12.10 The members of a commonhold association may choose to terminate their community and bring the commonhold to an end. They may choose to do so for whatever reason provided that sufficient clear majority support is obtained from the membership to proceed with this radical step. Essentially, voluntary liquidation is a way of collapsing the commonhold back into a single standard freehold title. A classic example will occur when a very attractive offer has been made for purchase of the whole commonhold, perhaps for redevelopment of the site. If the members of the commonhold are able to reach unanimous 100% agreement, they will be able to proceed in a straightforward manner. However, it will also be possible to terminate if 80% of the members agree to a winding-up resolution. There are a number of steps involved in the process. The members, having made a declaration of solvency, prepare a termination statement which will set out how the assets of the association are to be dealt with before the winding-up resolution is passed. A liquidator is appointed who makes an application to the court. Subsequently,

---

[9]   Under s 124 of the IA 1986.

the termination application is made to the Registrar who, once the procedure is complete, will register the commonhold association as proprietor of the freehold estate in each commonhold unit. The commonhold association will then be the registered proprietor of the whole of the commonhold land and so can make clean title on sale to a developer. No doubt the proceeds of sale will then be distributed among the members of the association in accordance with the termination statement.

Declaration of solvency

12.11   The first stage in the process is for the commonhold association to make a declaration of solvency.[10] This declaration must precede the winding-up resolution. It is defined to mean a director's statutory declaration made in accordance with s 89 of the IA 1986.[11] There should be no significant difficulty in making a declaration of solvency. In many situations, the commonhold association will have raised sufficient funds by way of commonhold assessment and levies on its members to ensure that there are funds held at the bank and in reserve funds for contingent liabilities such as repairs. If, however, the association has not met its obligations in this respect and debts do exceed assets but the members are determined to proceed to a voluntary winding up, it will be necessary to ensure that the association is solvent. This could be achieved by making fresh (and, if necessary, special) assessments from its members to clear any outstanding excess of liabilities over assets.

Termination statement

12.12   The second step in the process is for the commonhold association to agree a termination statement.[12] This termination statement must specify the association's proposals for the transfer of the commonhold land once the association is the freehold owner of the entirety of the commonhold.[13] For example, if the reason for termination is to transfer the estate to a developer for demolition and redevelopment, then the termination statement will so specify. No doubt an advantageous price will have been negotiated in such circumstances. The termination statement must then proceed to state how the

---

[10]   By resolution under CLRA 2002, s 43(1)(a).

[11]   Under CLRA 2002, s 43(2). IA 1986, s 89(2) and (3) requires this declaration of solvency to be in the five-week period immediately preceding the winding-up resolution and for a copy to be sent to the Registrar of Companies.

[12]   In accordance with CLRA 2002, s 47. In view of the time limits, work on preparing the termination statement may need to precede the declaration of solvency.

[13]   By virtue of CLRA 2002, s 48(3), at the end of the termination process, the commonhold association is entitled to be registered as the proprietor of the freehold estate in each of the commonhold units. Since it will be the proprietor of the freehold estate in the common parts already, this will mean that the association becomes the registered proprietor of the whole of the estate registered as a freehold estate in commonhold land.

assets of the association will be distributed.[14] The principle asset of the association will be the estate in commonhold land containing the complete commonhold, but will also include any reserve funds, cash at the bank and any other assets that are being sold separately, perhaps by recycling before demolition, for example. Essentially, the members must agree upon a division of the assets among themselves fairly and equitably in accordance with the value of their units prior to the termination of the commonhold.[15]

12.13   It may be that the commonhold community statement (CCS) makes provision for termination. The CLRA 2002 permits the CCS to make provision requiring a termination statement to make arrangements about the rights of unit-holders in the event of all the land ceasing to be commonhold land. These arrangements can be of a specified kind or may be determined in a specified manner.[16] It may be thought relatively unlikely that it will be common for a CCS to make express provision relating to its termination. If, however, such provisions are contained in the statement, and it may well be that such provisions will have been added some years after the commonhold was first set up, then the termination statement must comply with any such provision.[17]

12.14   It is possible that provisions in the CCS, even those agreed on in good faith many years before, may make it very difficult to proceed to a voluntary termination upon events that later happen. Therefore, the CLRA 2002 provides that the need to comply with any provision about termination in the CCS may be disapplied by order of the court.[18] An application for an order for disapplication may be made by any member of the commonhold association.[19]

12.15   Once a termination statement is agreed between the members, the final step in this part of the process is for the association to pass a termination statement resolution approving the terms of the termination statement.[20] Such a resolution must be passed before the association can move on to a winding-up resolution and must be passed with at least 80% of the members of the association voting in favour.[21]

---

[14]   CLRA 2002, s 47(1)(b).

[15]   It should be noted in this context that the draft articles of association of a commonhold association provide that, on the winding up of the association, any surplus after the satisfaction of debts and liabilities, and after compliance with any termination statement, is to be distributed among the members rateably in accordance with the percentages allocated to their units in the CCS: cl 82.

[16]   Ibid, s 47(2).

[17]   Ibid, s 47(3).

[18]   Ibid, s 47(4). Such disapplication may be generally or in respect of specified matters or for specified purposes.

[19]   Ibid, s 47(5).

[20]   Ibid, s 43(2).

[21]   Ibid, s 43(1)(b) and (c).

Resolution to wind up

12.16 Once a commonhold association has, through its directors, made a statutory declaration of solvency and agreed a termination statement (which might well be a tortuous process requiring considerable negotiation), the commonhold association can proceed with a resolution to wind up the commonhold voluntarily. Such a resolution must be passed with at least 80% of the members of the association voting in favour.[22] This significant barrier means that only in the most clear and generally accepted circumstances will it be possible to wind up a commonhold association voluntarily. Members will have to realise that the protection for monies held in a reserve fund ceases on the passing of a voluntary winding-up resolution.[23]

Appointment of liquidator

12.17 Following up the winding-up resolution, the association will need to appoint a liquidator.[24] The procedure taken by the liquidator, however, depends on whether the winding-up resolution and termination statement resolution were passed with at least 80% of the members being in favour, or whether each of those resolutions was passed with 100% of the members voting in favour.

80% agreement

12.18 Where the commonhold association has passed the winding-up resolution and the termination statement resolution with at least 80% of the members of the association voting in favour, then the procedure is that the liquidator must first apply to the court for an order.[25] This order of the court will determine the terms and conditions on which a termination application may be made and the terms of the termination statement to accompany a termination application.[26] Such an application will permit any dissenting members of the association who did not agree either with the termination statement resolution or with the winding up to argue before the court in the presence of the liquidator for different terms and conditions to apply to the

---

[22] CLRA 2002, s 43(1)(c). A 'winding-up resolution' is defined to mean a resolution for voluntary winding up within the meaning of s 84 of the IA 1986: CLRA 2002, s 43(2). Section 84 of the IA 1986 applies subject to CLRA 2002, s 43 – see ibid, Sch 5, para 6.

[23] By virtue of CLRA 2002, s 56(b), assets of a reserve fund established by virtue of s 34 can now be used for the enforcement of any debts of the association. Since, however, the association will have made a declaration of solvency, this should not normally be a concern.

[24] Under s 91 of the IA 1986 – CLRA 2002, ss 43(1)(b) and 44(1)(b). The liquidator must be an insolvency practitioner.

[25] The application will be within a time limit to be prescribed.

[26] A termination application is the application to the Registrar that all land should cease to be commonhold land – see below.

termination.[27] If the liquidator fails to make an application to the court within the prescribed period, then the application to the court can be made by a unit-holder or a person falling within a class prescribed for the purposes of the CLRA 2002.[28]

12.19   Once the order of the court is made, the liquidator then makes a termination application, namely an application to the Registrar that all the land in relation to which a particular commonhold association exercises functions should cease to be commonhold land. This application must be made within a period of three months starting with the date on which the court order is made.[29]

100% agreement

12.20   The procedure is slightly easier if every single member of the association has agreed with the termination statement resolution and with the winding-up resolution. In such a case, where each resolution has been passed with 100% of the association voting in favour, then the liquidator no longer needs to apply to the court. Instead, a termination application direct to the Registrar is made at any time within the period of six months beginning with the day on which the winding-up resolution is passed.[30] If the liquidator fails to make such a termination application within that six-month period, the termination application can be made either by a unit-holder or by a person falling within a class prescribed for the purposes of the Act.[31]

Termination application

12.21   A termination application is an application to the Registrar that all the land in relation to which a particular commonhold exercises its functions should cease to be commonhold land. The application must be accompanied by the termination statement and, on receipt of the application, the Registrar immediately notes the application in the register.[32]

12.22   Either at the same time as the liquidation or as soon as possible thereafter, the liquidator notifies the Registrar of his appointment.[33] If the termination statement resolution and the winding-up resolution were both passed with 100% agreement of the members, the liquidator must notify the

---

[27]   It should be noted that there is no express statutory provision permitting the dissident minority to challenge the merits of the majority decision to wind up.

[28]   Section 45(4).

[29]   CLRA 2002, ss 45(3), 46(1).

[30]   Ibid, s 44(2).

[31]   Ibid, s 44(3).

[32]   Ibid, s 46.

[33]   Ibid, s 48(2), (6). A liquidator is a person appointed under s 91 of the IA 1986 or a person acting as liquidator in accordance with s 100 of that Act in the case of a member's voluntary winding up which becomes a creditors' voluntary winding up – CLRA 2002, s 48(7).

Registrar that he is content with the termination statement that he submits with the termination application. This is necessary because in such a case there will have been no opportunity for the court to approve or amend the terms.[34] If the liquidator is not so content with the termination statement, even though it received unanimous support of the members, then he applies to the court to determine the terms of the termination statement.[35] Once again, the liquidator must make the application as soon as possible, and, when the determination of the court is available, he must send a copy of the determination to the Registrar.[36]

Termination

12.23 The termination of a commonhold occurs when the termination process is completed. This will happen in one of three ways.[37]

– A termination application was passed with at least 80% of the members voting in favour of the winding up, the termination statement resolutions have been made and the court has determined the terms and conditions of a termination application and the terms of a termination statement.[38]

– The two resolutions were passed with 100% agreement of the members, and the liquidator who has been appointed notified the Registrar that he was content with the termination statement.

– The two resolutions were passed with 100% agreement and the liquidator, not having declared that he was content with the termination statement, applied to the court and a determination was made under s 112 of the IA 1986.[39]

12.24 In any one of those three cases, and providing a termination application has been made,[40] then the commonhold association is entitled to be registered as the proprietor of the freehold estate in each commonhold unit.[41] At that point, the community terminates. There is no longer a variety of freehold owners of units with a commonhold association registered as proprietor of the common parts. Instead, the association, which was already registered proprietor of the common parts, is proprietor of all the units as well

---

34   CLRA 2002, s 48(3)(a).

35   Ibid, s 48(3)(b). The application is under s 112 of the IA 1986.

36   Ibid, s 48(4). This requirement is in addition to the requirement under IA 1986, s 112(3) – CLRA 2002, s 48(5). Section 112 requires a copy to be sent to the Registrar of Companies who enters it into the records relating to the company.

37   CLRA 2002, s 49(1) and (2).

38   Under CLRA 2002, s 45.

39   By virtue of CLRA 2002, s 48(3)(b).

40   Either under s 44 or s 45 of the CLRA 2002.

41   Ibid, s 49(3).

and therefore registered proprietor of the whole of the land registered as commonhold.

12.25   The final stage of the termination process of the commonhold will be de-registration by the Registrar. Much will depend on the details of the termination as set out in the termination statement, and therefore the CLRA 2002 merely provides that the Registrar shall take such action as appears to him to be appropriate for the purpose of giving effect to the termination statement.[42]

WINDING UP BY THE COURT

12.26   A commonhold association may be wound up compulsorily by the court. Since a commonhold association is a company limited by guarantee, the procedure is that set out in the IA 1986.[43] The normal IA 1986 procedures will apply except that there are additional requirements contained in the CLRA 2002. The most significant feature is the ability for the court to make a succession order so that the successor commonhold association can take over management of the commonhold and be registered as the proprietor of the freehold estates in the common parts. A successor association is not an absolute requirement, however desirable it may be.

An insolvent commonhold association

12.27   The CLRA 2002 assumes that a commonhold association may become insolvent even though an association always has the ability to raise funds by way of commonhold assessment on its members. The definition of an insolvent commonhold association is a functional one. It means an association in relation to which a winding-up petition has been presented under IA 1986, s 124.[44] Consequently, it will be in the interest of a commonhold association that has debts and is being pressed for payment to avoid the problems of facing a compulsory winding up and to make urgent arrangements to ensure that it has sufficient funds from its members to meet judgment debts. If this does not happen, then it becomes insolvent within the definition in the CLRA 2002 as soon as the winding-up petition is presented.

The 'Phoenix' commonhold association

12.28   Where a petition for winding up a commonhold association is presented, the procedure will follow the standard insolvency practice.[45]

---

[42]   CLRA 2002, s 49(4).

[43]   By way of petition presented under IA 1986, s 124 for winding up by the court.

[44]   CLRA 2002, s 50(2)(a).

[45]   For presentation of a petition under s 124 of the IA 1986, see, eg, *Palmer's Company Law* (Sweet & Maxwell), para 15.225.

However, wherever such a petition is presented, the provisions of the CLRA 2002 relating to a succession order apply.[46] Thus, at the hearing of a winding-up petition, an application may be made to the court for a succession order in relation to the insolvent commonhold association.[47] An application for such a succession order can be made only by either the insolvent commonhold association, or one or more of its members, or a provisional liquidator for the insolvent association who has been appointed under the IA 1986.[48] Such an application must be accompanied by prescribed evidence of the formation of the proposed successor association and a certificate given by its directors that its articles and memorandum comply with the standard regulations applicable to all such associations.[49] Thus it will be necessary to make such an application actually to incorporate such an association, and the successor association will need to specify exactly the same land as commonhold land as the insolvent association.

12.29   There is a statutory presumption in favour of granting an application. The aim will always be to transfer ownership of the common parts and management of the commonhold units to a successor association. Thus, the court is required to grant an application for a succession order unless the court thinks that the circumstances of the insolvent association make a succession order inappropriate.[50]

Transfer to the successor association

12.30   If the court makes a succession order in relation to an insolvent commonhold association on the making of a winding-up order, then at that point the insolvent commonhold association ceases to be treated as the proprietor of the freehold estate in the common parts.[51] Immediately, the successor commonhold association is entitled to be registered as the proprietor of the freehold estate in the common parts by way of replacement of the insolvent association.[52] The CLRA 2002 assumes that the succession order will normally direct the Registrar to make the change of registration. Certainly, the succession order is to make provision as to the treatment of any legal charge which exists over all or any part of the common parts and may require the Registrar to take action of whatever kind the court specifies.[53] A court has power to make supplemental or incidental provisions that may

---

[46]   Sections 50(1), 51.

[47]   CLRA 2002, s 51(1).

[48]   Ibid, s 51(2); the provisional liquidator will be appointed under s 135 of the IA 1986.

[49]   CLRA 2002, s 51(3).

[50]   Ibid, s 51(4).

[51]   Ibid, s 52(1) and (3).

[52]   Ibid, s 52(2).

[53]   Ibid, s 54(4)(a) and (b). This might include a transfer of any charge over the common parts to the title registered by the successor association.

include an order enabling the liquidator to require the Registrar to take specified action.[54]

12.31   From the making of the succession order, the successor association is treated as the commonhold association for the commonhold in respect of any matter which occurs after the making of the winding-up order.[55] The court can, and probably normally will, make an order requiring the liquidator of the insolvent association to make documents available to the successor association. The CLRA 2002 specifically requires that records, copies of records and information may be made available and the order can include terms as to the timing and payment of any sums.[56]

Consequences of the succession order

12.32   The aim of a succession order is to preserve the integrity of the commonhold and ensure that the common parts remain available to the freehold owners of the commonhold units. The successor commonhold association will be able to begin with a clean sheet. However, the members of the insolvent commonhold, who will become members of the successor association, will not be able to escape the consequences of the insolvency of the original association. The liquidator will have powers to realise all the assets of the commonhold association to pay creditors. This will include, it is apprehended, raising additional assessments where necessary to meet the debts and pursuing recalcitrant members who have not paid their commonhold assessment and might even involve the enforced sale of the freehold units of those recalcitrant members. Indeed, all members may find that additional assessments are made upon them to pay the not inconsiderable costs of an insolvency.

12.33   The aim of any commonhold association must be to avoid compulsory winding up. The biggest incentive to ensure judgment debts are paid and a compulsory winding up avoided is the provision in the CLRA 2002 that any reserve fund can be made available to the creditors of the insolvent association. Normally, the assets of a reserve fund which has been established and maintained for the repair and maintenance of either commonhold units or common parts is not to be used for the enforcement of any debt, except a judgment debt referable to a reserve fund activity.[57] However, this protection ceases to have effect in respect of debts, liabilities accruing at any time if the court makes a winding-up order in respect of the association.[58] It is likely that there will be a considerable value in those reserve funds and these funds will

---

[54]   CLRA 2002, s 52(4)(c) and (d).

[55]   Ibid, s 53(2).

[56]   Ibid, s 53(3) and (4).

[57]   See ibid, s 39(4), and **10.31**.

[58]   Ibid, s 56(a).

be taken for the payment of the debts of the insolvent association. The successor association will have to build up fresh reserves by levies on its members.

Termination without a succession order

12.34 Where, exceptionally, a court makes a winding-up order in respect of a commonhold association but refuses to make a succession order, then special provisions apply.[59] In such a case, the liquidator of a commonhold association notifies the Registrar as soon as possible of the position. There are a series of notification provisions which relate to applications, directions and notices that may be made or given by virtue of the IA 1986. The first action the liquidator must take is to notify the Registrar that s 54 of the CLRA 2002 now applies. Subsequently, the liquidator must notify the Registrar, where applicable, of any of the following under the IA 1986.[60]

(1) Any directions given under s 168 relating to the supplementary powers of the liquidator.
(2) Any notice given to the court and the Registrar of Companies in accordance with s 172(8) which relates to a liquidator vacating office after the final meeting.
(3) Any notice given to the Secretary of State under s 174(3) of the completion of the winding up.
(4) Any application made to the Registrar of Companies under s 202(2) relating to insufficient assets and early dissolution.
(5) Any notice given to the Registrar of Companies under s 205(1)(b) in relation to the winding up.
(6) Any other matter which in the liquidator's opinion is relevant to the Registrar.

12.35 In each case, notification to the Registrar must be accompanied by the relevant copy of directions notice or application concerned.[61] The Registrar is then under a general duty to make such arrangements as appear to him appropriate for ensuring that the freehold estate in the land in respect of which the commonhold association exercises functions ceases to be registered as a freehold estate in commonhold land as soon as reasonably practicable after notification that the winding up is completed. He must also take any such action as appears to him appropriate for the purpose of giving effect to a determination made by the liquidator in exercise of his functions.[62]

---

[59] CLRA 2002, s 54(1).

[60] Ibid, s 54(2).

[61] Ibid, s 54(3).

[62] Ibid, s 54(4).

TERMINATION BY THE COURT

12.36 There is one additional way that a commonhold association can be wound up by the court and the commonhold terminate. This power of termination by the court is a fairly limited jurisdiction arising in two particular circumstances and will apply, if relevant, early in the history of the commonhold concerned.

Registration in error

12.37 Wherever a commonhold has been registered by mistake or in error the court has power to grant a declaration that the freehold estate should not have been registered in the first place as a freehold estate in commonhold land.[63] Where such a declaration is made the CLRA 2002 gives the court wide powers, on granting a declaration, to make any order which appears to it to be appropriate. This, in particular, may include provision for the land to cease to be commonhold land.[64] In such a case, the court has power to make a winding-up order in respect of the commonhold association.[65]

Rectification of documents

12.38 A similar position occurs whenever a unit-holder applies to the court for a declaration that either the memorandum or articles of association of the relevant commonhold association does not comply with the statutory regulations or that the relevant CCS does not comply with any statutory regulatory requirement. If the court finds that the application is proved and makes a declaration[66] then the court has wide powers to make an order. Normally, it is likely that the court will require the documents to be amended to ensure that they conform in all respects to statutory requirements.

12.39 However, in extreme circumstances, it may be that rectification of the documents to ensure that the commonhold is properly established is not possible. Consequently, there is a long-stop provision that an order may include provision for land to cease to be commonhold land.[67] In such a case, the same power is given to the court[68] that the court would have had if it were making a winding-up order in respect of the commonhold association.

---

[63] By virtue of CLRA 2002, s 6(3); see **3.73**.

[64] Ibid, s 6(5) and (6)(c). Such an order is very unlikely where a commonhold has been established and unit-holders are in place.

[65] Ibid, s 55(1) and (2). The court has all the powers it would have if it were making a winding-up order.

[66] Under CLRA 2002, s 40(1) and (2).

[67] Ibid, s 40(3)(d).

[68] Under CLRA 2002, s 55(2).

Procedure for termination by the court

12.40   The procedure for termination in these two instances will be by the court appointing a liquidator. Such a liquidator has the powers and duties of a liquidator appointed under the IA 1986.[69] However, the order of the court can require the liquidator to exercise his functions in a particular way, or impose additional rights or duties or modify or remove those rights or duties that would normally apply to the liquidator in such a case.[70]

12.41   Once again, the reserve fund, if any, is then available in the winding up of the commonhold association by the court.[71] Termination in this way is likely to occur early on in the history of the commonhold, and it is relatively unlikely that large reserve funds have been built up. Indeed, winding up for errors, mistakes or after an application for rectification may only occur in the most exceptional cases once the commonhold is activated by the sale of the first unit. However, if there are reserve funds, they are always available in the winding up of the association.

COMPULSORY PURCHASE

12.42   A commonhold is not, of course, exempt from a compulsory purchase. Special provision is made for dealing with compulsory purchase of either the whole estate in commonhold land or of any part of it, whether units or common parts or parts of units or common parts. A compulsory purchase of part of a unit does not need the written consent of the commonhold association.[72] Where a freehold estate in commonhold land is transferred to a compulsory purchaser, the land so transferred will normally cease to be commonhold land.[73] This general rule does not apply if the Registrar is satisfied that the compulsory purchaser has indicated a desire for the transferred land to continue to be commonhold land.[74] Where part of the commonhold is purchased under compulsory powers, it may be appropriate for some or all of the rest of the commonhold land also to cease to be commonhold. For example, if all (or all but one) of the units have been so

---

[69]   See CLRA 2002, s 55(3) and IA 1986, s 125.

[70]   CLRA 2002, s 55(4).

[71]   Ibid, s 56(c).

[72]   Ibid, s 60(3). Consent would normally be required for a transfer of part of a unit – see **6.29**.

[73]   Ibid, s 60(1). A compulsory purchaser is a person acquiring land either by exercising a power given by virtue of an enactment or because there is a statutory obligation to make the acquisition – ibid, s 60(7).

[74]   Ibid, s 60(2). It is difficult to envisage circumstances where it will be appropriate for the land transferred, whether the whole of the commonhold or part, to continue as commonhold but, if desired, the purchaser only has to so indicate.

purchased, leaving only common parts and one unit at most, there can be no ongoing community.[75]

12.43 Compulsory purchase is yet another area where regulations may be needed to map out the detailed consequences of a transfer of commonhold land to a compulsory purchaser. The powers are wide, including the power to disapply or modify any existing legislation relating to compulsory purchase or to require the compulsory purchaser to acquire, in addition to the land compulsorily acquired, the freehold estate in the whole or any particular part of the commonhold.[76]

---

[75]   Regulations may include provision in respect of land which is not transferred for some or all of that land to cease to be commonhold land – CLRA 2002, s 60(6).

[76]   CLRA 2002, s 60(4) and (5). The powers listed, which also include the ability to make provision for compensation and confer jurisdiction on a court, are not exhaustive.

CHAPTER 13

COMMONHOLD – A PRELIMINARY ASSESSMENT

SCOPE FOR COMMONHOLD

13.1 The flexibility of the commonhold concept suggests that there will be a broad spectrum of possible uses for this new land tenure. In every case, the utility of commonhold will have to be tested against the merits of standard freehold or leasehold. In particular, some of the constraints of the statute may make commonhold less suitable than it might otherwise have been.

Residential flats

13.2 Commonhold will be particularly appropriate for a standard straightforward new development of residential flats, especially if the block consists of a number of residential units all of similar size.[1] In such a case, the common parts will consist primarily of the external structure of the building in which the flats are contained, the stairs, lifts and other access ways to the building, and the pipes and conduits of the services supplied to it. The only other common parts are likely to be a communal area for parking, and for storage of rubbish bins, the hanging of washing and so forth and, perhaps, a shared garden, if such facilities exist. The buyers of units can be assured of securing a freehold title to their unit and the consequent membership of the commonhold association. The management will be regulated by the filed documentation based on the standardised statutory framework. Members will be able to acquire documentation and advice on commonholds generally to assist them.[2]

13.3 Commonhold will be equally appropriate for up-market residential developments as for the provision of basic housing. In such developments, the common parts may be more extensive and offer greater leisure and ancillary facilities for use by the community as a whole. The common parts

---

[1] If the residential units differ in size, the principle of voting parity among members may disadvantage holders of larger units carrying a greater share of the commonhold assessment, see **4.16–4.20** and **13.20–13.24**.

[2] See CLRA 2002, s 62, authorising the Lord Chancellor to give financial assistance to permit advice to be given.

might even include a flat for use by a resident caretaker or for security staff, or a commonhold estate office.

Housing estates

13.4 Commonhold may also be a vehicle of choice for some freehold developments currently undertaken with standard freehold title. An estate of houses (whether detached, semi-detached or terraced) may be constructed where it is desired to have a small number of positive obligations imposed on the purchasers. Currently, the enforceability of these obligations against future purchasers usually depends on the reservation of, and payment of, an estate rent charge. Commonhold will permit an alternative format in such cases. The commonhold association will have a much reduced role in such circumstances compared with that in a block of flats. It will be responsible for a less extensive area of common parts and there will be fewer repairing or maintenance obligations. The repair, maintenance and insurance of the units will often be entirely in the hands of the unit-holder, as in a standard freehold development.

Properties constructed for letting at market rents

13.5 Commonhold may also be appropriate when the development is primarily to construct properties to be let at market rents. Commonhold will permit individual units, or groups of units within a larger development, to be sold on the open market to investors buying with the intention of renting out the units for income purposes. Indeed, commonhold could permit a group of such investors to share in the cost of development each taking a number of units for letting on the open market. There will be the flexibility to convert some or all of the units at a later date for sale to individuals for their own residence.

Retirement villages and sheltered accommodation

13.6 Commonhold will offer an alternative form of development vehicle for new retirement villages and sheltered accommodation for occupation by elderly persons. At present, such accommodation is, of necessity, developed by way of long leases. Purchasers buying into retirement villages and sheltered accommodation, having previously been freeholders in their own homes, will not always appreciate the complexities of the leasehold structure. In other jurisdictions, condominiums and strata title units are commonly used for provision of retirement homes. Commonhold will allow each unit-holder to have a freehold home and membership of the commonhold association while no doubt maintaining a professional management for the elderly residents.[3]

---

[3]   It will not be possible to restrict the persons to whom the retirement units are sold – CLRA 2002, s 20(1). But there is no objection to restricting the use of such units to individuals over a prescribed age as is found in leases of sheltered accommodation.

Holiday homes

13.7 In some holiday complexes, units are offered for sale where the nature of the development, with owners often away from their holiday residences, usually means that there are communal facilities and security arrangements which have to be paid for by the residents. Once again, commonhold offers an attractive alternative for such development. The fact that unit-holders are bound by the obligation to pay the commonhold assessment yet retain a freehold title with ultimate control over management of the holiday complex may prove to be more attractive to buyers. Commonhold will be significantly less appropriate for time-share developments.

Commercial commonholds

13.8 The potential for the use of commonhold for retail, industrial and other commercial use is considerable. Experience in overseas jurisdiction suggests that the commercial lease is unlikely to be displaced as the preferred form of development and vehicle for occupation by business users, although commonhold will offer niche uses in a variety of situations. Serviced office suites, small industrial or retail units, markets and food halls are all examples of development situations where commonhold may have attractions. It may be useful wherever there are to be shared facilities. Moreover, the development of a very large office building as a commonhold will not prevent all or indeed a majority of the space being let on commercial leases by the investors in the unit, subject to the terms of the commonhold community statement (CCS).[4]

Mixed developments

13.9 In principle, commonhold is available for mixed developments of residential and non-residential units. There is no doubt that it should be so available and there will be many situations where it might be valuable. The common situation where the ground floor of a building is used for retail and there is residential accommodation above can certainly be developed as a single commonhold. However, it is suggested that the current format of the legislation will not encourage mixed use commonholds given the difficulty of balancing the interests of the owners and occupiers of the retail units on the one hand and the residents of the residential commonhold units on the other. There is no mechanism for 'subsidiary' commonholds allowing the quite different interests of the residential unit-holders and those of the commercial unit-holders to be dealt with separately.[5] The value of the units is likely to differ significantly and, as we have seen,[6] each member of the commonhold

---

[4]   Some 17% of office space in Sydney, Australia is apparently developed by way of strata title.

[5]   See **2.19**.

[6]   See **4.16**.

has the same voting rights. It may be difficult to attract retail buyers or commercial tenants of units in a commonhold where the majority vote and therefore control of the association is held by residents.

COMMONHOLD AND LEASEHOLD

13.10   The differences between an estate in commonhold land and a leasehold are profound in legal theory. The commonhold, as a community of freehold units, offers titles of indefinite duration that can be freely bought, sold and mortgaged in the same way as any other freehold estate in land. A leasehold estate is by definition of limited duration and subjects the holder of the lease to a relationship of landlord and tenant, even if the lessor is a tenants' management company. A buyer of a commonhold unit will have the assurance that the rights and obligations as defined in the CCS equally affect all the other unit-holders in exactly the same way. There will be one filed document for the whole development. By way of contrast, a buyer into a leasehold block will have no guarantee that the terms of the other leases (which are not available to inspect as of right) in the development are exactly the same. Moreover, a buyer of a lease is heavily reliant on the skills of the conveyancer to advise as to the adequacy of the terms of the lease. Lease terms can only be changed by a complex statutory procedure. A commonholder will have the assurance of a statutory regulation of the basic fundamentals with the knowledge that the detailed rules of the commonhold can be changed in general meeting of the association when required. With regard to remedies, the leaseholder will be dependent upon the terms of the lease, and contractual remedies are directed to the immediate landlord or freehold reversioner, as the case may be. A commonholder will have the benefit of a statutory system of remedies set out in commonhold regulations ensuring informal internal mechanisms in the first instance with the statutory encouragement of arbitration and mediation to follow. The ultimate sanction of remedies through the courts is available if required. Above all, in this context, there can be no risk of forfeiture of a commonhold unit.

13.11   Nevertheless, it is by no means absolutely certain that developers will embrace commonhold as the preferred mechanism for developing flats for sale. Commonhold will succeed only if developers consider that the market will prefer freehold flats developed by way of commonhold rather than their leasehold counterparts. If a commonhold unit will sell for more than a similar flat offered by way of a lease, then commonhold will be preferred. On the other hand, if a long leasehold flat can command the same premium as the purchase price for a commonhold unit, then a developer may consider that there is some financial inducement to develop by way of leasehold. This is because, on the sale of the last unit, the freehold reversion can currently be transferred for value by the developer to a property management company. Developers will know that, by way of contrast, on the sale of the last commonhold unit they have no further direct property interest in the development. There is no interest left to sell. However, if, as is now possible, reversions to residential long leaseholds are perceived as a burden and the reversion has little value,[7] then development by way of commonhold may be perceived as an advantage.

COMMONHOLD AND STANDARD FREEHOLD

13.12   There may be situations where developers need to assess the use of a commonhold, or series of commonholds, to construct and market a development that could, alternatively, also be undertaken by way of standard freehold. Commonhold offers the ability for a developer to offer a range of communal services benefiting the residents which is secured and paid for by means of the commonhold assessment. Some developers may find there is a marketing advantage if communal control of open leisure spaces is to be regulated in future by the residents operating through a commonhold association. Gated freehold communities will be particularly suited to development by way of commonhold tenure. The main handicap may be the unwillingness of developers to embrace developments of large commonholds with a large number of units that such estates may involve.

LEGISLATIVE DEFECTS

13.13   It is too much to expect legislative perfection, even after 18 years of reflection and proposals.[8] Some of the concerns have been addressed in the analysis. Not many are serious. However, it is submitted that there are three significant defects which, in different ways, threaten to undermine the efficacy of the new legislation. These are:

(1)   the need for the consent of all registered proprietors of long leases in a block of flats when conversion is contemplated for long leasehold to commonhold;
(2)   the principle of community equality, namely the insistence of voting parity for each member;
(3)   the failure to provide for a first charge on a unit in respect of unpaid commonhold assessment and reserve fund levies.

---

[7]   This is a very possible consequence of the new right to manage introduced by CLRA 2002, Part 2, Chapter 1, and which will be in force by the time commonhold is implemented. If qualifying tenants can take over management at will and without payment, the value of reversions to such developments is likely to be low.

[8]   The Government Minister was of a rather different view when she concluded debate on commonhold with the words: 'When concluded, this will be one of the finest Bills to go through both houses': HL Deb, Vol 633, col 691 (Baroness Scotland of Asthal).

Consent of all long leaseholders required

13.14   When a group of long leaseholders meet to consider the possibility of converting their tenure for long leases to commonhold they will face a huge and possibly unsurmountable hurdle. The conversion will require the consent of every long leaseholder in the block.[9] So, where there is a desire to convert (say) the residue of 99-year lease terms into commonhold units, all of the leaseholders in the block, and their mortgagees if any, must consent. A straightforward example is a block of ten long leasehold flats let on 99-year lease terms. Perhaps nine of the long leaseholders can agree to act together. The first step – if not already taken – is that they will enfranchise collectively and purchase the freehold to their block. Subsequently, they wish to convert to commonhold title, perhaps believing that their flats will be more marketable and valuable if they are commonhold units rather than long leases. Unless they can get the tenth lessee to consent, and further obtain the consent of all the chargees and mortgagees, they will be unable to transfer to commonhold title. Even if the tenth leaseholder is acting unreasonably, unhelpfully or just cannot be bothered, there seems little prospect of dispensing with the required consent.[10]

13.15 This issue generated by far the most debate and concern within Parliament at each stage of the passage of the legislation. Members of all parties in the Lords and Commons urged the Government to be flexible and devise a scheme whereby less than 100% could convert.[11] At one point, it seemed that the Government might capitulate. The Lord Chancellor indicated that the Government would consider carefully any sensible scheme that was brought forward[12] – but a few weeks later the Minister decided that nothing could be done.[13] The main reason for opposing flexibility was that the commonhold concept required that every unit-holder was a member of the community with an equal part to play, and it would be contrary to principle to permit the continuance of long leases within the commonhold. Even if it were technically possible to construct a scheme to retain the non-consenting lessees

---

[9]   However, see **3.17**, where the possibility of proceeding by excluding any flats above the proposed commonhold is mooted.

[10]   See **3.40**, where it is suggested that the court's power to dispense with consent is unlikely to be used to override a refusal to consent.

[11]   Concerns on this issue were raised at most stages of the parliamentary process, for example, by the Conservative Shadow Minister at Second Reading in the Commons – see *Hansard*, Vol 377, col 443 (Mr William Cash). But the concerns were only developed into an amendment taken to a division at Report stage (11 March 2002).

[12]   At Second Reading in the House of Lords – see HL Deb, Vol 626, col 889 (5 July 2001): 'if a well-judged amendment for which there is substantial cross-party support is put forward to the effect that less that 100% of the prospective unit-holders should be necessary for the conversion of leasehold to commonhold, the government would consider it carefully'.

[13]   See Baroness Scotland of Asthal in the debates at Committee stage: HL Deb, Vol 627, cols 487–494 (16 October 2001).

within a commonhold structure, it would be too complex and difficult to do so.

13.16   Flexibility could be achieved in another manner. The only solution seriously discussed in Parliament was to permit the commonhold to be established by less than 100%, leaving the dissident long leaseholders continuing within the commonhold. The Government argued, rightly it is submitted, that this would be an unsatisfactory state of affairs.[14] The commonhold association would have to become the landlord of any remaining long lease. The terms of that lease might fit very unhappily with the rules, regulations and obligations for the members of the commonhold association set out in the CCS. There would need to be provision to permit the lessee to 'opt in' to the commonhold at a later date. The lessees would have no say in setting the level of the commonhold assessment or levies for reserves, but would lose some existing leasehold rights such as challenging the reasonableness of service charges unless special arrangements were made.[15]

13.17   The alternative solution, never discussed in Parliament, is to require any minority of long leaseholders to surrender their leases and receive in return a freehold title in the commonhold unit by way of substitution for the surrendered lease. Perhaps this option was not considered because of fear of a challenge under the human rights legislation.[16] There are two answers to such concerns. The CLRA 2002 already provides for compensation for the extinguishment of leases.[17] Property can be purchased compulsorily provided fair and full compensation is given. So the dissident long leaseholders could be offered either the full market value for their leasehold interest in the same way as other extinguished leases,[18] or the alternative of a commonhold unit in substitution for the extinguished lease. Those forced to change to the new tenure could have been given the additional opportunity to claim compensation in addition, if it could be shown that the value of the commonhold flat was somehow worth less than the long lease it replaced.

---

[14]   See, particularly, Baroness Scotland at HL Deb, Vol 627, col 489, and Mr Michael Wills in Standing Committee D, First Sitting, col 17 (the Ministers were certainly singing from the same songsheet as the wording is virtually identical). They stress that the remaining lease might have to be amended and the CCS would have to take account of the two distinct forms of occupiers.

[15]   A commonholder will not have power to challenge the amount of the commonhold assessment on the grounds that it is unreasonable. A long leaseholder left isolated in a commonhold would, unless the right was taken away, be able to do so.

[16]   Article 1 of the First Protocol of the European Convention for the Protection of Human Rights and Fundamental Freedoms 1950, incorporated by Sch 1 to the Human Rights Act 1998.

[17]   Indeed, it seems that compensation may be required in respect of an unregistered lease granted for more than 21 years and at a low rent if the holders of unregistered leases are not required to consent to the establishment of a commonhold – see **3.34** and **3.41**.

[18]   This possibility was briefly raised at Report stage in the Commons by Mr Adrian Sanders – see *Hansard*, Vol 381, col 651 (11 March 2002).

13.18   The unfortunate consequence of the 100% consent requirement from long leaseholders is that commonhold will normally only be used in new build and redevelopment situations.[19] Only in the very smallest blocks is it likely in practice that the 100% consent will be obtained for the conversion to commonhold. When challenged that this position did not meet the aspirations of existing residential long leaseholders, the Minister responded with an interesting assertion. It was contended that the greater availability of collective enfranchisement and the new right to manage[20] would enable existing long leaseholders to 'have an effective remedy against the problems' simply by purchasing the freehold reversion and continuing with their leasehold titles to their flats.[21] If this is correct one wonders why commonhold was established in the first place. If commonhold does not offer any greater benefits than arrangements where there are leasehold titles for 999 years at a peppercorn rent and the leaseholders control the freehold through a management company then much of the effort to establish this new form of title has been wasted. However, if (as it is contended) commonhold offers significant and vital other benefits, then the case for allowing easier conversion is a strong one.

13.19   In summary, the argument is that a majority group of long leaseholders should not be prevented from establishing commonhold simply because one or two other leaseholders refuse to consent or cannot be bothered to consider the benefits of the change. Provision could have been made to require such a minority to convert their long leasehold flats into units within a commonhold and with freehold title with suitable compensation provisions. Exchanging a lease of a flat for a freehold unit within a commonhold ought to be no bad bargain.

The need for voting parity

13.20   Every member of a commonhold has one vote.[22] Even if a single person holds more than one unit, that person will only have a vote in respect of each unit if there is a valid call for a poll.[23] This principle of equality has the merits of simplicity as any voting system weighted to reflect different sizes of

---

[19]   This is ironic given that the introduction of commonhold was delayed to permit the principle of leasehold enfranchisement for flats to be established first in the Leasehold Reform, Housing and Urban Development Act 1993. Existing leaseholders demanded this because it was seen as a step to achieving their ultimate goal of a freehold unit within a commonhold community.

[20]   By Chapters 2–4 of Part 2 of the CLRA 2002, a greater number of residential long leaseholders will qualify to purchase the freehold. The new right to manage, introduced by Chapter 1 of the Act, may reduce the incentives to invest in reversions to residential long leases with the result that more freeholds may be offered to long leaseholders to buy by private treaty.

[21]   Mr Michael Wills – see *Hansard*, Vol 381, col 666 (11 March 2002).

[22]   See **4.16**.

[23]   This is the provision proposed by the draft articles of association of a commonhold association, cls 31 and 32; see Appendix 1.

unit will of necessity be more complex. In a community where each unit-holder pays exactly the same level of commonhold assessment, there will be no difficulty.

13.21 In more complex situations, however, the principle of voting parity may militate against a development by way of commonhold. There is no mechanism for having different categories of unit-holder, so as to provide differently for commercial and residential units.[24] There can be no 'flying commonholds' so one residential commonhold cannot be developed separately on top of another.[25] When seen in this context, the need for voting parity makes it relatively unattractive to develop mixed commonholds with some retail or office units and some residential units. If this is the case, one situation that is an obvious candidate for a commonhold, namely the building with shops on the ground floor and residential accommodation above, is likely to continue to be developed by way of leasehold.

13.22 Similar considerations apply wherever the units are of very different size. It has already been argued that, even in an exclusively residential development, purchasers of more valuable units are unlikely to be content if that value, reflected in the amount of commonhold assessment demanded perhaps, is unable to be reflected in the weighting of votes in the meeting of the association.[26]

13.23 The straitjacket of voting parity may found to be irksome. Until it is changed, estates consisting of a wide variety of types of residential unit and mixed-use developments are unlikely to be developed as commonholds in large numbers.

Security for payments by unit-holders

13.24 This issue has been analysed in the discussion of remedies.[27] Although it is unlikely to be a factor featuring either in the mind of a developer or a buyer of a unit, it is submitted that the inability of a commonhold association to have security for unpaid assessment or reserve fund levies is a serious omission. Its absence may compromise the financial security of an association and promote community disharmony in a system whose main object is to provide a form of ownership that promotes community co-operation.

---

[24] The idea of subsidiary and master commonhold to facilitate mixed developments was not incorporated into the Act despite consultation on the issue – see **2.19**.

[25] See the discussion at **2.15–2.21** and **3.17–3.19**.

[26] See **4.19**.

[27] At **11.18–11.26**.

PROSPECTS

Some inherent limitations

13.25 Commonhold offers developers and land-owners a new choice alongside standard freehold and leasehold titles. However, we should not expect too much of the new tenure by expecting it to provide answers to problems it does not address. Commonhold is not, for example, the final answer to the problem of freehold covenants. That awaits the introduction of land obligations, for commonhold only solves the problem of positive obligations within the commonhold community.

13.26 Commonhold is no more than a framework for community living. It will not and cannot ensure more harmonious relationships within that community than any other form of property holding where people live or work in close proximity. No law could ever claim so much. But one test in due course when considering whether commonhold has been a success will be whether the new statutory scheme is more likely to promote well-being in circumstances of ownership of a property interest within a larger community.[28]

The need for further statutory provision and the role of regulations

13.27 Commonhold does have a future – a bright future – but there are undoubted limitations in the legislation. The insistence on the principle of unanimity and the requirement of 100% consent from all lessees and their mortgagees will mean that it will be rarely possible for existing developments of long leaseholders to convert to commonhold. Even where this does occur, it is likely to be in the smaller blocks of flats where the leasehold arrangements are not causing undue difficulty. If commonhold is to be a success in the long run, it is submitted that the problem of conversion will have to be addressed by future legislation. If new commonhold developments are perceived by the market to be successful for developer and occupier alike then the pressure from the many hundreds of thousands of existing long leaseholders for the ability to enjoy the benefits of commonhold will be very difficult to resist. The insistence on an equity and parity of interest between each unit-holder will make it very difficult for large commonholds to be established with a variety of sizes of units and types of housing. It will also be a very impractical feature for any mixed developments of commercial and residential units. The approach of the 1996 Bill was better in this respect, and change will be required if commonhold is to be widely used for larger and mixed-use

---

[28] One of the strongest arguments for retention of the leasehold system with an 'outside' landlord is that it does ensure that a single person makes decisions on such issues as painting and decorating covenants where the occupiers themselves have diverse views and cannot agree on a solution (eg pink or white paint?). However, commonhold has the significant advantage of offering owners what they appear to want – namely a say and ultimate control of the management of community affairs.

schemes. The concerns raised relating to the remedies available for the resolutions of disputes will probably not be sufficient to deter either developers or buyers of newly developed commonhold units. However, the failure of a legislation to recognise the importance of payment by unit-holders for the shared benefits received and the consequent refusal to allow a first charge on the property for unpaid assessment and levies is likely to be a significant disadvantage in commonhold management.

13.28 In the final parliamentary stages of the CLRA 2002, the Minister articulated a *raison d'être* for the legislation: 'The purpose of the Bill is for commonhold to take root'.[29] This expresses a rather limited parliamentary expectation at the end of such a prolonged process and suggests that even the Government recognises that further development will be necessary in due course.

13.29 Many of the unresolved problems relating to management and some of those relating to remedies may be addressed in regulations and rules yet to be made before implementation.[30] These regulations will have a significant part to play in ensuring that commonhold does take firm root and gains acceptance within the property community. However, to flourish and become as popular as strata titles and condominiums are in other jurisdictions it is likely that tinkering with regulations will be insufficient. Further legislative action to permit freer conversion from long leasehold to commonhold and to address the concerns about remedies and other issues discussed in this book is likely to be needed. This conclusion should not be viewed in a negative way. There has had to be extensive reformulation as strata title was developed in New South Wales and elsewhere. Commonhold will also need to be re-examined and improved in due course.

---

[29] Mr Michael Wills, Parliamentary Secretary, Lord Chancellor's Department: *Hansard*, Vol 381, col 666 (11 March 2002).

[30] At the time of writing, the implementation of commonhold is planned for late autumn 2003 at the earliest.

APPENDIX 1

DRAFT MEMORANDUM AND ARTICLES OF ASSOCIATION FOR A COMMONHOLD ASSOCIATION

The Lord Chancellor's Department requests that we make known that the following documents are at an early stage of development and are included in this volume for illustrative purposes only.

DRAFT 8 OCTOBER 2001

THE COMPANIES ACTS 1985 AND 1989

COMPANY LIMITED BY GUARANTEE AND NOT HAVING A SHARE CAPITAL

MEMORANDUM OF ASSOCIATION OF [NAME] COMMONHOLD ASSOCIATION LIMITED

1   The name of the Company (referred to in this document as 'the Commonhold Association') is '[name] Commonhold Association Limited'.

2   The registered office of the Commonhold Association will be situated in [England and Wales] [Wales].

3   The objects for which the Commonhold Association is established are to carry out the functions of a commonhold association in relation to the property known as [name] and any addition or alteration thereto which is identified in the commonhold community statement relating to the Commonhold Association as modified or amended from time to time ('the Commonhold' and 'the Commonhold Community Statement' respectively) in accordance with the Commonhold and Leasehold

Reform Act 2002 or any statutory modification or re-enactment thereof for the time being in force ('the 2002 Act').

4   In furtherance of its objects as set out in clause 3 above, but not otherwise, the Commonhold Association shall have power:

4.1   to acquire, hold as registered proprietor, manage and administer the freehold estate in the common parts of the Commonhold ('the Common Parts');

4.2   to co-operate with the developer for such purposes connected with any development business related to the Commonhold as may be specified in the Commonhold Community Statement;

4.3   to permit or facilitate so far as possible the exercise by holders of commonhold units forming part of the Commonhold from time to time ('Commonhold Units') of their rights and the enjoyment by each such unit-holder of the freehold estate in his Commonhold Unit;

4.4   subject to and in accordance with section 35 of the 2002 Act, to use any right, power or procedure, or take any other step available to the Commonhold Association to enforce compliance by unit-holders or tenants of Commonhold Units with any requirement or duty (whether arising under the 2002 Act, this Memorandum, the Articles of Association of the Commonhold Association, the Commonhold Community Statement or otherwise), or to prevent, remedy or curtail any failure by a unit-holder or tenant of a Commonhold Unit to comply with any such requirement or duty;

4.5   to make, administer and enforce provisions regulating or limiting the use of the Common Parts or any specified part or parts thereof;

4.6   to create interests in, exchange, let on lease or otherwise, mortgage, sell, dispose of, turn to account, grant licences, options, rights and privileges in respect of or otherwise deal in any lawful way with the Common Parts;

4.7   to purchase, acquire or accept a transfer of the freehold estate in any land for the purpose of adding that land to the Commonhold, and to pursue or participate in applications to add land to the Commonhold;

4.8   to acquire, hold as registered proprietor, manage and administer, create interests in, exchange, let on lease or otherwise, mortgage, charge, sell, dispose of, turn to account, grant licences, options, rights and privileges in respect of or otherwise deal in any way with the freehold estate in any Commonhold Unit which it may be thought advantageous for the Commonhold Association to acquire, hold or deal with as aforesaid from time to time, and to exercise all rights and perform all duties and obligations of a unit-holder in connection therewith;

4.9 to alter, improve, develop or construct any part or parts of the Commonhold of which the Commonhold Association is for the time being the registered proprietor, and in connection therewith to make or participate in applications to amend the Commonhold Community Statement;

4.10 to insure (and use the proceeds of insurance for the purposes of rebuilding or reinstating), repair and maintain the Commonhold or any part or parts thereof, including the Common Parts and any of the Commonhold Units;

4.11 to provide services and amenities (including advertising and marketing services) in relation to the Commonhold or any part or parts thereof, including the Common Parts and any of the Commonhold Units;

4.12 with the prior consent of the Commonhold Association in general meeting, to employ or enter into contracts with managing agents of the Commonhold;

4.13 (subject to the preceding sub-clause) from time to time to employ or enter into contracts with builders, decorators, cleaners, contractors, gardeners or any other such person, to consult and retain any professional advisers and to pay, reward or remunerate in any way any person, firm or company supplying goods or services to the Commonhold Association;

4.14 to issue and receive any notice, counter-notice, consent or other communication and to enter into any correspondence concerning or in any way affecting the Commonhold, the management of the Commonhold, the unit-holders, the Commonhold Association, any of its activities, or any member thereof;

4.15 to commence and pursue or defend or participate in any application to, or other proceeding before, any court, tribunal or ombudsman of any description;

4.16 to insure any property of the Commonhold Association or in which it has an interest against damage or destruction and such other risks as may be considered necessary, appropriate or desirable, and to insure the Commonhold Association against public liability and any other risks which it may consider prudent or desirable to insure against;

4.17 to make estimates from time to time of the income required by the Commonhold Association, whether to meet its expenses or otherwise, to allocate the same among the Commonhold Units, and to take all necessary and appropriate steps to collect in, receive and enforce payment of the amounts allocated to each unit at such times, in such amounts and in such manner as the Commonhold Association may think fit;

4.18 to establish and maintain capital reserves or funds of any description, including reserves or funds to finance the repair and maintenance of the Common Parts or the Commonhold Units or to pay or contribute towards all fees, costs and other expenses incurred in the implementation of the Commonhold Association's objects and its business, to set levies and to allocate the same among the Commonhold Units, and to take all necessary and appropriate steps to collect in, receive and enforce payment of the amounts allocated to each unit at such times, in such amounts and in such manner as the Commonhold Association may think fit;

4.19 to purchase, acquire or accept any interests, licences, options, rights and privileges in or over any property, real or personal;

4.20 to improve, manage, construct, repair, develop, exchange, let on lease or otherwise, mortgage, charge, sell, assign, transfer, surrender, turn to account, grant licences, options, rights and privileges in respect of, or otherwise dispose of or deal with all or any part of the property and rights of the Commonhold Association;

4.21 to enter into any agreements or arrangements with any government or authority (central, municipal, local, or otherwise) that may seem conducive to the attainment of the Commonhold Association's objects, and to obtain from any such government or authority any charters, decrees, rights, privileges or concessions which the Commonhold Association may think desirable, and to carry out, exercise, and comply with any such charters, decrees, rights, privileges, and concessions;

4.22 to establish, undertake and execute any trusts which may lawfully be, or which are required by law to be, undertaken by the Commonhold Association;

4.23 to invest any money of the Commonhold Association in the United Kingdom by depositing the same at interest with the Bank of England, or by depositing the same in the United Kingdom at interest with a person carrying on in the United Kingdom a deposit-taking business within the meaning of the Banking Act 1987, or by depositing the same at interest with, or investing in shares in, a building society within the meaning of the Building Societies Act 1986, or to invest the same in such other manner as the Commonhold Association in general meeting may authorise from time to time;

4.24 to lend and advance money or give credit on any terms and with or without security to any person, firm or company, to enter into guarantees, contracts of indemnity and suretyship of all kinds, to receive money on deposit or loan upon any terms, and to secure or guarantee in any manner and upon any terms the payment of any sum of money or the performance of any obligation by any person, body of persons, firm or company;

4.25 to borrow and raise money in any manner;

4.26 with the consent of the Commonhold Association in general meeting, to secure the repayment of any money borrowed, raised or owing by mortgage, charge, standard security, lien or other security upon the whole or any part of the Commonhold Association's property or assets (whether present or future), and also by a similar mortgage, charge, standard security, lien or other security to secure and guarantee the performance by the Commonhold Association of any obligation or liability it may undertake or which may become binding on it, provided that in no case shall the Commonhold Association charge or purport to create a charge over the Common Parts save in accordance with section 29 of the 2002 Act;

4.27 to operate bank accounts and to draw, make, accept, endorse, discount, negotiate, execute and issue cheques, bills of exchange, promissory notes, debentures, and other negotiable or transferable instruments;

4.28 to pay all or any expenses incurred in connection with the promotion, formation and incorporation of the Commonhold Association, or to contract with any person, firm or company to pay the same;

4.29 with the consent of the Commonhold Association in general meeting, to promote any other company, and to acquire and hold all or any part of the share or loan capital or other securities of any other company;

4.30 with the consent of the Commonhold Association in general meeting, to acquire and undertake all or any part of the business, property and liabilities of any person or company carrying on any business which may be conducive to the attainment of the objects of the Commonhold Association;

4.31 subject to regulations made under the 2002 Act in relation to amendment of the Commonhold Community Statement or otherwise, to amalgamate with any companies, institutions, societies or associations having objects wholly or in part similar to those of the Commonhold Association, whether in relation to the Commonhold or any other property, and to purchase or otherwise acquire and undertake all or any part of the property, assets, liabilities and engagements of any body with which the Commonhold Association is authorised to amalgamate;

4.32 to make a termination application in relation to the Commonhold and in connection therewith to prepare a termination statement;

4.33 to make an application for a succession order in relation to the Commonhold;

4.34 to do all such other things as may be authorised or required to be done by a commonhold association by and under the 2002 Act;

4.35 to do all things specified for the time being in the Articles of

Association of the Commonhold Association and the Commonhold Community Statement;

4.36 to do all such other things as may be necessary, incidental or conducive to the attainment of the Commonhold Association's objects; and

4.37 to do or procure or arrange for the doing of all or any of the things or matters aforesaid in any part of the world and either as principals, agents, contractors or otherwise, and by or through agents, brokers, sub-contractors or otherwise and either alone or in conjunction with others.

5. The income of the Commonhold Association, from wherever derived, shall be applied solely in promoting the above objects, and save in accordance with a termination statement or on a winding up of the Commonhold Association, no distribution shall be made to its members in cash or otherwise.

6. The liability of the members is limited.

7. Without prejudice to any further liability which he may have under or arising out the Commonhold Community Statement, every member of the Commonhold Association undertakes to contribute such amount as may be required, not exceeding £1, to the assets of the Commonhold Association in the event of the Commonhold Association being wound up while he is a member, or within one year after he ceases to be a member, for payment of the debts and liabilities of the Commonhold Association contracted before he ceases to be a member, and of the costs, charges, and expenses of winding up the Commonhold Association, and for the adjustment of the rights of the contributories among themselves.

8. If on a winding up of the Commonhold Association there remains any surplus after the satisfaction of all its debts and liabilities, and after compliance with the provisions of any termination statement in accordance with the 2002 Act, the surplus shall be paid to or distributed among the members of the Commonhold Association rateably in accordance with the percentages allocated to their Commonhold Units in the Commonhold Community Statement.

9. In this Memorandum:

9.1 words and expressions shall, unless the context otherwise requires, have the meaning given to them by the 2002 Act or the Companies Act 1985 or any statutory modification or re-enactment thereof for the time being in force;

9.2   words expressed in any gender shall include any other gender;

9.3   persons shall include bodies corporate and partnerships and other unincorporated bodies; and

9.4   words expressed in the singular shall, unless the context otherwise requires, include the plural, and vice versa.

10.   If there is any conflict between the provisions of this Memorandum and those of the Commonhold Community Statement, the provisions of this Memorandum shall prevail.

We, the subscribers to this Memorandum of Association, wish to be formed into a company pursuant to this Memorandum.

Names and addresses of subscribers:

Dated   20**

Witness to the above signatures

THE COMPANIES ACTS 1985 AND 1989

COMPANY LIMITED BY GUARANTEE AND NOT HAVING A SHARE CAPITAL

ARTICLES OF ASSOCIATION OF [NAME] COMMONHOLD ASSOCIATION LIMITED ('the Commonhold Association')

PRELIMINARY

1. The Regulations contained in the Schedule to the Companies (Tables A to F) Regulations 1985 as amended by the Companies (Tables A to F) (Amendment) Regulations 1985 shall not apply to the Commonhold Association.

INTERPRETATION

2. In these:

    'the 2002 Act' means the Commonhold and Leasehold Reform Act 2002 or any statutory modification or re-enactment thereof for the time being in force;

    'address' in relation to electronic communications includes any number or address used for the purposes of such communications;

    'clear days' in relation to the period of notice means that period excluding the day when the notice is given or deemed to be given and the day for which it is given or on which it is to take effect;

    'the Commonhold' means [name] and any addition or alteration thereto and any part or parts thereof which are identified in the Commonhold Community Statement;

    'the Commonhold Community Statement' means the commonhold community statement relating to the Commonhold Association as modified or amended from time to time;

    'communication' means the same as in the Electronic Communications Act 2000;

    'the Companies Act' means the Companies Act 1985 or any statutory modification or re-enactment thereof for the time being in force;

    'the developer' means the same as in section 58 of the 2002 Act;

'electronic communication' means the same as in the Electronic Communications Act 2000;

'the member' means the person whose name is entered in the register of members as a member;

'registered office' means the registered office of the Commonhold Association;

'the seal' means the common seal of the Commonhold Association;

'Secretary' means the secretary of the Commonhold Association or any other person appointed to perform the duties of the secretary of the Commonhold Association, including a joint, assistant or deputy secretary;

'the United Kingdom' means Great Britain and Northern Ireland.

3   Subject as aforesaid, words and expressions contained in these articles shall, unless the context otherwise requires, have the meaning given to them by the 2002 Act or the Companies Act.

4   In these articles:

4.1   words expressed in any gender shall include any other gender;

4.2   persons shall include bodies corporate and partnerships and other unincorporated bodies;

4.3   words expressed in the singular shall, unless the context otherwise requires, include the plural, and vice versa.

If there is any conflict between the provisions of these articles and those of the Commonhold Community Statement, the provisions of these articles shall prevail.

MEMBERS

5   Part 2 of Schedule 3 to the 2002 Act shall apply to determine the entitlement of any person or persons to membership of the Commonhold Association from time to time.

6   The Commonhold Association shall maintain a register of members and shall comply in all respects with regulations made in relation thereto from time to time pursuant to paragraph 14 of Schedule 3 to the 2002 Act.

GENERAL MEETINGS

7   All general meetings other than annual general meetings shall be called extraordinary general meetings.

8   The directors may call general meetings and, on the requisition of members pursuant to the provisions of the Companies Act, shall forthwith proceed to convene an extraordinary general meeting for a date not more than 28 days after the date of the notice convening the meeting. If there are not within the United Kingdom sufficient directors to call a general meeting, any director or any member of the Commonhold Association may call a general meeting.

9   In addition to its annual general meeting, the Commonhold Association shall hold at least one extraordinary general meeting each year at which, in addition to any other business, the directors shall present an interim review of the business and affairs of the Commonhold Association since the preceding annual general meeting. Such meeting shall not be held within three months of any annual general meeting of the Commonhold Association.

NOTICE OF GENERAL MEETINGS

10   An annual general meeting and an extraordinary general meeting called for the passing of a special resolution or a resolution appointing a person as a director shall be called by at least twenty-one clear days' notice. All other extraordinary general meetings shall be called by at least fourteen clear days' notice but a general meeting may be called by shorter notice if is so agreed:

10.1 in the case of an annual general meeting, by all the members entitled to attend and vote thereat; and

10.2 in the case of any other meeting by a majority in number of the members having a right to attend and vote being a majority together holding not less than ninety-five per cent of the total voting rights at the meeting of all the members.

11   The notice shall specify the time and place of the meeting and in the case of an annual general meeting, shall specify the meeting as such.

12   The notice shall also include or be accompanied by a statement of the agenda of the business to be transacted at the meeting, the text of any resolutions to be proposed at the meeting, and an explanation to be provided by the proposers of any resolution of the motivation for such resolution.

13   Subject to the provisions of these articles, the notice shall be given to all the members and to the directors and auditors.

14   The accidental omission to give notice of a meeting to, or the non-receipt of notice of a meeting by, any person entitled to receive notice shall not invalidate the proceedings at that meeting.

PROCEEDINGS AT GENERAL MEETINGS

15   No business shall be transacted at any general meeting unless details relating to it were included in the notice convening the meeting in accordance with Article 12 above. A proposal to amend an ordinary resolution may, however, be voted upon if the terms of the proposed amendment were received by the Commonhold Association at its registered office, or at any address specified in the notice convening the meeting for the purpose of receiving electronic communications, not less than 48 hours before the time for holding the meeting. The decision of the Chairman as to the admissibility of any proposed amendment shall be final and conclusive and shall not invalidate any proceedings on the substantive resolution.

16   At any general meeting, so far as practicable and subject to any contrary resolution of the meeting, any business arising from a requisition of members shall be transacted before any other business, and if there were more than one requisition, the business arising therefrom shall be transacted in the order in which the requisitions were received by the Commonhold Association.

17   No business shall be transacted at any general meeting unless a quorum is present. The quorum for the meeting shall be 20% of the members of the Commonhold Association entitled to vote upon the business to be transacted, or two members of the Commonhold Association so entitled (whichever is the greater) present in person or by proxy.

18   If such a quorum is not present within half an hour from the time appointed for the meeting, or if during a meeting such a quorum ceases to be present, the meeting shall stand adjourned to the same day in the next week at the same time and place or to such time and place as the directors may determine.

19   The chairman, if any, of the board of directors or in his absence some other director nominated by the directors shall preside as chairman of the meeting, but if neither the chairman nor such other director (if any) be present within fifteen minutes after the time appointed for holding the meeting and willing to act, the directors present shall elect one of their number to be chairman and, if there is only one director present and willing to act, he shall be chairman.

20   If no director is willing to act as chairman, or if no director is present within fifteen minutes after the time appointed for holding the meeting, the members present and entitled to vote shall choose one of their number to be chairman.

21   A director shall, notwithstanding that he is not a member, be entitled to attend, speak and propose (but, subject to article 27 below, not vote upon) a resolution at any general meeting of the Commonhold Association.

22   The chairman may, with the consent of a meeting at which a quorum is present (and shall if so directed by the meeting), adjourn the meeting from time to time and from place to place, but no business shall be transacted at an adjourned meeting other than business which might properly have been transacted at the meeting had the adjournment not taken place. When a meeting is adjourned for fourteen days or more, at least seven clear days' notice shall be given specifying the time and place of the adjourned meeting and the general nature of the business to be transacted. Otherwise it shall not be necessary to give any such notice.

23   A resolution put to the vote of a meeting shall be decided on a show of hands unless before, or on the declaration of the result of, the show of hands a poll is duly demanded. Subject to the provisions of the Companies Act, a poll may be demanded:

23.1 by the chairman; or
23.2 by at least five members having the right to vote at the meeting; or
23.3 by a member or members representing not less than one-tenth of the total voting rights of all the members having the right to vote at the meeting;

and a demand by a person as proxy for a member shall be the same as a demand by the member.

24   Unless a poll is duly demanded a declaration by the chairman that a resolution has been carried or carried unanimously, or by a particular majority, or lost, or not carried by a particular majority and an entry to that effect in the minutes of the meeting shall be conclusive evidence of the fact without proof of the number or proportion of the votes recorded in favour of or against the resolution.

25   The demand for a poll may, before the poll is taken, be withdrawn but only with the consent of the chairman and a demand so withdrawn shall not be taken to have invalidated the result of a show of hands declared before the demand was made.

26   A poll shall be taken in such manner as the chairman may direct, having particular regard to the convenience of members, and he may appoint scrutineers (who need not be members) and fix a time and place for declaring the result of the poll. The result of the poll shall be deemed to be the resolution of the meeting at which the poll was demanded.

27   In the case of an equality of votes, whether on a show of hands or on a poll, the chairman shall be entitled to a casting vote in addition to any other vote he may have.

28   A poll demanded on the election of a chairman or on a question of adjournment shall be taken forthwith. A poll demanded on any other question shall be taken either forthwith or at such time and place as the chairman may direct, having particular regard to the convenience of members, and not being more than thirty days after the poll is demanded. The demand for a poll shall not prevent the continuance of a meeting for the transaction of any business other than the question on which the poll was demanded. If a poll is demanded before the declaration of the result of a show of hands and the demand is duly withdrawn, the meeting shall continue as if the demand had not been made.

29   No notice need be given of a poll not taken forthwith if the time and place at which it is to be taken are announced at the meeting at which it is demanded. In any other case at least seven clear days' notice shall be given specifying the time and place at which the poll is to be taken.

30   A resolution in writing executed by or on behalf of each member who would have been entitled to vote upon it if it had been proposed at a general meeting at which he was present shall be as effectual as if it had been passed at a general meeting duly convened and held and may consist of several instruments in the like form each executed by or on behalf of one or more members.

VOTES OF MEMBERS

31   Subject to articles 33 and 34 below, on a show of hands, every member who (being an individual) is present in person or (being a corporation) is present by a duly authorised representative, not being himself a member entitled to vote, shall have one vote.

32   Subject to articles 33 and 34 below, on a poll, every member shall have one vote, provided that a member who is a unit-holder of more than one commonhold unit shall have one vote for every commonhold unit in respect of which he is entitled to have his name entered in the register of members of the Commonhold Association.

33   Members of the Commonhold Association other than the developer shall
       not be entitled to vote upon a resolution for the removal from office of a
       director appointed by the developer pursuant to article 44 below.

34   At any time at which the developer is entitled to exercise the power to
       appoint and remove directors pursuant to article 44 below, the developer
       shall not be entitled to vote upon a resolution fixing the number of
       directors of the Commonhold Association, or upon a resolution for the
       appointment or removal from office of any director not appointed by
       him, or upon any resolution concerning the remuneration of any director
       not appointed by him, or upon a special resolution giving a direction to
       the directors.

35   A member in respect of whom an order has been made by any court
       having jurisdiction (whether in the United Kingdom or elsewhere) in
       matters concerning mental disorder may vote, whether on a show of
       hands or on a poll, by his receiver, curator bonis or other person
       authorised in that behalf appointed by that court, and any such receiver,
       curator bonis or other person may, on a poll, vote by proxy. Evidence to
       the satisfaction of the directors of the authority of the person claiming to
       exercise the right to vote shall be deposited at the registered office, or at
       such other place as is specified in accordance with the articles for the
       deposit of instruments of proxy, not less than 48 hours before the time
       appointed for holding the meeting or adjourned meeting at which the
       right to vote is to be exercised and in default the right to vote shall not
       be exercisable.

36   No objection shall be raised to the qualification of any voter except at the
       meeting or adjourned meeting at which the vote objected to is tendered,
       and every vote not disallowed at the meeting shall be valid. Any objection
       made in due time shall be referred to the chairman whose decision shall
       be final and conclusive.

37   On a poll votes may be given either personally or by proxy. A member
       may appoint more than one proxy to attend on the same occasion.

38   The appointment of a proxy shall be in writing, executed by or on behalf
       of the appointor and shall be in the following form (or in a form as near
       thereto as circumstances allow or in any other form which is usual or
       which the directors may approve):

[Name] Commonhold Association Limited

[I] *******, of ********, being a member of the above-named company, hereby appoint(s) ***** of ******, or failing him, ******* of ******* , as my/its proxy to vote in my/its name and on my/its behalf at the annual/extraordinary general meeting of the company to be held on ***** 20**, and at any adjournment thereof

Signed on *********** 20**

39   Where it is desired to afford members an opportunity of instructing the proxy how he shall act the appointment of a proxy shall be in the following form (or in a form as near thereto as circumstances allow or in any other form which is usual or which the directors may approve):

[Name] Commonhold Association Limited

[I], *******, of **********, being a member/members of the above-named company, hereby appoint(s) **** of ****** or failing him ********* of ********, as my/its proxy to vote in my/its name and on my/its behalf at the annual/extraordinary general meeting of the company, to be held on ********* 20**, and at any adjournment thereof.

This form is to be used in respect of the resolutions mentioned below as follows:

Resolution No 1 [for][against]
Resolution No 2 [for][against]

[Strike out whichever is not desired]

Unless otherwise instructed, the proxy may vote as he thinks fit or abstain from voting.

Signed on *********** 20**

40   The appointment of a proxy and any authority under which it is executed or a copy of such authority certified notarially or in some other way approved by the directors may:

40.1   in the case of an instrument in writing be deposited at the office or at such other place within the United Kingdom as is specified in the notice convening the meeting or in any instrument of proxy sent out by the Commonhold Association in relation to the meeting not less than 48 hours before the time for holding the meeting or adjourned meeting at which the person named in the instrument proposes to vote; or

40.2 in the case of an appointment contained in an electronic communication, where an address has been specified for the purpose of receiving electronic communications –

(i) in the notice convening the meeting, or

(ii) in any instrument of proxy sent out by the Commonhold Association in relation to the meeting, or

(iii) in any invitation contained in an electronic communication to appoint a proxy issued by the Commonhold Association in relation to the meeting,

be received at such address not less than 48 hours before the time for holding the meeting or adjourned meeting at which the person named in the appointment proposes to vote;

40.3 in the case of a poll taken more than 48 hours after it is demanded, be deposited or received as aforesaid after the poll has been demanded and not less than 24 hours before the time appointed for the taking of the poll; or

40.4 where the poll is not taken forthwith but is taken not more than 48 hours after it was demanded, be delivered at the meeting at which the poll was demanded to the chairman or to the secretary or to any director;

and an instrument of proxy which is not deposited, delivered or received in a manner so permitted shall be invalid.

41 A vote given or poll demanded by proxy or by the duly authorised representative of a corporation shall be valid notwithstanding the previous determination of the authority of the person voting or demanding a poll unless notice of the determination was received by the Commonhold Association at the registered office or at such other place at which the instrument of proxy was duly deposited or, where the appointment of the proxy was contained in an electronic communication, at the address at which such appointment was duly received before the commencement of the meeting or adjourned meeting at which the vote is given or the poll demanded or (in the case of a poll taken otherwise than on the same day as the meeting or adjourned meeting) the time appointed for taking the poll.

QUALIFICATION OF DIRECTORS

42 A director need not be a member of the Commonhold Association.

NUMBER OF DIRECTORS

43 The maximum number of directors of the Commonhold Association shall be as determined by ordinary resolution of the Commonhold

Association, and if not so determined, shall be six. The minimum number of directors shall be two.

APPOINTMENT AND REMOVAL OF DIRECTORS

44 This article shall apply if the Commonhold Community Statement confers upon the developer the right to appoint and remove directors of the Commonhold Association. In such event:

44.1 during the transitional period the developer shall be entitled to appoint a maximum of two directors in addition to any directors appointed by the subscriber or subscribers to the Memorandum of Association of the Commonhold Association, and shall be entitled to remove or replace any director so appointed;

44.2 after the end of the transitional period and for so long as the developer is the unit-holder of more than one quarter of the total number of units in the Commonhold, he shall be entitled to appoint a total of one quarter (or the nearest whole number exceeding one quarter) of the maximum number of directors of the Commonhold Association, and shall be entitled to remove or replace any director so appointed;

44.3 references hereinafter to a 'developer's director' are references to a director appointed under article 44.1 or 44.2 above;

44.4 every such appointment and removal of a developer's director shall be effected by notice in writing signed by or on behalf of the developer and shall take effect immediately upon receipt of such notice at the registered office of the Commonhold Association or by the Secretary or as and from any date thereafter as may be specified in such notice;

44.5 if at any time the Commonhold Association resolves to reduce the maximum number of directors, and as a consequence the number of developer's directors in office exceeds the number permitted under article 44.2 above, the developer shall immediately reduce the number of developer's directors accordingly. If such reduction has not been effected by the commencement of the next directors' meeting, the longest in office of the developer's directors shall cease to hold office immediately as to achieve the required reduction in numbers;

44.6 if the developer ceases to be the unit-holder of more than one quarter of the total number of units in the Commonhold, he shall thereupon cease to be entitled to appoint, remove or replace any director of the Commonhold Association, and any developer's directors previously appointed by him under this article shall cease to hold office immediately; and

44.7 a developer's director who is removed from office or who ceases to hold office under this article shall not have any claim against the Commonhold Association in respect thereof.

45   At the first annual general meeting after the end of the transitional period, all of the directors other than any developer's directors shall retire from office, and at every subsequent annual general meeting one-third of the directors who are subject to retirement by rotation or, if their number is not three or a multiple of three, the number nearest to one-third shall retire from office; but if there is only one director who is subject to retirement by rotation, he shall retire.

46   A developer's director shall not be subject to retirement by rotation. Subject to the provisions of the Companies Act, the directors to retire by rotation shall be those who have been longest in office since their last appointment or reappointment, but as between persons who became or who were last reappointed directors on the same day those to retire shall (unless they otherwise agree among themselves) be determined by lot.

47   If the Commonhold Association, at the meeting at which a director retires by rotation, does not fill the vacancy, the retiring director shall, if willing to act, be deemed to have been reappointed unless at the meeting it is resolved not to fill the vacancy or unless a resolution for the reappointment of the director is put to the meeting and lost.

48   No person other than a director retiring by rotation shall be appointed or reappointed as a director at any general meeting unless:

48.1 he is recommended by the directors; or
48.2 not less than fourteen nor more than thirty-five clear days before the date appointed for the meeting, notice executed by a member qualified to vote at the meeting has been given to the Commonhold Association of the intention to propose that person for appointment or reappointment stating the particulars which would, if he were so appointed or reappointed, be required to be included in the Commonhold Association's register of directors together with notice executed by that person of his willingness to be appointed or reappointed.

49   Not less than seven nor more than twenty-eight clear days before the date appointed for holding a general meeting notice shall be given to all who are entitled to receive notice of the meeting of any person who is recommended by the directors for appointment or reappointment as a director at the meeting or in respect of whom notice has been duly given to the Commonhold Association of the intention to propose him at the

meeting for appointment or reappointment as a director. The notice shall give the particulars of that person which would, if he were so appointed or reappointed be required to be included in the Commonhold Association's register of directors.

50   Subject as aforesaid, the Commonhold Association may by ordinary resolution appoint a person who is willing to act to be a director either to fill a vacancy (other than a vacancy in respect of a developer's director), or as an additional director and may also determine the rotation in which any additional directors are to retire.

51   The directors may appoint a person who is willing to act to be a director, either to fill a vacancy (other than a vacancy in respect of a developer's director) or as an additional director, provided that the appointment does not cause the number of directors to exceed any number fixed by or in accordance with the articles as the maximum number of directors. A director so appointed shall hold office only until the next following annual general meeting. If not reappointed at such annual general meeting, he shall vacate office at the conclusion thereof.

52   Subject as aforesaid, a director who retires at an annual general meeting may, if willing to act, be reappointed. If he is not reappointed, he shall retain office until the meeting appoints someone in his place, or if it does not do so, until the end of the meeting.

ALTERNATE DIRECTORS

53   Any director (other than an alternate director) may appoint any other director, or any other person approved by resolution of the directors and willing to act, to be an alternate director to attend meetings of directors in the event that the director is unable to do so. If the director is a member of the Commonhold Association, his alternate must also be a member of the Commonhold Association. The director may remove from office an alternate director so appointed by him.

54   An alternate director shall be entitled to receive notice of all meetings of directors and of all meetings of committees of directors of which his appointor is a member, to attend and vote at any such meeting at which the director appointing him is not personally present and generally to perform all the functions of his appointor as a director in his absence but shall not be entitled to receive any remuneration from the Commonhold Association for his service as an alternate director. But it shall not be necessary to give notice of such a meeting to an alternate director who is absent from the United Kingdom.

55 An alternate director shall cease to be an alternate director if his appointor ceases to be a director. If a director retires but is reappointed or deemed to have been reappointed at the meeting at which he retires, any appointment of an alternate director made by him which was in force immediately prior to his retirement shall continue after his reappointment.

56 Any appointment or removal of an alternate director shall be by notice to the Commonhold Association signed by the director making or revoking the appointment or in any other manner approved by the directors.

57 Save as otherwise provided in the articles, an alternate director shall be deemed for all purposes to be a director and shall alone be responsible for his own acts and defaults and he shall not be deemed to be the agent of the director appointing him.

DISQUALIFICATION AND VACATION OF OFFICE OF DIRECTORS

58 The office of a director shall be vacated if:

58.1 having been a member of the Commonhold Association when appointed a director, he ceases to be a member of the Commonhold Association;

58.2 he ceases to be a director by virtue of any provision of the Companies Act or he becomes prohibited by law from being a director; or

58.3 he becomes bankrupt or makes any arrangement or composition with his creditors generally; or

58.4 he is, or may be, suffering from mental disorder and either:

58.4.1 he is admitted to hospital in pursuance of an application for admission for treatment under the Mental Health Act 1983 or, in Scotland, an application for admission under the Mental Health (Scotland) Act 1960, or

58.4.2 an order is made by a court having jurisdiction (whether in the United Kingdom or elsewhere) in matters concerning mental disorder for his, detention or for the appointment of a receiver, curator bonis or other person to exercise powers with respect to his property or affairs; or

58.5 he resigns his office by notice to the Commonhold Association; or

58.6 he shall for more than six consecutive months have been absent without permission of the directors from meetings of directors held during that period and the directors resolve that his office be vacated.

POWERS OF DIRECTORS

59   Subject to the provisions of the Companies Act, the memorandum and the articles, and to any directions given by special resolution, the business of the Commonhold Association shall be managed by the directors who may exercise all the powers of the Commonhold Association. No alteration of the memorandum or articles and no such direction shall invalidate any prior act of the directors which would have been valid if that alteration had not been made or that direction had not been given. The powers given by this article shall not be limited by any special power given to the directors by the articles and a meeting of directors at which a quorum is present may exercise all powers exercisable by the directors.

AGENTS

60   The directors shall have the power on behalf of the Commonhold Association to appoint and enter into contracts with managing agents of the Commonhold on such terms as they shall think fit, but shall not exercise such power unless the terms of such appointment or contract (including those as to remuneration) shall first have been approved by the Commonhold Association in general meeting.

61   Subject to the preceding article, the directors may, by power of attorney or otherwise, appoint any person to be the agent of the Commonhold Association for such purposes and on such conditions as they determine, including authority for the agent to delegate all or any of his powers.

DELEGATION OF DIRECTORS' POWERS

62   The directors may delegate any of their powers to any committee consisting of two or more directors, members of the Commonhold Association and others as they shall think fit, provided that the majority of the members of any such committee from time to time shall be members of the Commonhold Association. They may also delegate to any managing director or any director holding any other executive office or any managing agent such of their powers as they consider desirable to be exercised by him. Any such delegation shall be made subject to any provisions of the Commonhold Community Statement, may be made subject to any conditions the directors may impose, may be made either collaterally with or to the exclusion of their own powers, and may be revoked or altered. Subject to any such conditions, the proceedings of a committee with two or more members shall be governed by the articles

regulating the proceedings of directors so far as they are capable of applying.

REMUNERATION OF DIRECTORS

63   The developer's directors shall not be entitled to any remuneration from the Commonhold Association. Save with the consent of the Commonhold Association in general meeting, the directors other than the developer's director shall not be entitled to any remuneration. Any resolution giving such consent shall specify the amount of remuneration to be paid to the directors, and unless the resolution provides otherwise, the remuneration shall be deemed to accrue from day to day.

DIRECTORS' EXPENSES

64   The directors may be paid all travelling, hotel, and other expenses properly incurred by them in connection with their attendance at meetings of directors or committees of directors or general meetings or separate meetings of the members of the Commonhold Association or otherwise in connection with the discharge of their duties.

DIRECTORS' APPOINTMENTS AND INTERESTS

65   Subject to the provisions of the Companies Act, and provided that the terms of any such appointment, agreement or arrangement have been approved in advance by the Commonhold Association in general meeting, the directors may appoint one or more of their number to the office of managing director or to any other executive office under the Commonhold Association and may enter into an agreement or arrangement with any director for his employment by the Commonhold Association or for the provision by him of any services outside the scope of the ordinary duties of a director. Any appointment of a director to an executive office shall terminate if he ceases to be a director but without prejudice to any claim to damages for breach of the contract of service between the director and the Commonhold Association.

66   Subject to the provisions of the Companies Act, and provided that he has disclosed to the directors the nature and extent of any material interest of his, a director notwithstanding his office:

66.1   may be a party to, or otherwise interested in, any transaction or arrangement with the Commonhold Association or in which the Commonhold Association is otherwise interested; and

66.2 may be a director or other officer of, or employed by, or a party to any transaction or arrangement with, or otherwise interested in, any body corporate promoted by the Commonhold Association or in which the Commonhold Association is otherwise interested; and

66.3 shall not, by reason of his office, be accountable to the Commonhold Association for any benefit which he derives from any such office or employment or from any such transaction or arrangement or from any interest in any such body corporate and no such transaction or arrangement shall be liable to be avoided on the ground of any such interest or benefit.

67 For the purposes of the foregoing article:

67.1 a general notice given to the directors that a director is to be regarded as having an interest of the nature and extent specified in the notice in any transaction or arrangement in which a specified person or class of persons is interested shall be deemed to be a disclosure that the director has an interest in any such transaction of the nature and extent so specified; and

67.2 an interest of which a director has no knowledge and of which it is unreasonable to expect him to have knowledge shall not be treated as an interest of his.

68 A developer's director may provide to the developer any information which he receives by virtue of his being a director.

PROCEEDINGS OF DIRECTORS

69 Subject to the provisions of the articles, the directors may regulate their proceedings as they think fit. A director may, and the secretary at the request of a director shall, call a meeting of the directors. It shall not be necessary to give notice of a meeting to a director who is absent from the United Kingdom unless he has given to the Commonhold Association an address to which notices may be sent using electronic communications. In such case the director shall be entitled to have notices given to him at that address. Questions arising at a meeting shall be decided by a majority of votes. In the case of an equality of votes, the chairman shall have a second or casting vote. A director who is also an alternate director shall be entitled in the absence of his appointor to a separate vote on behalf of his appointor in addition to his own vote.

70 The quorum for the transaction of the business of the directors may be fixed by the directors and unless so fixed at any other greater number, shall be the greater of 50% of the number of appointed directors for the time being, or two. At least one of the persons present at the meeting

must be a director other than a developer's director. A person who holds office only as an alternate director shall, if his appointor is not present, be counted in the quorum. A person who holds office both as a director and as an alternate director shall only be counted once in the quorum.

71   The continuing directors or a sole continuing director may act notwithstanding any vacancies in their number, but, if the number of directors is less than the number fixed as the quorum, the continuing director may act only for the purpose of filling vacancies or of calling a general meeting.

72   The directors may appoint one of their number to be the chairman of the board of directors and may at any time remove him from that office. Unless he is unwilling to do so, the director so appointed shall preside at every meeting of directors at which he is present. But if there is no director holding that office, or if the director holding it is unwilling to preside or is not present within fifteen minutes after the time appointed for the meeting, the directors present may appoint one of their number to be chairman of the meeting.

73   All acts done by a meeting of directors, or of a committee, or by a person acting as a director shall, notwithstanding that it be afterwards discovered that there was a defect in the appointment of any director or that any of them were disqualified from holding office, or had vacated office, or were not entitled to vote, be as valid as if every such person had been duly appointed and was qualified and had continued to be a director and had been entitled to vote.

74   A resolution in writing signed by all the directors entitled to receive notice of a meeting of directors or of a committee of directors shall be as valid and effectual as if it had been passed at a meeting of directors or (as the case, may be) a committee of directors duly convened and held and may consist of several documents in the like form each signed by one or more directors; but a resolution signed by an alternate director need not also be signed by his appointor and, if it is signed by a director who has appointed an alternate director, it need not be signed by the alternate director in that capacity.

75   A director who is not a member of the Commonhold Association shall not vote at a meeting of directors or of a committee of directors on any resolution concerning a matter in which he has, directly or indirectly, an interest or duty which is material and which conflicts or may conflict with the interests of the Commonhold Association. For the purposes of this article, an interest of a person who is, for any purpose of the Companies Act (excluding any statutory modification thereof not in

force when this regulation becomes binding on the Commonhold Association), connected with a director shall be treated as an interest of the director and, in relation to an alternate director, an interest of his appointor shall be treated as an interest of the alternate director without prejudice to any interest which the alternate director has otherwise. A director shall not be counted in the quorum present at a meeting in relation to a resolution on which he is not entitled to vote.

76   A director who is a member of the Commonhold Association may vote at any meeting of directors or of any committee of directors of which he is a member notwithstanding that it in any way concerns or relates to a matter in which he has any interest whatsoever, directly or indirectly, and if he votes on such a resolution, his vote shall be counted; and in relation to any such resolution, he shall (whether or not he votes on the same) be taken into account in calculating the quorum present at the meeting.

77   If a question arises at a meeting of directors or of a committee of directors as to the right of a director to vote, the question may, before the conclusion of the meeting, be referred to the chairman of the meeting and his ruling in relation to any director other than himself shall be final and conclusive.

SECRETARY

78   Subject to the provisions of the Companies Act, the secretary shall be appointed by the directors for such terms, at such remuneration and upon such conditions as they may think fit; and any secretary so appointed may be removed by them.

MINUTES

79   The directors shall cause minutes to be made in books kept for the purpose:

79.1 of all appointments of officers made by the directors or by the developer; and

79.2 of all proceedings at meetings of the Commonhold Association, of members and of the directors, and of committees, including the names of the persons present at each such meeting.

THE SEAL

80   The seal shall only be used by the authority of the directors or of a committee authorised by the directors. The directors may determine who shall sign any instrument to which the seal is affixed and unless otherwise

so determined it shall be signed by a director and by the secretary or by a second director.

NO DISTRIBUTION OF PROFITS

81 Save in accordance with a termination statement or in a winding up, the Commonhold Association shall not make any distribution to its members of its profits or assets, whether in cash or otherwise.

WINDING UP

82 If on a winding up of the Commonhold Association there remains any surplus after the satisfaction of all its debts and liabilities, and after compliance with the provisions of any termination statement in accordance with the 2002 Act, the surplus shall be paid to or distributed among the members of the Commonhold Association rateably in accordance with the percentages allocated to their Commonhold Units in the Commonhold Community Statement.

INSPECTION AND COPYING OF BOOKS AND RECORDS

83 In addition to, and without derogation from, any right conferred by statute or by the Commonhold Community Statement, any member shall have the right, on reasonable notice, at such time and place as shall be convenient to the Commonhold Association, to inspect any book, minute, document or accounting record of the Commonhold Association, and to be provided with a copy of the same upon payment of any reasonable charge for copying. Such rights shall be subject to any resolution of the Commonhold Association in general meeting, and, in the case of any book, minute, document or accounting record which the directors reasonably consider contains confidential material the disclosure of which would be contrary to the interests of the Commonhold Association, to any reasonable conditions or redactions which the directors may impose or make.

NOTICES

84 Any notice to be given to or by any person pursuant to the articles shall be in writing or shall be given using electronic communications to an address for the time being notified for that purpose to the person giving the notice. A notice calling a meeting of the directors need not be in writing or given using electronic communications if there is insufficient

time to give such notice having regard to the urgency of the business to be conducted thereat.

85   The Commonhold Association may give any notice to a member either personally or by sending it by first class post in a prepaid envelope addressed to the member at his registered address or by leaving it at that address or by giving it using electronic communications in accordance with any of the methods described in subsections (4A)–(4D) of section 369 of the Companies Act. A member whose registered address is not within the United Kingdom and who gives to the Commonhold Association an address within the United Kingdom at which notices may be given to him, or an address to which notices may be sent by electronic communications, shall be entitled to have notices given to him at that address, but otherwise no such member shall be entitled to receive any notice from the Commonhold Association.

86   A member present, either in person or by proxy, at any meeting of the Commonhold Association shall be deemed to have received notice of the meeting and, where requisite, of the purposes for which it was called.

87   Proof that an envelope containing a notice was properly addressed, prepaid and posted by first class post shall be conclusive evidence that the notice was given. Proof that a notice contained in an electronic communication was sent in accordance with guidance issued by the Institute of Chartered Secretaries and Administrators shall be conclusive evidence that the notice was given. A notice sent by first class post shall be deemed to be given at the expiration of 48 hours after the envelope containing it was posted. A notice contained in an electronic communication sent in accordance with section 369(4A) of the Companies Act shall be deemed to be given at the expiration of 48 hours after the time it was sent. A notice contained in an electronic communication given in accordance with section 369(4B) of the Companies Act shall be deemed to be given when treated as having been so given in accordance with that subsection.

INDEMNITY

88   Subject to the provisions of the Companies Act but without prejudice to any indemnity to which a director may otherwise be entitled, every director or other officer or auditor of the Commonhold Association shall be indemnified out of the assets of the Commonhold Association against any liability incurred by him in defending any proceedings, whether civil or criminal, in which judgment is given in his favour or in which he is acquitted or in connection with any application in which relief is granted to him by the court from liability for negligence, default, breach of duty

or breach of trust in relation to the affairs of the Commonhold Association.

Names and Addresses of Members:

APPENDIX 2

DRAFT COMMONHOLD COMMUNITY STATEMENT FOR A COMMONHOLD ASSOCIATION

The Lord Chancellor's Department requests that we make known that the following documents are at an early stage of development and are included in this volume for illustrative purposes only.

DRAFT 8 OCTOBER 2001

COMMONHOLD AND LEASEHOLD REFORM ACT 2002

COMMONHOLD COMMUNITY STATEMENT

[*NAME*] COMMONHOLD ASSOCIATION LIMITED

This Commonhold Community Statement (referred to as 'this Statement') is to be read together with the Memorandum and Articles of Association of the company referred to above (referred to in this Statement as the 'Memorandum', the 'Articles' and the 'Commonhold Association' respectively). In the event of any conflict between the provisions of this Statement and the Memorandum and Articles, the provisions of the Memorandum and Articles shall prevail.

Capitalised terms have the same meaning as in Part 1 of the Commonhold and Leasehold Reform Act 2002 (referred to in this Statement as 'the Act').

Wherever permitted or required by regulations made under section 13(6) of the Act, references in this Statement to Unit-holders include joint Unit-holders.

This Statement may only be amended in accordance with sections 23, 24, 30 and 33 of the Act and regulations made thereunder (as applicable).

The Statement must be signed by or on behalf of the applicant for registration.

FURTHER INFORMATION ABOUT THE COMMONHOLD [ENTER NAME OF COMMONHOLD] MAY BE FOUND IN THE MEMORANDUM AND ARTICLES OF ASSOCIATION OF THE [   ] COMMONHOLD ASSOCIATION AND BY LOOKING AT THE RELEVANT REGISTERS KEPT BY HM LAND REGISTRY.

PART I: THE COMMONHOLD LAND, THE COMMONHOLD ASSOCIATION AND THE APPLICANT FOR REGISTRATION

The Land

1   Address(es) of the Commonhold:

The Commonhold Association

2   Name of the company:

3   Registered number of the company at the Companies Registry:

4   Date of incorporation:

5   Registered office:

The Applicant for Registration (the Developer)

6   Name

7   Address

8   Company registration number (if applicable)

PART II: THE COMMONHOLD

In the event of any inconsistency between any of the descriptions given below and the plan or plans of the Commonhold attached hereto, the plans will prevail.

The Commonhold

1   Description of the type of Commonhold (residential only, commercial only, or mixed use):

The Commonhold Units

2   The total number of Commonhold Units in the Commonhold:

3   Identification of the Commonhold Units (in words) by reference to the plans attached hereto, including in each case:

   (a)   a description and the distinctive address(es) of the unit;
   (b)   a description of any excluded structures, fittings, apparatus or appurtenances;
   (c)   whether the unit is a residential unit as provided for in Section C of the Rules in Part IV below:
   (d)   the relevant percentage or percentages allocated to the unit for the purposes of the payment of the Commonhold Assessment and any levies under sections 38 and 39 of the Act.

Limited Use Areas[1]

4   Identification of the Limited Use Areas, if any, including in the case of each area:

   (a)   a description of the area; and
   (b)   a statement of the classes of person who may use it and the kind of use to which the area may be put.

---

[1]   Section 24(1) of the Act contains a definition of the Common Parts and should be read in conjunction with the plans attached hereto.

<u>The Plans</u>

5   A plan or plans of the Commonhold showing each Commonhold Unit, the Common Parts and any Limited Use Areas is/are attached to this Statement.

PART III: DEVELOPMENT RIGHTS

This Part of the Statement is subject to section 58 of the Act and regulations made thereunder.

If no development rights of the types mentioned below are to be conferred on the Developer, the relevant paragraph should be deleted.

The Developer's rights to carry out Development Business on the Commonhold

1   The Developer has the right to add the following land to the Commonhold:

2   The right conferred by 1 above will expire on: [date]

3   The Developer has the right to remove the following land from the Commonhold:

4   The right conferred by 3 above will expire on: [date]

5   The Developer has the right to redefine the Commonhold Units in the following respects:

6   The right conferred by 5 above will expire on: [date]

7   The Developer has the right to complete the following works on the Commonhold and on any added or removed land:

8   The works specified in 7 above will be completed by: [date]

The extent and effect of the Development Business

9   A plan or plans of the Commonhold showing the effect and extent of the Development Business is/are attached to this Statement.

The Developer's rights to market the Commonhold Units

10   The Developer has the right to carry out the following transactions in Commonhold Units which he owns:

11   The Developer has the right to conduct the following advertising and other activities designed to promote transactions in the Commonhold Units:

The Developer's rights to appoint and remove directors of the Commonhold Association

12   The Developer has the right to appoint and remove directors in accordance with the articles of association of the Commonhold Association.

PART IV: THE RULES OF THE COMMONHOLD ASSOCIATION

References to the 'Rules' are to these rules of the Commonhold Association.

Rules or parts of Rules shown in italics are optional and are provided by way of illustration only.

INDEX TO THE RULES

SECTION A: GENERAL

Effect of the Memorandum and Articles and the Rules

1 The Memorandum and Articles shall be binding on the members of the Commonhold Association and upon the Commonhold Association in accordance with the provisions thereof and of section 14 of the Companies Act 1985.

2 These Rules shall be binding on the Commonhold Association and upon all Unit-holders holding Commonhold Units in the Commonhold ('Unit-holders'). The Commonhold Association and all Unit-holders undertake to do, or to refrain from doing, all such things as are necessary to give effect to these Rules.

Amendment of the Rules

3 These Rules may only be amended in accordance with sections 23, 24, 30 and 33 of the Act and regulations made thereunder (as applicable).

Non-discrimination

4   Subject to any applicable law, and except as specifically permitted or required by these Rules, the Commonhold Association shall not discriminate in its application of these Rules or in its treatment of any Unit-holder on the grounds of sex, race or physical or mental capacity.

SECTION B: DEALINGS WITH COMMONHOLD UNITS AND THE COMMON PARTS

Transfer of Commonhold Units

5   The Commonhold Association shall not prevent or restrict the transfer of a Commonhold Unit.

6   On transfer of a Commonhold Unit the new Unit-holder shall notify the Commonhold Association of the transfer in the form and manner, and within the time prescribed by regulations made under section 15(4) of the Act.

7   Subject to and in accordance with section 16 of the Act, upon transfer of a Commonhold Unit, the new Unit-holder shall become subject to the Rules.

Leases of Commonhold Units

8   A Unit-holder of a Commonhold Unit designated as a residential unit in Part II above may only create a term of years absolute in his Commonhold Unit in accordance with such regulations as may be prescribed from time to time under sections 17 and 19 of the Act.

9   A Unit-holder of a Commonhold Unit which is not designated as a residential unit in Part II above may only create a term of years absolute in his Commonhold Unit in accordance with such regulations as may be prescribed from time to time under section 19 of the Act.

10   To the extent provided by the Act and by such regulations, and with such minor modifications as the context requires, references in this Statement to a 'Unit-holder' shall be construed as applying also to a tenant of a Commonhold Unit.

Other transactions relating to Commonhold Units

11   Subject to Rules 8 and 9 above, a Unit-holder may only create, grant or transfer an interest in the whole or part of his Commonhold Unit, or create a charge over his Commonhold Unit in accordance with sections

20, 21 and 22 [?] of the Act and such regulations as may be prescribed from time to time under sections 21 and 22. [?]

12 To the extent provided by the Act and by such regulations and with such minor modifications as the context requires, references in this Statement to a 'Unit-holder' shall be construed as applying also to the holder of such interest or charge in a Commonhold Unit.

Licences etc of Commonhold Units

13 A Unit-holder may only create or grant any licence or other right over, or part with possession of, his Commonhold Unit or any part thereof, with the prior written consent of the board of directors of the Commonhold Association (the 'Board of Directors') and subject to such terms and conditions as the Board of Directors may specify.

14 To the extent provided by such terms and conditions and with such minor modifications as the context requires, references in this Statement to a 'Unit-holder' shall be construed as applying also to a licensee, grantee or occupier of a Commonhold Unit.

Mortgages of the Common Parts

15 Save that the Commonhold Association may create a legal mortgage over the Common Parts in accordance with section 29 of the Act, the Commonhold Association may not create a charge over the Common Parts.

SECTION C: USE OF THE COMMONHOLD

Use of residential units

16 *The Commonhold Units designated as residential units in Part II above ('residential units') shall be used only for residential purposes, or for residential purposes and other incidental purposes.*[2]

17 *A garage included in a residential unit shall only be used as a private garage.*

18 *A parking space included in a residential unit shall only be used for parking vehicles and shall be for the exclusive use of the Unit-holder of that unit and his invitees.*

General restriction on the use of Commonhold Units

19 No Commonhold Unit may be used for any illegal or immoral purpose.

---

[2] This Rule must be included if the Commonhold has any residential units.

Use of Common Parts

20   Subject to any applicable Rules, the Common Parts may be used by all Unit-holders (including any Unit-holder who has created or granted a lease, licence or other right in or over their Commonhold Unit or parted with possession of the same in accordance with these Rules) and their invitees.

Limited Use Areas

21   *The areas of the Common Parts which are specified as Limited Use Areas in Part II of this Statement may only be used by the classes of persons set out therein and for the kind of use specified therein.*

SECTION D: INSURANCE, REPAIR AND MAINTENANCE

Insurance

22   *Every Unit-holder shall take out and maintain buildings and contents insurance, including public liability insurance, in respect of his Commonhold Unit in a form satisfactory to the Board of Directors. Any buildings insurance which is in a form satisfactory to the mortgagee of a Commonhold Unit shall be deemed to be in a form satisfactory to the Board of Directors.*[3]

OR

Every Unit-holder shall take out and maintain contents insurance, including public liability insurance, in respect of his Commonhold Unit in a form satisfactory to the Board of Directors. The Commonhold Association shall take out and maintain buildings insurance, including public liability insurance, in respect of the Commonhold Units.[4]

23   If default is made by any Unit-holder in effecting the insurance required by these Rules, the Commonhold Association shall be entitled to arrange and effect such insurance as the Board of Directors shall consider appropriate in respect of the Commonhold Unit.

24   The Commonhold Association shall take out and maintain appropriate insurance, including public liability insurance, in respect of the Common Parts.

---

[3]   This option must be used for commonholds which are not, or which do not include, blocks of flats.

[4]   This option must be used for commonholds which are, or which include, blocks of flats.

Repair and Maintenance of the Commonhold Units

25   Each Unit-holder shall be responsible for the repair and maintenance of the interior of his Commonhold Unit. *The Commonhold Association shall be responsible for the repair and maintenance of the exterior of the Commonhold Units.*[5]

26   If default is made by any Unit-holder in repairing or maintaining his Commonhold Unit as required by these Rules, the Commonhold Association shall be entitled to effect such repairs or maintenance as the Board of Directors shall consider appropriate in respect of the Commonhold Unit and for that purpose shall be entitled to use and enforce rights of access to the Commonhold Unit in accordance with Rule 46 below.

Alterations

27   Any alterations to the structure or external appearance of a Commonhold Unit may only be made with the written consent of the Board of Directors, and subject to the provisions of sections 23 and 24 of the Act (if applicable).

Prohibited works

28   No Unit-holder shall do or cause to be done any of the following works in or upon his Commonhold Unit, namely [specify].

Repair and Maintenance of the Common Parts

29   The Commonhold Association shall be responsible for the repair and maintenance of the Common Parts in accordance with such specifications and standards as may be set by the Board of Directors and published to Unit-holders from time to time.

SECTION E: THE COMMONHOLD ASSESSMENT AND OTHER FINANCIAL MATTERS

Commonhold Assessment

30   At least once a year, and at any other time as they may think necessary or appropriate, the Board of Directors shall prepare an estimate of the income required by the Commonhold Association to meet its expenses (including the remuneration, if any, of the directors). The amount so determined shall be allocated among the Commonhold Units in

---

[5]   The words in italics are recommended in the case of commonholds which are, or which include, blocks of flats.

accordance with the relevant percentages for the units as set out in Part II above.

Reserve study

31   At least every [ten][6] years, and at any other time as they may think necessary or appropriate, the Board of Directors shall prepare, on the basis of an inspection and with the assistance of such surveyors, engineers or other professional advisers as may be appropriate, a written study listing all of the major assets, equipment, fixtures or fittings which the Commonhold Association owns or maintains with a remaining life of less than [number] years (a 'reserve study'). The reserve study must estimate in the case of each such item, (i) the remaining life of the item, (ii) the costs of maintaining and replacing the item, and (iii) the annual contribution required to maintain such costs.

Reserve funds and levies

32   The Board of Directors may from time to time, and having regard to any relevant reserve study, resolve to establish and maintain reserve funds in accordance with, and for the purposes specified in, section 39 of the Act.

33   For the purpose of obtaining the necessary monies for such reserve funds, the Board of Directors may from time to time set levies which shall be allocated among the Commonhold Units in accordance with the relevant percentages for the units as set out in Part II above.

Notices and payment of commonhold assessment and levies

34   Within 28 days after any amounts have been determined and allocated among Commonhold Units as aforesaid, the Board of Directors shall serve notices on each Unit-holder specifying the payment required to be made by him. The notice shall specify the date upon which payment is due and may, if the Board of Directors think fit, give the Unit-holder the option of paying the specified sum in instalments in such amounts and on such dates as shall be specified. Except where earlier payment by Unit-holders is necessary to enable the Commonhold Association to pay its debts as and when they fall due, the notice shall not specify a date for payment of any sum which is less than 28 days after service of the notice.

35   Upon receipt of any such notice, the Unit-holders shall pay the amount(s) specified therein by the date(s) specified therein.

---

[6]   Note for peers and working group. Members of the commonhold working group commented that undertaking a reserve study every 5 years may be too onerous a task for the Board of Directors. We invite suggestions on the appropriate period between reserve studies and the life-span of assets to be listed in the reserve study.

Annual report and budget

36   In addition to, and at the same time as circulating or laying before the
      members of the Commonhold Association in general meeting its annual
      accounts and its directors' report as required by the Companies Act 1985,
      the Board of Directors shall also circulate or lay before the members a
      written report comparing the results of the Commonhold Association
      against its estimated budget for the year and setting out an estimated
      budget for the forthcoming year.

SECTION F: COMPLAINTS PROCEDURE, DEFAULT PROCEDURES
AND ENFORCEMENT

37   Subject to section 35 of the Act, in the event of any breach (including any
      alleged, suspected or threatened breach) of the Articles or these Rules,
      Rule 40 below sets out a procedure to be followed by Unit-holders (the
      'Complaints Procedure') and Rules 41–45 below set out a procedure to
      be followed by the Commonhold Association (the 'Default Procedure').

38   Subject to Rule 39 below:

      (a)   the Complaints Procedure must be followed prior to the Unit-
             holder (i) taking any legal proceedings against another Unit-holder
             or the Commonhold Association, or (ii) referring any matter to an
             ombudsman appointed pursuant to section 42 of the Act (an
             'Ombudsman'); and
      (b)   the Default Procedure must be followed prior to the Commonhold
             Association (i) exercising any of the rights given under Rules 23 or
             26 above, (ii) serving any indemnity notice under Rule 49 below, (iii)
             taking any legal proceedings against a Unit-holder, or (iv) referring
             any matter to an Ombudsman.

39   A Unit-holder shall be entitled to depart from the Complaints Procedure
      in whole or in part, and the Commonhold Association shall be entitled to
      depart from the Default Procedure in whole or in part, in any case in
      which the urgency of the matter or other special circumstances make it
      unreasonable for the Complaints Procedure or the Default Procedure to
      be implemented in accordance with their terms.

Complaints Procedure

40   Any Unit-holder having grounds for complaint in relation to any breach
      (including any alleged, suspected or threatened breach) of the Articles or
      the Rules and being unable to achieve a resolution of his complaint by
      agreement with the other party or parties concerned, shall notify the

Board of Directors of his complaint in writing and provide them with all necessary information as they may reasonably require to enable them to take appropriate steps in an effort to resolve the matter in accordance with their duties under section 35 of the Act and under the Default Procedure.

Default Procedure

41 If the Board of Directors have reason to believe that any person (the 'alleged defaulter') has breached, is breaching, or may breach any of the Articles or these Rules, they shall first attempt to resolve the matter by informal means.

42 If the Board of Directors are unable to resolve the matter by informal means, they shall serve upon the alleged defaulter a notice in writing (a 'default notice') before taking any other action in respect thereof.

43 The default notice shall specify the alleged breach or anticipated breach of the Articles or these Rules in sufficient detail to enable the alleged defaulter to understand how it is contended that the Articles or Rules have been, are being or might be breached.

44 The default notice shall specify a reasonable period within which the alleged defaulter (i) must cease and/or remedy the breach, or (ii) give assurances satisfactory to the Board of Directors that a breach will not occur, or (iii) show that there is no breach or anticipated breach as specified in the default notice.

45 The default notice shall contain a prominent warning that in the event that the alleged defaulter does not comply with the default notice within the required period, the Commonhold Association may take action without any further notice to him, including exercising its rights under Rules 23 or 26, serving an indemnity notice under Rule 49, referring the dispute to an Ombudsman, or taking legal proceedings, and that any such action may result in orders being made against the alleged defaulter for compensation, costs and interest.

Rights of Access to Commonhold Units

46 In addition to any other rights of access which may exist or be enforceable at law, every Unit-holder hereby grants to the Commonhold Association, acting by its officers or other duly appointed agents for the purpose,

(a) the right to enter upon his Commonhold Unit in the event of emergency or risk of harm, whether by fire, flood, escape of noxious substances, electricity or otherwise, to the Commonhold or to the health or well-being of any person upon the Commonhold or in adjoining premises; and

(b)   the right to enter upon his Commonhold Unit to carry out any repairs or maintenance in accordance with Rule 26 above, provided that such right of access shall only be enforceable with the consent of the Unit-holder, or pursuant to the order of a court of competent jurisdiction.

Enforcement of Rules relating to the parking of vehicles

47   *Without prejudice to its other rights to ensure compliance with the Rules, the Commonhold Association may take such lawful steps as are necessary to enforce any Rules relating to the parking of vehicles on any part of the Commonhold, including arranging for the immobilisation or removal of vehicles parked in contravention of the Rules.*

Indemnity

48   Without prejudice to any other remedy to which the Commonhold Association or any other Unit-holder may be entitled, any Unit-holder who is in breach of any provision of the Articles or the Rules or any statutory requirement (the 'defaulter') shall indemnify and hold harmless the Commonhold Association and any other Unit-holder against any costs arising from such breach, including, if appropriate, the costs of remedying the breach or of acting in the stead of the defaulter as permitted by the Rules.

49   If the Board of Directors are of the opinion that the Commonhold Association or any Unit-holder has incurred any costs arising from such breach as aforesaid which the defaulter ought to pay, they shall serve a notice (an 'indemnity notice') on the defaulter requiring him to pay the amount of such costs to the Commonhold Association or to the other Unit-holder within a specified period being not less than 14 days.

50   Upon receipt of such notice, the defaulter shall have 14 days within which to pay the amount specified in the notice, or serve a notice upon the Commonhold Association disputing his liability to pay and/or the amount specified in the notice. If any such dispute cannot be resolved by agreement within 28 days, either the Commonhold Association or the defaulter may refer the dispute to an Ombudsman.

51   Subject to any judgment or award by a court of competent jurisdiction or by an Ombudsman to the contrary, interest shall be payable upon any amounts due or found to be due and not paid by the date specified in the

indemnity notice at the rate specified for the time being in regulations made under section 37 of the Act.

SECTION G: MEETINGS, ACCESS TO DOCUMENTS *AND COMMITTEES*

Meetings of the Commonhold Association

52   All meetings of the Commonhold Association shall be held on the Commonhold or at such other suitable place as is nearby and reasonably accessible to all members.

Maintenance and inspection of books and records etc

53   The Commonhold Association must retain and make available for inspection at its registered office a copy of the original and any amended versions of the Commonhold Community Statement, together with a list of the date(s) upon which such documents were registered.

54   All Unit-holders shall be entitled to and shall be given the same rights of access to, and inspection of the books, documents and accounting records of the Commonhold Association as members of the Commonhold Association.

Committees

55   *The Commonhold Association shall have the following committees established pursuant to the Articles and for the purposes specified below, together with such other functions and subject to such other powers and restrictions as may be placed upon them from time to time by the Board of Directors. Such committees shall report to, and be subject at all times to control and supervision by, the Board of Directors. The members of such committees shall be elected by the members of the Commonhold Association at the annual general meeting in each year to serve until the conclusion of the next annual general meeting. The committees are:*

(a)   *the executive committee, consisting of [number] members, and having [specify functions];*

(b)   *the finance committee, consisting of [number] members, and having [specify functions];*

(c)   *the buildings committee, consisting of [number] members, and having [specify functions];*

(d)   *the residents' committee, consisting of [number] members who shall be Unit-holders of residential units in the Commonhold and having [specify functions];*

(e)   the commercial committee, consisting of [number] members who shall be Unit-
       holders of non-residential units in the Commonhold, and having [specify
       functions].

SECTION H: MISCELLANEOUS RULES

Access

56   No Unit-holder or his invitees shall do any thing or leave or permit to be
      left any goods, rubbish or other object which obstructs or hinders lawful
      access to any part of the Commonhold.

Aerials and satellite dishes

*57   No Unit-holder or his invitees shall erect or permit to project outside his Commonhold
      Unit or into the Common Parts any radio or television aerial or satellite dish.*

Behaviour

58   A Unit-holder must not, and must take reasonable steps to ensure that
      his invitees do not, behave in any way or create any sound or noise which
      causes or is likely to cause any annoyance, nuisance, injury or disturbance
      to other Unit-holders, or to any other person lawfully on the
      Commonhold, or to the occupiers of adjoining buildings or premises.

Cleaning of Common Parts, exterior and windows

59   The Commonhold Association shall be responsible for the regular
      cleaning of the Common Parts *and the exterior of the Commonhold, including
      windows.*

Cleaning of Commonhold Units

60   Each Unit-holder shall be responsible for the regular cleaning of his
      Commonhold Unit, *including the exterior and windows thereof.*

Drainage and water pipes

61   Every Unit-holder shall take adequate steps to prevent the leakage of
      pipes or escape of water from his Commonhold Unit, including lagging
      all pipes and tanks against freezing.

Hanging of clothes

62   Save in the areas specifically made available for the same by the
      Commonhold Association, no Unit-holder or his invitees may hang or
      expose any clothes or other articles outside his Commonhold Unit or in
      the Common Parts.

Hazardous materials

63   A Unit-holder or his invitees may not, without the written consent of the Board of Directors, bring onto the Commonhold or store in any part thereof, any flammable, hazardous or noxious substance. This does not apply to the storage of fuel in the fuel tank of a vehicle or in a small reserve tank for use in connection with the vehicle.

Mechanical, scientific or electrical items

64   Except with the written consent of the Board of Directors, no Unit-holder of a residential unit or his invitees shall have or install in his Commonhold Unit any mechanical, scientific or electrical apparatus other than ordinary domestic appliances.

Notices

65   Any notice to be given to or by any person pursuant to these Rules shall be in writing. The Commonhold Association may give any notice to a Unit-holder either personally or by sending it by first class post in a prepaid envelope addressed to the Unit-holder at his Commonhold Unit or by leaving it at that address. Proof that an envelope containing a notice was properly addressed, prepaid and posted by first class post shall be conclusive evidence that the notice was given. A notice sent by first class post shall be deemed to be given at the expiration of 48 hours after the envelope containing it was posted.

Pets

66   No animals may be kept or brought onto the Commonhold without the written consent of the Board of Directors.

Signs

67   No Unit-holder or his invitees shall post or permit to be posted any notice or sign in the Common Parts, except upon any notice-board or other facility provided for the same by the Commonhold Association.

Smoke detectors

68   Each Unit-holder shall install in his Commonhold Unit and maintain in working order a smoke detector or smoke detection system of a type specified by the Board of Directors and complying with any applicable health and safety or building regulations.

69   The Commonhold Association shall install in the Common Parts and maintain in working order a smoke detector or smoke detection system of a type complying with any applicable health and safety or building regulations.

Window boxes

70   No flower pot or other like object shall be placed outside the Commonhold Units or in the Common Parts except where provided by or with the written consent of the Commonhold Association.

PART V: ADDITIONAL INFORMATION

This section should include any additional information concerning the Commonhold.

Any special or unusual features or facilities which are to be found in or provided as part of the Commonhold, the Commonhold Units or the Common Parts may be mentioned here.

PART VI: EXECUTION AND AMENDMENT OF THIS STATEMENT

This Statement is signed by or on behalf of the Applicant for Registration by

          Name

          Address

          Name[7]

          Address

on _____ 2_____

This Statement has been amended as set out below.

Amendment number	Date of resolution amending the Statement
1	
2	
3	
4	
5	

---

[7] If a body corporate, the Statement should be signed by two officers.

APPENDIX 3

EXTRACTS FROM THE COMMONHOLD AND LEASEHOLD REFORM ACT 2002

2002 c 15

PART 1
COMMONHOLD

Nature of commonhold

1 Commonhold land

(1) Land is commonhold land if—

    (a)   the freehold estate in the land is registered as a freehold estate in commonhold land,

    (b)   the land is specified in the memorandum of association of a commonhold association as the land in relation to which the association is to exercise functions, and

    (c)   a commonhold community statement makes provision for rights and duties of the commonhold association and unit-holders (whether or not the statement has come into force).

(2) In this Part a reference to a commonhold is a reference to land in relation to which a commonhold association exercises functions.

(3) In this Part—

    'commonhold association' has the meaning given by section 34,
    'commonhold community statement' has the meaning given by section 31,
    'commonhold unit' has the meaning given by section 11,
    'common parts' has the meaning given by section 25, and
    'unit-holder' has the meaning given by sections 12 and 13.

(4) Sections 7 and 9 make provision for the vesting in the commonhold association of the fee simple in possession in the common parts of a commonhold.

Registration

2 Application

(1) The Registrar shall register a freehold estate in land as a freehold estate in commonhold land if—

(a)   the registered freeholder of the land makes an application under this section, and

(b)   no part of the land is already commonhold land.

(2)   An application under this section must be accompanied by the documents listed in Schedule 1.

(3)   A person is the registered freeholder of land for the purposes of this Part if—

(a)   he is registered as the proprietor of a freehold estate in the land with absolute title, or

(b)   he has applied, and the Registrar is satisfied that he is entitled, to be registered as mentioned in paragraph (a).

3   Consent

(1)   An application under section 2 may not be made in respect of a freehold estate in land without the consent of anyone who—

(a)   is the registered proprietor of the freehold estate in the whole or part of the land,

(b)   is the registered proprietor of a leasehold estate in the whole or part of the land granted for a term of more than than 21 years,

(c)   is the registered proprietor of a charge over the whole or part of the land, or

(d)   falls within any other class of person which may be prescribed.

(2)   Regulations shall make provision about consent for the purposes of this section; in particular, the regulations may make provision—

(a)   prescribing the form of consent;

(b)   about the effect and duration of consent (including provision for consent to bind successors);

(c)   about withdrawal of consent (including provision preventing withdrawal in specified circumstances);

(d)   for consent given for the purpose of one application under section 2 to have effect for the purpose of another application;

(e)   for consent to be deemed to have been given in specified circumstances;

(f)   enabling a court to dispense with a requirement for consent in specified circumstances.

(3)   An order under subsection (2)(f) dispensing with a requirement for consent—

(a)   may be absolute or conditional, and

(b)   may make such other provision as the court thinks appropriate.

4   Land which may not be commonhold

Schedule 2 (which provides that an application under section 2 may not relate wholly or partly to land of certain kinds) shall have effect.

5   Registered details

(1)   The Registrar shall ensure that in respect of any commonhold land the following are kept in his custody and referred to in the register—

    (a)   the prescribed details of the commonhold association;

    (b)   the prescribed details of the registered freeholder of each commonhold unit;

    (c)   a copy of the commonhold community statement;

    (d)   a copy of the memorandum and articles of association of the commonhold association.

(2)   The Registrar may arrange for a document or information to be kept in his custody and referred to in the register in respect of commonhold land if the document or information—

    (a)   is not mentioned in subsection (1), but

    (b)   is submitted to the Registrar in accordance with a provision made by or by virtue of this Part.

(3)   Subsection (1)(b) shall not apply during a transitional period within the meaning of section 8.

6   Registration in error

(1)   This section applies where a freehold estate in land is registered as a freehold estate in commonhold land and—

    (a)   the application for registration was not made in accordance with section 2,

    (b)   the certificate under paragraph 7 of Schedule 1 was inaccurate, or

    (c)   the registration contravened a provision made by or by virtue of this Part.

(2)   The register may not be altered by the Registrar under Schedule 4 to the Land Registration Act 2002 (alteration of register).

(3)   The court may grant a declaration that the freehold estate should not have been registered as a freehold estate in commonhold land.

(4)   A declaration under subsection (3) may be granted only on the application of a person who claims to be adversely affected by the registration.

(5)   On granting a declaration under subsection (3) the court may make any order which appears to it to be appropriate.

(6)   An order under subsection (5) may, in particular—

    (a)   provide for the registration to be treated as valid for all purposes;

    (b)   provide for alteration of the register;

    (c)   provide for land to cease to be commonhold land;

    (d)   require a director or other specified officer of a commonhold association to take steps to alter or amend a document;

    (e)   require a director or other specified officer of a commonhold association to take specified steps;

(f)   make an award of compensation (whether or not contingent upon the occurrence or non-occurrence of a specified event) to be paid by one specified person to another;

(g)   apply, disapply or modify a provision of Schedule 8 to the Land Registration Act 2002 (indemnity).

Effect of registration

7   Registration without unit-holders

(1)   This section applies where—

(a)   a freehold estate in land is registered as a freehold estate in commonhold land in pursuance of an application under section 2, and

(b)   the application is not accompanied by a statement under section 9(1)(b).

(2)   On registration—

(a)   the applicant shall continue to be registered as the proprietor of the freehold estate in the commonhold land, and

(b)   the rights and duties conferred and imposed by the commonhold community statement shall not come into force (subject to section 8(2)(b)).

(3)   Where after registration a person other than the applicant becomes entitled to be registered as the proprietor of the freehold estate in one or more, but not all, of the commonhold units—

(a)   the commonhold association shall be entitled to be registered as the proprietor of the freehold estate in the common parts,

(b)   the Registrar shall register the commonhold association in accordance with paragraph (a) (without an application being made),

(c)   the rights and duties conferred and imposed by the commonhold community statement shall come into force, and

(d)   any lease of the whole or part of the commonhold land shall be extinguished by virtue of this section.

(4)   For the purpose of subsection (3)(d) 'lease' means a lease which—

(a)   is granted for any term, and

(b)   is granted before the commonhold association becomes entitled to be registered as the proprietor of the freehold estate in the common parts.

8   Transitional period

(1)   In this Part 'transitional period' means the period between registration of the freehold estate in land as a freehold estate in commonhold land and the event mentioned in section 7(3).

(2)   Regulations may provide that during a transitional period a relevant provision—

(a)   shall not have effect, or

(b)   shall have effect with specified modifications.

(3)   In subsection (2) 'relevant provision' means a provision made—

(a)   by or by virtue of this Part,

(b)   by a commonhold community statement, or

(c)   by the memorandum or articles of the commonhold association.

(4)   The Registrar shall arrange for the freehold estate in land to cease to be registered as a freehold estate in commonhold land if the registered proprietor makes an application to the Registrar under this subsection during the transitional period.

(5)   The provisions about consent made by or under sections 2 and 3 and Schedule 1 shall apply in relation to an application under subsection (4) as they apply in relation to an application under section 2.

(6)   A reference in this Part to a commonhold association exercising functions in relation to commonhold land includes a reference to a case where a commonhold association would exercise functions in relation to commonhold land but for the fact that the time in question falls in a transitional period.

9   Registration with unit-holders

(1)   This section applies in relation to a freehold estate in commonhold land if—

(a)   it is registered as a freehold estate in commonhold land in pursuance of an application under section 2, and

(b)   the application is accompanied by a statement by the applicant requesting that this section should apply.

(2)   A statement under subsection (1)(b) must include a list of the commonhold units giving in relation to each one the prescribed details of the proposed initial unit-holder or joint unit-holders.

(3)   On registration—

(a)   the commonhold association shall be entitled to be registered as the proprietor of the freehold estate in the common parts,

(b)   a person specified by virtue of subsection (2) as the initial unit-holder of a commonhold unit shall be entitled to be registered as the proprietor of the freehold estate in the unit,

(c)   a person specified by virtue of subsection (2) as an initial joint unit-holder of a commonhold unit shall be entitled to be registered as one of the proprietors of the freehold estate in the unit,

(d)   the Registrar shall make entries in the register to reflect paragraphs (a) to (c) (without applications being made),

(e)   the rights and duties conferred and imposed by the commonhold community statement shall come into force, and

(f)   any lease of the whole or part of the commonhold land shall be extinguished by virtue of this section.

(4)   For the purpose of subsection (3)(f) 'lease' means a lease which—

(a)   is granted for any term, and

(b)   is granted before the commonhold association becomes entitled to be registered as the proprietor of the freehold estate in the common parts.

10 Extinguished lease: liability

(1) This section applies where—

    (a)   a lease is extinguished by virtue of section 7(3)(d) or 9(3)(f), and

    (b)   the consent of the holder of that lease was not among the consents required by section 3 in respect of the application under section 2 for the land to become commonhold land.

(2) If the holder of a lease superior to the extinguished lease gave consent under section 3, he shall be liable for loss suffered by the holder of the extinguished lease.

(3) If the holders of a number of leases would be liable under subsection (2), liability shall attach only to the person whose lease was most proximate to the extinguished lease.

(4) If no person is liable under subsection (2), the person who gave consent under section 3 as the holder of the freehold estate out of which the extinguished lease was granted shall be liable for loss suffered by the holder of the extinguished lease.

Commonhold unit

11 Definition

(1) In this Part 'commonhold unit' means a commonhold unit specified in a commonhold community statement in accordance with this section.

(2) A commonhold community statement must—

    (a)   specify at least two parcels of land as commonhold units, and

    (b)   define the extent of each commonhold unit.

(3) In defining the extent of a commonhold unit a commonhold community statement—

    (a)   must refer to a plan which is included in the statement and which complies with prescribed requirements,

    (b)   may refer to an area subject to the exclusion of specified structures, fittings, apparatus or appurtenances within the area,

    (c)   may exclude the structures which delineate an area referred to, and

    (d)   may refer to two or more areas (whether or not contiguous).

(4) A commonhold unit need not contain all or any part of a building.

12 Unit-holder

A person is the unit-holder of a commonhold unit if he is entitled to be registered as the proprietor of the freehold estate in the unit (whether or not he is registered).

13 Joint unit-holders

(1) Two or more persons are joint unit-holders of a commonhold unit if they are entitled to be registered as proprietors of the freehold estate in the unit (whether or not they are registered).

(2)   In the application of the following provisions to a unit with joint unit-holders a reference to a unit-holder is a reference to the joint unit-holders together—

    (a)   section 14(3),
    (b)   section 15(1) and (3),
    (c)   section 19(2) and (3),
    (d)   section 20(1),
    (e)   section 23(1),
    (f)   section 35(1)(b),
    (g)   section 38(1),
    (h)   section 39(2), and
    (i)   section 47(2).

(3)   In the application of the following provisions to a unit with joint unit-holders a reference to a unit-holder includes a reference to each joint unit-holder and to the joint unit-holders together—

    (a)   section 1(1)(c),
    (b)   section 16,
    (c)   section 31(1)(b), (3)(b), (5)(j) and (7),
    (d)   section 32(4)(a) and (c),
    (e)   section 35(1)(a), (2) and (3),
    (f)   section 37(2),
    (g)   section 40(1), and
    (h)   section 58(3)(a).

(4)   Regulations under this Part which refer to a unit-holder shall make provision for the construction of the reference in the case of joint unit-holders.

(5)   Regulations may amend subsection (2) or (3).

(6)   Regulations may make provision for the construction in the case of joint unit-holders of a reference to a unit-holder in—

    (a)   an enactment,
    (b)   a commonhold community statement,
    (c)   the memorandum or articles of association of a commonhold association, or
    (d)   another document.

14   Use and maintenance

(1)   A commonhold community statement must make provision regulating the use of commonhold units.

(2)   A commonhold community statement must make provision imposing duties in respect of the insurance, repair and maintenance of each commonhold unit.

(3)   A duty under subsection (2) may be imposed on the commonhold association or the unit-holder.

15   Transfer

(1)   In this Part a reference to the transfer of a commonhold unit is a reference to the transfer of a unit-holder's freehold estate in a unit to another person—

(a)   whether or not for consideration,

(b)   whether or not subject to any reservation or other terms, and

(c)   whether or not by operation of law.

(2)   A commonhold community statement may not prevent or restrict the transfer of a commonhold unit.

(3)   On the transfer of a commonhold unit the new unit-holder shall notify the commonhold association of the transfer.

(4)   Regulations may—

(a)   prescribe the form and manner of notice under subsection (3);

(b)   prescribe the time within which notice is to be given;

(c)   make provision (including provision requiring the payment of money) about the effect of failure to give notice.

16   Transfer: effect

(1)   A right or duty conferred or imposed—

(a)   by a commonhold community statement, or

(b)   in accordance with section 20,

shall affect a new unit-holder in the same way as it affected the former unit-holder.

(2)   A former unit-holder shall not incur a liability or acquire a right—

(a)   under or by virtue of the commonhold community statement, or

(b)   by virtue of anything done in accordance with section 20.

(3)   Subsection (2)—

(a)   shall not be capable of being disapplied or varied by agreement, and

(b)   is without prejudice to any liability or right incurred or acquired before a transfer takes effect.

(4)   In this section—

'former unit-holder' means a person from whom a commonhold unit has been transferred (whether or not he has ceased to be the registered proprietor), and

'new unit-holder' means a person to whom a commonhold unit is transferred (whether or not he has yet become the registered proprietor).

17   Leasing: residential

(1)   It shall not be possible to create a term of years absolute in a residential commonhold unit unless the term satisfies prescribed conditions.

(2)   The conditions may relate to—

(a)   length;

(b)   the circumstances in which the term is granted;

(c)   any other matter.

(3)   Subject to subsection (4), an instrument or agreement shall be of no effect to the extent that it purports to create a term of years in contravention of subsection (1).

(4)   Where an instrument or agreement purports to create a term of years in contravention of subsection (1) a party to the instrument or agreement may apply to the court for an order—

(a)   providing for the instrument or agreement to have effect as if it provided for the creation of a term of years of a specified kind;

(b)   providing for the return or payment of money;

(c)   making such other provision as the court thinks appropriate.

(5)   A commonhold unit is residential if provision made in the commonhold community statement by virtue of section 14(1) requires it to be used only—

(a)   for residential purposes, or

(b)   for residential and other incidental purposes.

18   Leasing: non-residential

An instrument or agreement which creates a term of years absolute in a commonhold unit which is not residential (within the meaning of section 17) shall have effect subject to any provision of the commonhold community statement.

19   Leasing: supplementary

(1)   Regulations may—

(a)   impose obligations on a tenant of a commonhold unit;

(b)   enable a commonhold community statement to impose obligations on a tenant of a commonhold unit.

(2)   Regulations under subsection (1) may, in particular, require a tenant of a commonhold unit to make payments to the commonhold association or a unit-holder in discharge of payments which—

(a)   are due in accordance with the commonhold community statement to be made by the unit-holder, or

(b)   are due in accordance with the commonhold community statement to be made by another tenant of the unit.

(3)   Regulations under subsection (1) may, in particular, provide—

(a)   for the amount of payments under subsection (2) to be set against sums owed by the tenant (whether to the person by whom the payments were due to be made or to some other person);

(b)   for the amount of payments under subsection (2) to be recovered from the unit-holder or another tenant of the unit.

(4)   Regulations may modify a rule of law about leasehold estates (whether deriving from the common law or from an enactment) in its application to a term of years in a commonhold unit.

(5)   Regulations under this section—

(a)   may make provision generally or in relation to specified circumstances, and

(b)   may make different provision for different descriptions of commonhold land or commonhold unit.

20   Other transactions

(1)   A commonhold community statement may not prevent or restrict the creation, grant or transfer by a unit-holder of—

    (a)   an interest in the whole or part of his unit, or

    (b)   a charge over his unit.

(2)   Subsection (1) is subject to sections 17 to 19 (which impose restrictions about leases).

(3)   It shall not be possible to create an interest of a prescribed kind in a commonhold unit unless the commonhold association—

    (a)   is a party to the creation of the interest, or

    (b)   consents in writing to the creation of the interest.

(4)   A commonhold association may act as described in subsection (3)(a) or (b) only if—

    (a)   the association passes a resolution to take the action, and

    (b)   at least 75 per cent of those who vote on the resolution vote in favour.

(5)   An instrument or agreement shall be of no effect to the extent that it purports to create an interest in contravention of subsection (3).

(6)   In this section 'interest' does not include—

    (a)   a charge, or

    (b)   an interest which arises by virtue of a charge.

21   Part-unit: interests

(1)   It shall not be possible to create an interest in part only of a commonhold unit.

(2)   But subsection (1) shall not prevent—

    (a)   the creation of a term of years absolute in part only of a residential commonhold unit where the term satisfies prescribed conditions,

    (b)   the creation of a term of years absolute in part only of a non-residential commonhold unit, or

    (c)   the transfer of the freehold estate in part only of a commonhold unit where the commonhold association consents in writing to the transfer.

(3)   An instrument or agreement shall be of no effect to the extent that it purports to create an interest in contravention of subsection (1).

(4)   Subsection (5) applies where—

    (a)   land becomes commonhold land or is added to a commonhold unit, and

    (b)   immediately before that event there is an interest in the land which could not be created after that event by reason of subsection (1).

(5)   The interest shall be extinguished by virtue of this subsection to the extent that it could not be created by reason of subsection (1).

(6)   Section 17(2) and (4) shall apply (with any necessary modifications) in relation to subsection (2)(a) and (b) above.

(7)   Where part only of a unit is held under a lease, regulations may modify the application of a provision which—

    (a)   is made by or by virtue of this Part, and

    (b)   applies to a unit-holder or a tenant or both.

(8)   Section 20(4) shall apply in relation to subsection (2)(c) above.

(9)   Where the freehold interest in part only of a commonhold unit is transferred, the part transferred—

    (a)   becomes a new commonhold unit by virtue of this subsection, or

    (b)   in a case where the request for consent under subsection (2)(c) states that this paragraph is to apply, becomes part of a commonhold unit specified in the request.

(10)   Regulations may make provision, or may require a commonhold community statement to make provision, about—

    (a)   registration of units created by virtue of subsection (9);

    (b)   the adaptation of provision made by or by virtue of this Part or by or by virtue of a commonhold community statement to a case where units are created or modified by virtue of subsection (9).

22   Part-unit: charging

(1)   It shall not be possible to create a charge over part only of an interest in a commonhold unit.

(2)   An instrument or agreement shall be of no effect to the extent that it purports to create a charge in contravention of subsection (1).

(3)   Subsection (4) applies where—

    (a)   land becomes commonhold land or is added to a commonhold unit, and

    (b)   immediately before that event there is a charge over the land which could not be created after that event by reason of subsection (1).

(4)   The charge shall be extinguished by virtue of this subsection to the extent that it could not be created by reason of subsection (1).

23   Changing size

(1)   An amendment of a commonhold community statement which redefines the extent of a commonhold unit may not be made unless the unit-holder consents—

    (a)   in writing, and

    (b)   before the amendment is made.

(2)   But regulations may enable a court to dispense with the requirement for consent on the application of a commonhold association in prescribed circumstances.

24   Changing size: charged unit

(1)   This section applies to an amendment of a commonhold community statement which redefines the extent of a commonhold unit over which there is a registered charge.

(2)   The amendment may not be made unless the registered proprietor of the charge consents—

  (a)   in writing, and
  (b)   before the amendment is made.

(3)   But regulations may enable a court to dispense with the requirement for consent on the application of a commonhold association in prescribed circumstances.

(4)   If the amendment removes land from the commonhold unit, the charge shall by virtue of this subsection be extinguished to the extent that it relates to the land which is removed.

(5)   If the amendment adds land to the unit, the charge shall by virtue of this subsection be extended so as to relate to the land which is added.

(6)   Regulations may make provision—

  (a)   requiring notice to be given to the Registrar in circumstances to which this section applies;
  (b)   requiring the Registrar to alter the register to reflect the application of subsection (4) or (5).

Common parts

25   Definition

(1)   In this Part 'common parts' in relation to a commonhold means every part of the commonhold which is not for the time being a commonhold unit in accordance with the commonhold community statement.

(2)   A commonhold community statement may make provision in respect of a specified part of the common parts (a 'limited use area') restricting—

  (a)   the classes of person who may use it;
  (b)   the kind of use to which it may be put.

(3)   A commonhold community statement—

  (a)   may make provision which has effect only in relation to a limited use area, and
  (b)   may make different provision for different limited use areas.

26   Use and maintenance

A commonhold community statement must make provision—

  (a)   regulating the use of the common parts;
  (b)   requiring the commonhold association to insure the common parts;
  (c)   requiring the commonhold association to repair and maintain the common parts.

27   Transactions

(1)   Nothing in a commonhold community statement shall prevent or restrict—

  (a)   the transfer by the commonhold association of its freehold estate in any part of the common parts, or

     (b)   the creation by the commonhold association of an interest in any part of the common parts.

(2)   In this section 'interest' does not include—

     (a)   a charge, or

     (b)   an interest which arises by virtue of a charge.

28   Charges: general prohibition

(1)   It shall not be possible to create a charge over common parts.

(2)   An instrument or agreement shall be of no effect to the extent that it purports to create a charge over common parts.

(3)   Where by virtue of section 7 or 9 a commonhold association is registered as the proprietor of common parts, a charge which relates wholly or partly to the common parts shall be extinguished by virtue of this subsection to the extent that it relates to the common parts.

(4)   Where by virtue of section 30 land vests in a commonhold association following an amendment to a commonhold community statement which has the effect of adding land to the common parts, a charge which relates wholly or partly to the land added shall be extinguished by virtue of this subsection to the extent that it relates to that land.

(5)   This section is subject to section 29 (which permits certain mortgages).

29   New legal mortgages

(1)   Section 28 shall not apply in relation to a legal mortgage if the creation of the mortgage is approved by a resolution of the commonhold association.

(2)   A resolution for the purposes of subsection (1) must be passed—

     (a)   before the mortgage is created, and

     (b)   unanimously.

(3)   In this section 'legal mortgage' has the meaning given by section 205(1)(xvi) of the Law of Property Act 1925 (interpretation).

30   Additions to common parts

(1)   This section applies where an amendment of a commonhold community statement—

     (a)   specifies land which forms part of a commonhold unit, and

     (b)   provides for that land (the 'added land') to be added to the common parts.

(2)   The amendment may not be made unless the registered proprietor of any charge over the added land consents—

     (a)   in writing, and

     (b)   before the amendment is made.

(3)   But regulations may enable a court to dispense with the requirement for consent on the application of a commonhold association in specified circumstances.

(4)   On the filing of the amended statement under section 33—

    (a)   the commonhold association shall be entitled to be registered as the proprietor of the freehold estate in the added land, and

    (b)   the Registrar shall register the commonhold association in accordance with paragraph (a) (without an application being made).

Commonhold community statement

31   Form and content: general

(1)   A commonhold community statement is a document which makes provision in relation to specified land for—

    (a)   the rights and duties of the commonhold association, and

    (b)   the rights and duties of the unit-holders.

(2)   A commonhold community statement must be in the prescribed form.

(3)   A commonhold community statement may—

    (a)   impose a duty on the commonhold association;

    (b)   impose a duty on a unit-holder;

    (c)   make provision about the taking of decisions in connection with the management of the commonhold or any other matter concerning it.

(4)   Subsection (3) is subject to—

    (a)   any provision made by or by virtue of this Part, and

    (b)   any provision of the memorandum or articles of the commonhold association.

(5)   In subsection (3)(a) and (b) 'duty' includes, in particular, a duty—

    (a)   to pay money;

    (b)   to undertake works;

    (c)   to grant access;

    (d)   to give notice;

    (e)   to refrain from entering into transactions of a specified kind in relation to a commonhold unit;

    (f)   to refrain from using the whole or part of a commonhold unit for a specified purpose or for anything other than a specified purpose;

    (g)   to refrain from undertaking works (including alterations) of a specified kind;

    (h)   to refrain from causing nuisance or annoyance;

    (i)   to refrain from specified behaviour;

    (j)   to indemnify the commonhold association or a unit-holder in respect of costs arising from the breach of a statutory requirement.

(6)   Provision in a commonhold community statement imposing a duty to pay money (whether in pursuance of subsection (5)(a) or any other provision made by or by virtue of this Part) may include provision for the payment of interest in the case of late payment.

(7)   A duty conferred by a commonhold community statement on a commonhold association or a unit-holder shall not require any other formality.

(8)   A commonhold community statement may not provide for the transfer or loss of an interest in land on the occurrence or non-occurrence of a specified event.

(9)   Provision made by a commonhold community statement shall be of no effect to the extent that—

  (a)   it is prohibited by virtue of section 32,
  (b)   it is inconsistent with any provision made by or by virtue of this Part,
  (c)   it is inconsistent with anything which is treated as included in the statement by virtue of section 32, or
  (d)   it is inconsistent with the memorandum or articles of association of the commonhold association.

32   Regulations

(1)   Regulations shall make provision about the content of a commonhold community statement.

(2)   The regulations may permit, require or prohibit the inclusion in a statement of—

  (a)   specified provision, or
  (b)   provision of a specified kind, for a specified purpose or about a specified matter.

(3)   The regulations may—

  (a)   provide for a statement to be treated as including provision prescribed by or determined in accordance with the regulations;
  (b)   permit a statement to make provision in place of provision which would otherwise be treated as included by virtue of paragraph (a).

(4)   The regulations may—

  (a)   make different provision for different descriptions of commonhold association or unit-holder;
  (b)   make different provision for different circumstances;
  (c)   make provision about the extent to which a commonhold community statement may make different provision for different descriptions of unit-holder or common parts.

(5)   The matters to which regulations under this section may relate include, but are not limited to—

  (a)   the matters mentioned in sections 11, 14, 15, 20, 21, 25, 26, 27, 38, 39 and 58, and
  (b)   any matter for which regulations under section 37 may make provision.

33   Amendment

(1)   Regulations under section 32 shall require a commonhold community statement to make provision about how it can be amended.

(2)   The regulations shall, in particular, make provision under section 32(3)(a) (whether or not subject to provision under section 32(3)(b)).

(3)   An amendment of a commonhold community statement shall have no effect unless and until the amended statement is registered in accordance with this section.

(4)   If the commonhold association makes an application under this subsection the Registrar shall arrange for an amended commonhold community statement to be kept in his custody, and referred to in the register, in place of the unamended statement.

(5)   An application under subsection (4) must be accompanied by a certificate given by the directors of the commonhold association that the amended commonhold community statement satisfies the requirements of this Part.

(6)   Where an amendment of a commonhold community statement redefines the extent of a commonhold unit, an application under subsection (4) must be accompanied by any consent required by section 23(1) or 24(2) (or an order of a court dispensing with consent).

(7)   Where an amendment of a commonhold community statement has the effect of changing the extent of the common parts, an application under subsection (4) must be accompanied by any consent required by section 30(2) (or an order of a court dispensing with consent).

(8)   Where the Registrar amends the register on an application under subsection (4) he shall make any consequential amendments to the register which he thinks appropriate.

Commonhold association

34   Constitution

(1)   A commonhold association is a private company limited by guarantee the memorandum of which—

    (a)   states that an object of the company is to exercise the functions of a commonhold association in relation to specified commonhold land, and

    (b)   specifies £1 as the amount required to be specified in pursuance of section 2(4) of the Companies Act 1985 (members' guarantee).

(2)   Schedule 3 (which makes provision about the constitution of a commonhold association) shall have effect.

35   Duty to manage

(1)   The directors of a commonhold association shall exercise their powers so as to permit or facilitate so far as possible—

    (a)   the exercise by each unit-holder of his rights, and

    (b)   the enjoyment by each unit-holder of the freehold estate in his unit.

(2)   The directors of a commonhold association shall, in particular, use any right, power or procedure conferred or created by virtue of section 37 for the purpose of preventing, remedying or curtailing a failure on the part of a unit-holder to comply with a requirement or duty imposed on him by virtue of the commonhold community statement or a provision of this Part.

(3)   But in respect of a particular failure on the part of a unit-holder (the 'defaulter') the directors of a commonhold association—

(a)   need not take action if they reasonably think that inaction is in the best interests of establishing or maintaining harmonious relationships between all the unit-holders, and that it will not cause any unit-holder (other than the defaulter) significant loss or significant disadvantage, and

(b)   shall have regard to the desirability of using arbitration, mediation or conciliation procedures (including referral under a scheme approved under section 42) instead of legal proceedings wherever possible.

(4)   A reference in this section to a unit-holder includes a reference to a tenant of a unit.

36   Voting

(1)   This section applies in relation to any provision of this Part (a 'voting provision') which refers to the passing of a resolution by a commonhold association.

(2)   A voting provision is satisfied only if every member is given an opportunity to vote in accordance with any relevant provision of the memorandum or articles of association or the commonhold community statement.

(3)   A vote is cast for the purposes of a voting provision whether it is cast in person or in accordance with a provision which—

(a)   provides for voting by post, by proxy or in some other manner, and
(b)   is contained in the memorandum or articles of association or the commonhold community statement.

(4)   A resolution is passed unanimously if every member who casts a vote votes in favour.

Operation of commonhold

37   Enforcement and compensation

(1)   Regulations may make provision (including provision conferring jurisdiction on a court) about the exercise or enforcement of a right or duty imposed or conferred by or by virtue of—

(a)   a commonhold community statement;
(b)   the memorandum or articles of a commonhold association;
(c)   a provision made by or by virtue of this Part.

(2)   The regulations may, in particular, make provision—

(a)   requiring compensation to be paid where a right is exercised in specified cases or circumstances;
(b)   requiring compensation to be paid where a duty is not complied with;
(c)   enabling recovery of costs where work is carried out for the purpose of enforcing a right or duty;
(d)   enabling recovery of costs where work is carried out in consequence of the failure to perform a duty;
(e)   permitting a unit-holder to enforce a duty imposed on another unit-holder, on a commonhold association or on a tenant;

(f)   permitting a commonhold association to enforce a duty imposed on a unit-holder or a tenant;

(g)   permitting a tenant to enforce a duty imposed on another tenant, a unit-holder or a commonhold association;

(h)   permitting the enforcement of terms or conditions to which a right is subject;

(i)   requiring the use of a specified form of arbitration, mediation or conciliation procedure before legal proceedings may be brought.

(3)   Provision about compensation made by virtue of this section shall include—

(a)   provision (which may include provision conferring jurisdiction on a court) for determining the amount of compensation;

(b)   provision for the payment of interest in the case of late payment.

(4)   Regulations under this section shall be subject to any provision included in a commonhold community statement in accordance with regulations made by virtue of section 32(5)(b).

38   Commonhold assessment

(1)   A commonhold community statement must make provision—

(a)   requiring the directors of the commonhold association to make an annual estimate of the income required to be raised from unit-holders to meet the expenses of the association,

(b)   enabling the directors of the commonhold association to make estimates from time to time of income required to be raised from unit-holders in addition to the annual estimate,

(c)   specifying the percentage of any estimate made under paragraph (a) or (b) which is to be allocated to each unit,

(d)   requiring each unit-holder to make payments in respect of the percentage of any estimate which is allocated to his unit, and

(e)   requiring the directors of the commonhold association to serve notices on unit-holders specifying payments required to be made by them and the date on which each payment is due.

(2)   For the purpose of subsection (1)(c)—

(a)   the percentages allocated by a commonhold community statement to the commonhold units must amount in aggregate to 100;

(b)   a commonhold community statement may specify 0 per cent in relation to a unit.

39   Reserve fund

(1)   Regulations under section 32 may, in particular, require a commonhold community statement to make provision—

(a)   requiring the directors of the commonhold association to establish and maintain one or more funds to finance the repair and maintenance of common parts;

(b)   requiring the directors of the commonhold association to establish and maintain one or more funds to finance the repair and maintenance of commonhold units.

(2)   Where a commonhold community statement provides for the establishment and maintenance of a fund in accordance with subsection (1) it must also make provision—

(a)   requiring or enabling the directors of the commonhold association to set a levy from time to time,

(b)   specifying the percentage of any levy set under paragraph (a) which is to be allocated to each unit,

(c)   requiring each unit-holder to make payments in respect of the percentage of any levy set under paragraph (a) which is allocated to his unit, and

(d)   requiring the directors of the commonhold association to serve notices on unit-holders specifying payments required to be made by them and the date on which each payment is due.

(3)   For the purpose of subsection (2)(b)—

(a)   the percentages allocated by a commonhold community statement to the commonhold units must amount in aggregate to 100;

(b)   a commonhold community statement may specify 0 per cent in relation to a unit.

(4)   The assets of a fund established and maintained by virtue of this section shall not be used for the purpose of enforcement of any debt except a judgment debt referable to a reserve fund activity.

(5)   For the purpose of subsection (4)—

(a)   'reserve fund activity' means an activity which in accordance with the commonhold community statement can or may be financed from a fund established and maintained by virtue of this section,

(b)   assets are used for the purpose of enforcement of a debt if, in particular, they are taken in execution or are made the subject of a charging order under section 1 of the Charging Orders Act 1979, and

(c)   the reference to a judgment debt includes a reference to any interest payable on a judgment debt.

40   Rectification of documents

(1)   A unit-holder may apply to the court for a declaration that—

(a)   the memorandum or articles of association of the relevant commonhold association do not comply with regulations under paragraph 2(1) of Schedule 3;

(b)   the relevant commonhold community statement does not comply with a requirement imposed by or by virtue of this Part.

(2)   On granting a declaration under this section the court may make any order which appears to it to be appropriate.

(3)   An order under subsection (2) may, in particular—

(a)   require a director or other specified officer of a commonhold association to take steps to alter or amend a document;

(b)   require a director or other specified officer of a commonhold association to take specified steps;

(c)   make an award of compensation (whether or not contingent upon the occurrence or non-occurrence of a specified event) to be paid by the commonhold association to a specified person;

(d)   make provision for land to cease to be commonhold land.

(4)   An application under subsection (1) must be made—

(a)   within the period of three months beginning with the day on which the applicant became a unit-holder,

(b)   within three months of the commencement of the alleged failure to comply, or

(c)   with the permission of the court.

41   Enlargement

(1)   This section applies to an application under section 2 if the commonhold association for the purposes of the application already exercises functions in relation to commonhold land.

(2)   In this section—

(a)   the application is referred to as an 'application to add land', and

(b)   the land to which the application relates is referred to as the 'added land'.

(3)   An application to add land may not be made unless it is approved by a resolution of the commonhold association.

(4)   A resolution for the purposes of subsection (3) must be passed—

(a)   before the application to add land is made, and

(b)   unanimously.

(5)   Section 2(2) shall not apply to an application to add land; but the application must be accompanied by—

(a)   the documents specified in paragraph 6 of Schedule 1,

(b)   an application under section 33 for the registration of an amended commonhold community statement which makes provision for the existing commonhold and the added land, and

(c)   a certificate given by the directors of the commonhold association that the application to add land satisfies Schedule 2 and subsection (3).

(6)   Where sections 7 and 9 have effect following an application to add land—

(a)   the references to 'the commonhold land' in sections 7(2)(a) and (3)(d) and 9(3)(f) shall be treated as references to the added land, and

(b)   the references in sections 7(2)(b) and (3)(c) and 9(3)(e) to the rights and duties conferred and imposed by the commonhold community statement shall be treated as a reference to rights and duties only in so far as they affect the added land.

(7)   In the case of an application to add land where the whole of the added land is to form part of the common parts of a commonhold—

  (a)   section 7 shall not apply,

  (b)   on registration the commonhold association shall be entitled to be registered (if it is not already) as the proprietor of the freehold estate in the added land,

  (c)   the Registrar shall make any registration required by paragraph (b) (without an application being made), and

  (d)   the rights and duties conferred and imposed by the commonhold community statement shall, in so far as they affect the added land, come into force on registration.

42   Ombudsman

(1)   Regulations may provide that a commonhold association shall be a member of an approved ombudsman scheme.

(2)   An 'approved ombudsman scheme' is a scheme which is approved by the Lord Chancellor and which—

  (a)   provides for the appointment of one or more persons as ombudsman,

  (b)   provides for a person to be appointed as ombudsman only if the Lord Chancellor approves the appointment in advance,

  (c)   enables a unit-holder to refer to the ombudsman a dispute between the unit-holder and a commonhold association which is a member of the scheme,

  (d)   enables a commonhold association which is a member of the scheme to refer to the ombudsman a dispute between the association and a unit-holder,

  (e)   requires the ombudsman to investigate and determine a dispute referred to him,

  (f)   requires a commonhold association which is a member of the scheme to co-operate with the ombudsman in investigating or determining a dispute, and

  (g)   requires a commonhold association which is a member of the scheme to comply with any decision of the ombudsman (including any decision requiring the payment of money).

(3)   In addition to the matters specified in subsection (2) an approved ombudsman scheme—

  (a)   may contain other provision, and

  (b)   shall contain such provision, or provision of such a kind, as may be prescribed.

(4)   If a commonhold association fails to comply with regulations under subsection (1) a unit-holder may apply to the High Court for an order requiring the directors of the commonhold association to ensure that the association complies with the regulations.

(5)   A reference in this section to a unit-holder includes a reference to a tenant of a unit.

Termination: voluntary winding-up

43   Winding-up resolution

(1)   A winding-up resolution in respect of a commonhold association shall be of no effect unless—

    (a)   the resolution is preceded by a declaration of solvency,

    (b)   the commonhold association passes a termination-statement resolution before it passes the winding-up resolution, and

    (c)   each resolution is passed with at least 80 per cent of the members of the association voting in favour.

(2)   In this Part—

    'declaration of solvency' means a directors' statutory declaration made in accordance with section 89 of the Insolvency Act 1986,

    'termination-statement resolution' means a resolution approving the terms of a termination statement (within the meaning of section 47), and

    'winding-up resolution' means a resolution for voluntary winding-up within the meaning of section 84 of that Act.

44   100 per cent agreement

(1)   This section applies where a commonhold association—

    (a)   has passed a winding-up resolution and a termination-statement resolution with 100 per cent of the members of the association voting in favour, and

    (b)   has appointed a liquidator under section 91 of the Insolvency Act 1986.

(2)   The liquidator shall make a termination application within the period of six months beginning with the day on which the winding-up resolution is passed.

(3)   If the liquidator fails to make a termination application within the period specified in subsection (2) a termination application may be made by—

    (a)   a unit-holder, or

    (b)   a person falling within a class prescribed for the purposes of this subsection.

45   80 per cent agreement

(1)   This section applies where a commonhold association—

    (a)   has passed a winding-up resolution and a termination-statement resolution with at least 80 per cent of the members of the association voting in favour, and

    (b)   has appointed a liquidator under section 91 of the Insolvency Act 1986.

(2)   The liquidator shall within the prescribed period apply to the court for an order determining—

    (a)   the terms and conditions on which a termination application may be made, and

    (b)   the terms of the termination statement to accompany a termination application.

(3)   The liquidator shall make a termination application within the period of three months starting with the date on which an order under subsection (2) is made.

(4)   If the liquidator fails to make an application under subsection (2) or (3) within the period specified in that subsection an application of the same kind may be made by—

(a)   a unit-holder, or

(b)   a person falling within a class prescribed for the purposes of this subsection.

46   Termination application

(1)   A 'termination application' is an application to the Registrar that all the land in relation to which a particular commonhold association exercises functions should cease to be commonhold land.

(2)   A termination application must be accompanied by a termination statement.

(3)   On receipt of a termination application the Registrar shall note it in the register.

47   Termination statement

(1)   A termination statement must specify—

(a)   the commonhold association's proposals for the transfer of the commonhold land following acquisition of the freehold estate in accordance with section 49(3), and

(b)   how the assets of the commonhold association will be distributed.

(2)   A commonhold community statement may make provision requiring any termination statement to make arrangements—

(a)   of a specified kind, or

(b)   determined in a specified manner,

about the rights of unit-holders in the event of all the land to which the statement relates ceasing to be commonhold land.

(3)   A termination statement must comply with a provision made by the commonhold community statement in reliance on subsection (2).

(4)   Subsection (3) may be disapplied by an order of the court—

(a)   generally,

(b)   in respect of specified matters, or

(c)   for a specified purpose.

(5)   An application for an order under subsection (4) may be made by any member of the commonhold association.

48   The liquidator

(1)   This section applies where a termination application has been made in respect of particular commonhold land.

(2)   The liquidator shall notify the Registrar of his appointment.

(3)   In the case of a termination application made under section 44 the liquidator shall either—

> (a)   notify the Registrar that the liquidator is content with the termination statement submitted with the termination application, or
>
> (b)   apply to the court under section 112 of the Insolvency Act 1986 to determine the terms of the termination statement.

(4)   The liquidator shall send to the Registrar a copy of a determination made by virtue of subsection (3)(b).

(5)   Subsection (4) is in addition to any requirement under section 112(3) of the Insolvency Act 1986.

(6)   A duty imposed on the liquidator by this section is to be performed as soon as possible.

(7)   In this section a reference to the liquidator is a reference—

> (a)   to the person who is appointed as liquidator under section 91 of the Insolvency Act 1986, or
>
> (b)   in the case of a members' voluntary winding up which becomes a creditors' voluntary winding up by virtue of sections 95 and 96 of that Act, to the person acting as liquidator in accordance with section 100 of that Act.

49   Termination

(1)   This section applies where a termination application is made under section 44 and—

> (a)   a liquidator notifies the Registrar under section 48(3)(a) that he is content with a termination statement, or
>
> (b)   a determination is made under section 112 of the Insolvency Act 1986 by virtue of section 48(3)(b).

(2)   This section also applies where a termination application is made under section 45.

(3)   The commonhold association shall by virtue of this subsection be entitled to be registered as the proprietor of the freehold estate in each commonhold unit.

(4)   The Registrar shall take such action as appears to him to be appropriate for the purpose of giving effect to the termination statement.

Termination: winding-up by court

50   Introduction

(1)   Section 51 applies where a petition is presented under section 124 of the Insolvency Act 1986 for the winding up of a commonhold association by the court.

(2)   For the purposes of this Part—

(a)   an 'insolvent commonhold association' is one in relation to which a winding-up petition has been presented under section 124 of the Insolvency Act 1986,

(b)   a commonhold association is the 'successor commonhold association' to an insolvent commonhold association if the land specified for the purpose of section 34(1)(a) is the same for both associations, and

(c)   a 'winding-up order' is an order under section 125 of the Insolvency Act 1986 for the winding up of a commonhold association.

51   Succession order

(1)   At the hearing of the winding-up petition an application may be made to the court for an order under this section (a 'succession order') in relation to the insolvent commonhold association.

(2)   An application under subsection (1) may be made only by—

(a)   the insolvent commonhold association,

(b)   one or more members of the insolvent commonhold association, or

(c)   a provisional liquidator for the insolvent commonhold association appointed under section 135 of the Insolvency Act 1986.

(3)   An application under subsection (1) must be accompanied by—

(a)   prescribed evidence of the formation of a successor commonhold association, and

(b)   a certificate given by the directors of the successor commonhold association that its memorandum and articles of association comply with regulations under paragraph 2(1) of Schedule 3.

(4)   The court shall grant an application under subsection (1) unless it thinks that the circumstances of the insolvent commonhold association make a succession order inappropriate.

52   Assets and liabilities

(1)   Where a succession order is made in relation to an insolvent commonhold association this section applies on the making of a winding-up order in respect of the association.

(2)   The successor commonhold association shall be entitled to be registered as the proprietor of the freehold estate in the common parts.

(3)   The insolvent commonhold association shall for all purposes cease to be treated as the proprietor of the freehold estate in the common parts.

(4)   The succession order—

(a)   shall make provision as to the treatment of any charge over all or any part of the common parts;

(b)   may require the Registrar to take action of a specified kind;

(c)   may enable the liquidator to require the Registrar to take action of a specified kind;

(d)   may make supplemental or incidental provision.

53   Transfer of responsibility

(1)   Where a succession order is made in relation to an insolvent commonhold association this section applies on the making of a winding-up order in respect of the association.

(2)   The successor commonhold association shall be treated as the commonhold association for the commonhold in respect of any matter which relates to a time after the making of the winding-up order.

(3)   On the making of the winding-up order the court may make an order requiring the liquidator to make available to the successor commonhold association specified—

    (a)   records;

    (b)   copies of records;

    (c)   information.

(4)   An order under subsection (3) may include terms as to—

    (a)   timing;

    (b)   payment.

54   Termination of commonhold

(1)   This section applies where the court—

    (a)   makes a winding-up order in respect of a commonhold association, and

    (b)   has not made a succession order in respect of the commonhold association.

(2)   The liquidator of a commonhold association shall as soon as possible notify the Registrar of—

    (a)   the fact that this section applies,

    (b)   any directions given under section 168 of the Insolvency Act 1986 (liquidator: supplementary powers),

    (c)   any notice given to the court and the registrar of companies in accordance with section 172(8) of that Act (liquidator vacating office after final meeting),

    (d)   any notice given to the Secretary of State under section 174(3) of that Act (completion of winding-up),

    (e)   any application made to the registrar of companies under section 202(2) of that Act (insufficient assets: early dissolution),

    (f)   any notice given to the registrar of companies under section 205(1)(b) of that Act (completion of winding-up), and

    (g)   any other matter which in the liquidator's opinion is relevant to the Registrar.

(3)   Notification under subsection (2)(b) to (f) must be accompanied by a copy of the directions, notice or application concerned.

(4)   The Registrar shall—

    (a)   make such arrangements as appear to him to be appropriate for ensuring that the freehold estate in land in respect of which a commonhold association exercises functions ceases to be registered as a freehold estate in commonhold land as soon as is reasonably practicable after he receives notification under subsection (2)(c) to (f), and

    (b)   take such action as appears to him to be appropriate for the purpose of giving effect to a determination made by the liquidator in the exercise of his functions.

Termination: miscellaneous

55   Termination by court

(1)   This section applies where the court makes an order by virtue of section 6(6)(c) or 40(3)(d) for all the land in relation to which a commonhold association exercises functions to cease to be commonhold land.

(2)   The court shall have the powers which it would have if it were making a winding-up order in respect of the commonhold association.

(3)   A person appointed as liquidator by virtue of subsection (2) shall have the powers and duties of a liquidator following the making of a winding-up order by the court in respect of a commonhold association.

(4)   But the order of the court by virtue of section 6(6)(c) or 40(3)(d) may—

    (a)   require the liquidator to exercise his functions in a particular way;
    (b)   impose additional rights or duties on the liquidator;
    (c)   modify or remove a right or duty of the liquidator.

56   Release of reserve fund

Section 39(4) shall cease to have effect in relation to a commonhold association (in respect of debts and liabilities accruing at any time) if—

    (a)   the court makes a winding-up order in respect of the association,
    (b)   the association passes a voluntary winding-up resolution, or
    (c)   the court makes an order by virtue of section 6(6)(c) or 40(3)(d) for all the land in relation to which the association exercises functions to cease to be commonhold land.

Miscellaneous

57   Multiple site commonholds

(1)   A commonhold may include two or more parcels of land, whether or not contiguous.

(2)   But section 1(1) of this Act is not satisfied in relation to land specified in the memorandum of association of a commonhold association unless a single commonhold community statement makes provision for all the land.

(3)   Regulations may make provision about an application under section 2 made jointly by two or more persons, each of whom is the registered freeholder of part of the land to which the application relates.

(4)   The regulations may, in particular—

(a)   modify the application of a provision made by or by virtue of this Part;

(b)   disapply the application of a provision made by or by virtue of this Part;

(c)   impose additional requirements.

58   Development rights

(1)   In this Part—

'the developer' means a person who makes an application under section 2, and 'development business' has the meaning given by Schedule 4.

(2)   A commonhold community statement may confer rights on the developer which are designed—

(a)   to permit him to undertake development business, or

(b)   to facilitate his undertaking of development business.

(3)   Provision made by a commonhold community statement in reliance on subsection (2) may include provision—

(a)   requiring the commonhold association or a unit-holder to co-operate with the developer for a specified purpose connected with development business;

(b)   making the exercise of a right conferred by virtue of subsection (2) subject to terms and conditions specified in or to be determined in accordance with the commonhold community statement;

(c)   making provision about the effect of breach of a requirement by virtue of paragraph (a) or a term or condition imposed by virtue of paragraph (b);

(d)   disapplying section 41(2) and (3).

(4)   Subsection (2) is subject—

(a)   to regulations under section 32, and

(b)   in the case of development business of the kind referred to in paragraph 7 of Schedule 4, to the memorandum and articles of association of the commonhold association.

(5)   Regulations may make provision regulating or restricting the exercise of rights conferred by virtue of subsection (2).

(6)   Where a right is conferred on a developer by virtue of subsection (2), if he sends to the Registrar a notice surrendering the right—

(a)   the Registrar shall arrange for the notice to be kept in his custody and referred to in the register,

(b)   the right shall cease to be exercisable from the time when the notice is registered under paragraph (a), and

(c)   the Registrar shall inform the commonhold association as soon as is reasonably practicable.

59   Development rights: succession

(1)   If during a transitional period the developer transfers to another person the freehold estate in the whole of the commonhold, the successor in title shall be treated as the developer in relation to any matter arising after the transfer.

(2)   If during a transitional period the developer transfers to another person the freehold estate in part of the commonhold, the successor in title shall be treated as the developer for the purpose of any matter which—

(a)   arises after the transfer, and

(b)   affects the estate transferred.

(3)   If after a transitional period or in a case where there is no transitional period—

(a)   the developer transfers to another person the freehold estate in the whole or part of the commonhold (other than by the transfer of the freehold estate in a single commonhold unit), and

(b)   the transfer is expressed to be inclusive of development rights,

the successor in title shall be treated as the developer for the purpose of any matter which arises after the transfer and affects the estate transferred.

(4)   Other than during a transitional period, a person shall not be treated as the developer in relation to commonhold land for any purpose unless he—

(a)   is, or has been at a particular time, the registered proprietor of the freehold estate in more than one of the commonhold units, and

(b)   is the registered proprietor of the freehold estate in at least one of the commonhold units.

60   Compulsory purchase

(1)   Where a freehold estate in commonhold land is transferred to a compulsory purchaser the land shall cease to be commonhold land.

(2)   But subsection (1) does not apply to a transfer if the Registrar is satisfied that the compulsory purchaser has indicated a desire for the land transferred to continue to be commonhold land.

(3)   The requirement of consent under section 21(2)(c) shall not apply to transfer to a compulsory purchaser.

(4)   Regulations may make provision about the transfer of a freehold estate in commonhold land to a compulsory purchaser.

(5)   The regulations may, in particular—

(a)   make provision about the effect of subsections (1) and (2) (including provision about that part of the commonhold which is not transferred);

(b)   require the service of notice;

(c)   confer power on a court;

(d)   make provision about compensation;

(e)   make provision enabling a commonhold association to require a compulsory purchaser to acquire the freehold estate in the whole, or a particular part, of the commonhold;

(f)   provide for an enactment relating to compulsory purchase not to apply or to apply with modifications.

(6)   Provision made by virtue of subsection (5)(a) in respect of land which is not transferred may include provision—

(a)   for some or all of the land to cease to be commonhold land;

(b)   for a provision of this Part to apply with specified modifications.

(7)   In this section 'compulsory purchaser' means—

(a)   a person acquiring land in respect of which he is authorised to exercise a power of compulsory purchase by virtue of an enactment, and

(b)   a person acquiring land which he is obliged to acquire by virtue of a prescribed enactment or in prescribed circumstances.

61   Matrimonial rights

In the following provisions of this Part a reference to a tenant includes a reference to a person who has matrimonial home rights (within the meaning of section 30(2) of the Family Law Act 1996 (matrimonial home)) in respect of a commonhold unit—

(a)   section 19,

(b)   section 35, and

(c)   section 37.

62   Advice

(1)   The Lord Chancellor may give financial assistance to a person in relation to the provision by that person of general advice about an aspect of the law of commonhold land, so far as relating to residential matters.

(2)   Financial assistance under this section may be given in such form and on such terms as the Lord Chancellor thinks appropriate.

(3)   The terms may, in particular, require repayment in specified circumstances.

63   The Crown

This Part binds the Crown.

General

64   Orders and regulations

(1)   In this Part 'prescribed' means prescribed by regulations.

(2)   Regulations under this Part shall be made by the Lord Chancellor.

(3)   Regulations under this Part—

(a)   shall be made by statutory instrument,

(b)   may include incidental, supplemental, consequential and transitional provision,

(c)   may make provision generally or only in relation to specified cases,

(d)   may make different provision for different purposes, and

(e)   shall be subject to annulment in pursuance of a resolution of either House of Parliament.

65   Registration procedure

(1)   The Lord Chancellor may make rules about—

     (a)   the procedure to be followed on or in respect of commonhold registration documents, and

     (b)   the registration of freehold estates in commonhold land.

(2)   Rules under this section—

     (a)   shall be made by statutory instrument in the same manner as land registration rules within the meaning of the Land Registration Act 2002,

     (b)   may make provision for any matter for which provision is or may be made by land registration rules, and

     (c)   may provide for land registration rules to have effect in relation to anything done by virtue of or for the purposes of this Part as they have effect in relation to anything done by virtue of or for the purposes of that Act.

(3)   Rules under this section may, in particular, make provision—

     (a)   about the form and content of a commonhold registration document;

     (b)   enabling the Registrar to cancel an application by virtue of this Part in specified circumstances;

     (c)   enabling the Registrar, in particular, to cancel an application by virtue of this Part if he thinks that plans submitted with it (whether as part of a commonhold community statement or otherwise) are insufficiently clear or accurate;

     (d)   about the order in which commonhold registration documents and general registration documents are to be dealt with by the Registrar;

     (e)   for registration to take effect (whether or not retrospectively) as from a date or time determined in accordance with the rules.

(4)   The rules may also make provision about satisfaction of a requirement for an application by virtue of this Part to be accompanied by a document; in particular the rules may—

     (a)   permit or require a copy of a document to be submitted in place of or in addition to the original;

     (b)   require a copy to be certified in a specified manner;

     (c)   permit or require the submission of a document in electronic form.

(5)   A commonhold registration document must be accompanied by such fee (if any) as is specified for that purpose by order under section 102 of the Land Registration Act 2002 (fee orders).

(6)   In this section—

     'commonhold registration document' means an application or other document sent to the Registrar by virtue of this Part, and

     'general registration document' means a document sent to the Registrar under a provision of the Land Registration Act 2002.

66 Jurisdiction

(1)   In this Part 'the court' means the High Court or a county court.

(2)   Provision made by or under this Part conferring jurisdiction on a court shall be subject to provision made under section 1 of the Courts and Legal Services Act 1990 (allocation of business between High Court and county courts).

(3)   A power under this Part to confer jurisdiction on a court includes power to confer jurisdiction on a tribunal established under an enactment.

(4)   Rules of court or rules of procedure for a tribunal may make provision about proceedings brought—

> (a)   under or by virtue of any provision of this Part, or
> (b)   in relation to commonhold land.

67   The register

(1)   In this Part—

> 'the register' means the register of title to freehold and leasehold land kept under section 1 of the Land Registration Act 2002,
> 'registered' means registered in the register, and
> 'the Registrar' means the Chief Land Registrar.

(2)   Regulations under any provision of this Part may confer functions on the Registrar (including discretionary functions).

(3)   The Registrar shall comply with any direction or requirement given to him or imposed on him under or by virtue of this Part.

(4)   Where the Registrar thinks it appropriate in consequence of or for the purpose of anything done or proposed to be done in connection with this Part, he may—

> (a)   make or cancel an entry on the register;
> (b)   take any other action.

(5)   Subsection (4) is subject to section 6(2).

68   Amendments

Schedule 5 (consequential amendments) shall have effect.

69   Interpretation

(1)   In this Part—

> 'instrument' includes any document, and
> 'object' in relation to a commonhold association means an object stated in the association's memorandum of association in accordance with section 2(1)(c) of the Companies Act 1985.

(2)   In this Part—

> (a)   a reference to a duty to insure includes a reference to a duty to use the proceeds of insurance for the purpose of rebuilding or reinstating, and
> (b)   a reference to maintaining property includes a reference to decorating it and to putting it into sound condition.

(3)   A provision of the Law of Property Act 1925 , the Companies Act 1985 or the Land Registration Act 2002 defining an expression shall apply to the use of the expression in this Part unless the contrary intention appears.

70   Index of defined expressions

In this Part the expressions listed below are defined by the provisions specified.

Expression	*Interpretation provision*
Common parts	Section 25
A commonhold	Section 1
Commonhold association	Section 34
Commonhold community statement	Section 31
Commonhold land	Section 1
Commonhold unit	Section 11
Court	Section 66
Declaration of solvency	Section 43
Developer	Section 58
Development business	Section 58
Exercising functions	Section 8
Insolvent commonhold association	Section 50
Instrument	Section 69
Insure	Section 69
Joint unit-holder	Section 13
Liquidator (sections 44 to 49)	Section 44
Maintenance	Section 69
Object	Section 69
Prescribed	Section 64
The register	Section 67
Registered	Section 67
Registered freeholder	Section 2
The Registrar	Section 67
Regulations	Section 64
Residential commonhold unit	Section 17

Expression	Interpretation provision
Succession order	Section 51
Successor commonhold association	Section 50
Termination application	Section 46
Termination-statement resolution	Section 43
Transfer (of unit)	Section 15
Transitional period	Section 8
Unit-holder	Section 12
Winding-up resolution	Section 43

...

PART 3
SUPPLEMENTARY

180 Repeals

Schedule 14 (repeals) has effect.

181 Commencement etc

(1) Apart from section 104 and sections 177 to 179, the preceding provisions (and the Schedules) come into force in accordance with provision made by order made by the appropriate authority.

(2) The appropriate authority may by order make any transitional provisions or savings in connection with the coming into force of any provision in accordance with an order under subsection (1).

(3) The power to make orders under subsections (1) and (2) is exercisable by statutory instrument.

(4) In this section 'the appropriate authority' means—

    (a) in relation to any provision of Part 1 or section 180 and Schedule 14 so far as relating to section 104, the Lord Chancellor, and

    (b) in relation to any provision of Part 2 or section 180 and Schedule 14 so far as otherwise relating, the Secretary of State (as respects England) and the National Assembly for Wales (as respects Wales).

182 Extent

This Act extends to England and Wales only.

183   Short title

This Act may be cited as the Commonhold and Leasehold Reform Act 2002.

SCHEDULE 1

Section 2

APPLICATION FOR REGISTRATION: DOCUMENTS

Introduction

1   This Schedule lists the documents which are required by section 2 to accompany an application for the registration of a freehold estate as a freehold estate in commonhold land.

Commonhold association documents

2   The commonhold association's certificate of incorporation under section 13 of the Companies Act 1985 (c 6).

3   Any altered certificate of incorporation issued under section 28 of that Act.

4   The memorandum and articles of association of the commonhold association.

Commonhold community statement

5   The commonhold community statement.

Consent

6 (1)   Where consent is required under or by virtue of section 3—

    (a)   the consent,

    (b)   an order of a court by virtue of section 3(2)(f) dispensing with the requirement for consent, or

    (c)   evidence of deemed consent by virtue of section 3(2)(e).

(2)   In the case of a conditional order under section 3(2)(f), the order must be accompanied by evidence that the condition has been complied with.

Certificate

7   A certificate given by the directors of the commonhold association that—

    (a)   the memorandum and articles of association submitted with the application comply with regulations under paragraph 2(1) of Schedule 3,

    (b)   the commonhold community statement submitted with the application satisfies the requirements of this Part,

    (c)   the application satisfies Schedule 2,

    (d)   the commonhold association has not traded, and

    (e)   the commonhold association has not incurred any liability which has not been discharged.

SCHEDULE 2

Section 4

LAND WHICH MAY NOT BE COMMONHOLD LAND

'Flying freehold'

1   (1)   Subject to sub-paragraph (2), an application may not be made under section 2 wholly or partly in relation to land above ground level ('raised land') unless all the land between the ground and the raised land is the subject of the same application.

(2)   An application for the addition of land to a commonhold in accordance with section 41 may be made wholly or partly in relation to raised land if all the land between the ground and the raised land forms part of the commonhold to which the raised land is to be added.

Agricultural land

2   An application may not be made under section 2 wholly or partly in relation to land if—

    (a)   it is agricultural land within the meaning of the Agriculture Act 1947 (c. 48),

    (b)   it is comprised in a tenancy of an agricultural holding within the meaning of the Agricultural Holdings Act 1986 (c. 5), or

    (c)   it is comprised in a farm business tenancy for the purposes of the Agricultural Tenancies Act 1995 (c. 8).

Contingent title

3   (1)   An application may not be made under section 2 if an estate in the whole or part of the land to which the application relates is a contingent estate.

(2)   An estate is contingent for the purposes of this paragraph if (and only if)—

    (a)   it is liable to revert to or vest in a person other than the present registered proprietor on the occurrence or non-occurrence of a particular event, and

    (b)   the reverter or vesting would occur by operation of law as a result of an enactment listed in sub-paragraph (3).

(3)   The enactments are—

    (a)   the School Sites Act 1841 (c. 38) (conveyance for use as school),

    (b)   the Lands Clauses Acts (compulsory purchase),

    (c)   the Literary and Scientific Institutions Act 1854 (c. 112) (sites for institutions), and

    (d)   the Places of Worship Sites Act 1873 (c. 50) (sites for places of worship).

(4)   Regulations may amend sub-paragraph (3) so as to—

    (a)   add an enactment to the list, or

    (b)   remove an enactment from the list.

SCHEDULE 3

Section 34

COMMONHOLD ASSOCIATION

PART 1

MEMORANDUM AND ARTICLES OF ASSOCIATION

Introduction

1   In this Schedule—

    (a)   'memorandum' means the memorandum of association of a commonhold association, and

    (b)   'articles' means the articles of association of a commonhold association.

Form and content

2   (1)   Regulations shall make provision about the form and content of the memorandum and articles.

(2)   A commonhold association may adopt provisions of the regulations for its memorandum or articles.

(3)   The regulations may include provision which is to have effect for a commonhold association whether or not it is adopted under sub-paragraph (2).

(4)   A provision of the memorandum or articles shall have no effect to the extent that it is inconsistent with the regulations.

(5)   Regulations under this paragraph shall have effect in relation to a memorandum or articles—

    (a)   irrespective of the date of the memorandum or articles, but

    (b)   subject to any transitional provision of the regulations.

Alteration

3   (1)   An alteration of the memorandum or articles of association shall have no effect until the altered version is registered in accordance with this paragraph.

(2)   If the commonhold association makes an application under this sub-paragraph the Registrar shall arrange for an altered memorandum or altered articles to be kept in his custody, and referred to in the register, in place of the unaltered version.

(3)   An application under sub-paragraph (2) must be accompanied by a certificate given by the directors of the commonhold association that the altered memorandum or articles comply with regulations under paragraph 2(1).

(4)   Where the Registrar amends the register on an application under sub-paragraph (2) he shall make any consequential amendments to the register which he thinks appropriate.

Disapplication of Companies Act 1985

4   (1)   The following provisions of the Companies Act 1985 (c 6) shall not apply to a commonhold association—

    (a)   sections 2(7) and 3 (memorandum), and

    (b)   section 8 (articles of association).

(2)   No application may be made under paragraph 3(2) for the registration of a memorandum altered by special resolution in accordance with section 4(1) of the Companies Act 1985 (objects) unless—

    (a)   the period during which an application for cancellation of the alteration may be made under section 5(1) of that Act has expired without an application being made,

    (b)   any application made under that section has been withdrawn, or

    (c)   the alteration has been confirmed by the court under that section.

PART 2
MEMBERSHIP

Pre-commonhold period

5   During the period beginning with incorporation of a commonhold association and ending when land specified in its memorandum becomes commonhold land, the subscribers (or subscriber) to the memorandum shall be the sole members (or member) of the association.

Transitional period

6   (1)   This paragraph applies to a commonhold association during a transitional period.

(2)   The subscribers (or subscriber) to the memorandum shall continue to be members (or the member) of the association.

(3)   A person who for the time being is the developer in respect of all or part of the commonhold is entitled to be entered in the register of members of the association.

Unit-holders

7   A person is entitled to be entered in the register of members of a commonhold association if he becomes the unit-holder of a commonhold unit in relation to which the association exercises functions—

    (a)   on the unit becoming commonhold land by registration with unit-holders under section 9, or

    (b)   on the transfer of the unit.

Joint unit-holders

8   (1)   This paragraph applies where two or more persons become joint unit-holders of a commonhold unit—

(a) on the unit becoming commonhold land by registration with unit-holders under section 9, or

(b) on the transfer of the unit.

(2) If the joint unit-holders nominate one of themselves for the purpose of this sub-paragraph, he is entitled to be entered in the register of members of the commonhold association which exercises functions in relation to the unit.

(3) A nomination under sub-paragraph (2) must—

(a) be made in writing to the commonhold association, and

(b) be received by the association before the end of the prescribed period.

(4) If no nomination is received by the association before the end of the prescribed period the person whose name appears first in the proprietorship register is on the expiry of that period entitled to be entered in the register of members of the association.

(5) On the application of a joint unit-holder the court may order that a joint unit-holder is entitled to be entered in the register of members of a commonhold association in place of a person who is or would be entitled to be registered by virtue of sub-paragraph (4).

(6) If joint unit-holders nominate one of themselves for the purpose of this sub-paragraph, the nominated person is entitled to be entered in the register of members of the commonhold association in place of the person entered by virtue of—

(a) sub-paragraph (2),

(b) sub-paragraph (5), or

(c) this sub-paragraph.

Self-membership

9 A commonhold association may not be a member of itself.

No other members

10 A person may not become a member of a commonhold association otherwise than by virtue of a provision of this Schedule.

Effect of registration

11 A person who is entitled to be entered in the register of members of a commonhold association becomes a member when the company registers him in pursuance of its duty under section 352 of the Companies Act 1985 (c. 6) (duty to maintain register of members).

Termination of membership

12 Where a member of a commonhold association ceases to be a unit-holder or joint unit-holder of a commonhold unit in relation to which the association exercises functions—

(a) he shall cease to be a member of the commonhold association, but

(b)   paragraph (a) does not affect any right or liability already acquired or incurred in respect of a matter relating to a time when he was a unit-holder or joint unit-holder.

13   A member of a commonhold association may resign by notice in writing to the association if (and only if) he is a member by virtue of paragraph 5 or 6 of this Schedule (and not also by virtue of any other paragraph).

Register of members

14   (1)   Regulations may make provision about the performance by a commonhold association of its duty under section 352 of the Companies Act 1985 (c. 6) (duty to maintain register of members) where a person—

(a)   becomes entitled to be entered in the register by virtue of paragraphs 5 to 8, or

(b)   ceases to be a member by virtue of paragraph 12 or on resignation.

(2)   The regulations may in particular require entries in the register to be made within a specified period.

(3)   A period specified under sub-paragraph (2) may be expressed to begin from—

(a)   the date of a notification under section 15(3),

(b)   the date on which the directors of the commonhold association first become aware of a specified matter, or

(c)   some other time.

(4)   A requirement by virtue of this paragraph shall be treated as a requirement of section 352 for the purposes of section 352(5) (fines).

Companies Act 1985

15   (1)   Section 22(1) of the Companies Act 1985 (initial members) shall apply to a commonhold association subject to this Schedule.

(2)   Sections 22(2) and 23 of that Act (members: new members and holding company) shall not apply to a commonhold association.

PART 3
MISCELLANEOUS

Name

16   Regulations may provide-

(a)   that the name by which a commonhold association is registered under the Companies Act 1985 must satisfy specified requirements;

(b)   that the name by which a company other than a commonhold association is registered may not include a specified word or expression.

Statutory declaration

17   For the purposes of section 12 of the Companies Act 1985 (registration: compliance with Act) as it applies to a commonhold association, a reference to the

requirements of that Act shall be treated as including a reference to a provision of or made under this Schedule.

SCHEDULE 4

Section 58

DEVELOPMENT RIGHTS

Introductory

1   This Schedule sets out the matters which are development business for the purposes of section 58.

Works

2   The completion or execution of works on—
     (a)   a commonhold,
     (b)   land which is or may be added to a commonhold, or
     (c)   land which has been removed from a commonhold.

Marketing

3   (1)   Transactions in commonhold units.

(2)   Advertising and other activities designed to promote transactions in commonhold units.

Variation

4   The addition of land to a commonhold.

5   The removal of land from a commonhold.

6   Amendment of a commonhold community statement (including amendment to redefine the extent of a commonhold unit).

Commonhold association

7   Appointment and removal of directors of a commonhold association.

SCHEDULE 5

Section 68

COMMONHOLD: CONSEQUENTIAL AMENDMENTS

Law of Property Act 1922 (c 16)

1   At the end of paragraph 5 of Schedule 15 to the Law of Property Act 1922 (perpetually renewable leases) (which becomes sub-paragraph (1)) there shall be added—

'(2)   Sub-paragraph (3) applies where a grant—

(a)   relates to commonhold land, and

(b)   would take effect by virtue of sub-paragraph (1) as a demise for a term of two thousand years or a subdemise for a fixed term.

(3)   The grant shall be treated as if it purported to be a grant of the term referred to in sub-paragraph (2)(b) (and sections 17 and 18 of the Commonhold and Leasehold Reform Act 2002 (residential and non-residential leases) shall apply accordingly).'

Law of Property Act 1925 (c 20)

2   After section 101(1) of the Law of Property Act 1925 (mortgagee's powers) there shall be added—

'(1A)   Subsection (1)(i) is subject to section 21 of the Commonhold and Leasehold Reform Act 2002 (no disposition of part-units)'.

3   At the end of section 149 of that Act (90-year term in place of certain determinable terms) there shall be added—

'(7)   Subsection (8) applies where a lease, underlease or contract—

(a)   relates to commonhold land, and

(b)   would take effect by virtue of subsection (6) as a lease, underlease or contract of the kind mentioned in that subsection.

(8)   The lease, underlease or contract shall be treated as if it purported to be a lease, underlease or contract of the kind referred to in subsection (7)(b) (and sections 17 and 18 of the Commonhold and Leasehold Reform Act 2002 (residential and non-residential leases) shall apply accordingly).'

Limitation Act 1980 (c 58)

4   After section 19 of the Limitation Act 1980 (actions for rent) there shall be inserted—

'Commonhold

19A   Actions for breach of commonhold duty

An action in respect of a right or duty of a kind referred to in section 37(1) of the Commonhold and Leasehold Reform Act 2002 (enforcement) shall not be brought after the expiration of six years from the date on which the cause of action accrued.'

Housing Act 1985 (c 68)

5   At the end of section 118 of the Housing Act 1985 (the right to buy) there shall be added—

'(3)   For the purposes of this Part, a dwelling-house which is a commonhold unit (within the meaning of the Commonhold and Leasehold Reform Act 2002) shall be treated as a house and not as a flat.'

Insolvency Act 1986 (c 45)

6   At the end of section 84 of the Insolvency Act 1986 (voluntary winding-up) there shall be added—

> '(4)   This section has effect subject to section 43 of the Commonhold and Leasehold Reform Act 2002.'

Law of Property (Miscellaneous Provisions) Act 1994 (c 36)

7   (1)   Section 5 of the Law of Property (Miscellaneous Provisions) Act 1994 (discharge of obligations) shall be amended as follows.

(2)   In subsection (1) for the words 'or of leasehold land' substitute 'of leasehold land or of a commonhold unit'.

(3)   After subsection (3) insert—

> '(3A)   If the property is a commonhold unit, there shall be implied a covenant that the mortgagor will fully and promptly observe and perform all the obligations under the commonhold community statement that are for the time being imposed on him in his capacity as a unit-holder or as a joint unit-holder.'

(4)   For subsection (4) substitute—

> '(4)   In this section—
>
> (a)   "commonhold community statement", "commonhold unit", "joint unit-holder" and "unit-holder" have the same meanings as in the Commonhold and Leasehold Reform Act 2002, and
>
> (b)   "mortgage" includes charge, and "mortgagor" shall be construed accordingly.'

Trusts of Land and Appointment of Trustees Act 1996 (c 47)

8   At the end of section 7 of the Trusts of Land and Appointment of Trustees Act 1996 (partition by trustees) there shall be added—

> '(6)   Subsection (1) is subject to sections 21 (part-unit: interests) and 22 (part-unit: charging) of the Commonhold and Leasehold Reform Act 2002.'

INDEX

References are to paragraph and Appendix numbers.